Carol Anderson (signature)

The Piscator Notebook

D1547988

"Piscator is the greatest theatre man of our time.

Bertolt Brecht

"The Living Theatre produced some of the greatest theatre ever."

Al Pacino

Judith Malina and The Living Theatre have been icons of political theatre for over six decades. What few realise is that she originally studied under another giant of 20th century culture, Erwin Piscator, in his Dramatic Workshop at The New School in New York. Piscator founded the Workshop after emigrating to New York, having collaborated with Brecht to create "Epic Theatre" in Germany.

The Piscator Notebook documents Malina's intensive and idiosyncratic training at Piscator's school. Part diary, part theatrical treatise, this unique and inspiring volume combines:

- complete transcriptions of Malina's notes from her first year at The Dramatic Workshop, as well as reproductions of various of Piscator's teaching materials, syllabi and lectures;
- notes on Malina's teachers, fellow students – including Marlon Brando and Tennessee Williams – and New School productions;
- studies of Piscator's process and influence, along with new essays on the relationship between his teaching, Malina's work with The Living Theatre and "The Ongoing Epic";
- a foreword by performance pioneer Richard Schechner.

The Piscator Notebook is a striking record of the genealogy of political theatre practice in the 20th century, from Europe to the US. But it is also a stunningly personal reflection on the pleasures and challenges of learning about theatre, charged with essential insights for the student and teacher, actor and director.

Judith Malina is the daughter of Rabbi Max Malina and Rose Malina, who gave up her own acting career to prepare Judith for a life of theatrical and political commitment. Judith founded The Living Theatre in 1947 with Julian Beck, continuing with Hanon Reznikov after Beck's death, until Reznikov passed away in 2008. After 64 years, she continues her political and experimental theatre work in downtown New York City and worldwide. She has been recognised with lifetime achievement awards by the Southern Eastern Theatre Conference, National Theatre Conference, Association for Theatre in Higher Education, New York Innovative Theatre Awards, and the OBIE Awards, and is a member of the Theatre Hall of Fame. In 2008, President Lula da Silva awarded her the Ordem de Merito for her theatre work in Brazil in the 1970s.

The Piscator Notebook

BY JUDITH MALINA

Routledge
Taylor & Francis Group

LONDON AND NEW YORK

First published 2012
by Routledge
2 Park Square, Milton Park, Abingdon, Oxon OX14 4RN

Simultaneously published in the USA and Canada
by Routledge
711 Third Avenue, New York, NY 10017

Routledge is an imprint of the Taylor & Francis Group, an informa business

British Library Cataloguing in Publication Data
A catalogue record for this book is available from the British Library

Library of Congress Cataloguing in Publication Data
Malina, Judith, 1926-
  The Piscator notebook / By Judith Malina.
     p. cm.
  Includes index.
  1. Piscator, Erwin, 1893-1966--Criticism and interpretation.
  2. Theatrical producers and directors--United States--Biography.
  3. New School for Social Research (New York, N.Y.). Dramatic Workshop.
  4. Malina, Judith, 1926--Diaries. 5. Actors--United States--Biography.
  6. Theater--United States--History--20th century. 7. Theater--Political
  aspects. I. Title.
  PN2658.P5M35 2012
  792.02'33092--dc23   2011050034

ISBN: 978-0-415-60073-6 (hbk)
ISBN: 978-0-415-60074-3 (pbk)
ISBN: 978-0-203-12816-9 (ebk)

Typeset in Univers and Sabon
by Keystroke, Station Road, Codsall, Wolverhampton

Printed and bound in the United States of America
by Edwards Brothers Malloy, Inc.

Contents

Plates

Plate Section I

Plates can be found between pp. 34–35.

Plate 1. Piscator in tweed jacket. Collection Alfred J. Balcombe, Institut für Theaterwissenschaft der Freien Universität Berlin. Copyright © Michael J. Balcombe.

Plate 2. 1942 Dramatic Workshop program cover. Taken from *Erwin Piscator: Das politische Theater*, courtesy of Officina Edizioni, Teatrino dei Fondi.

Plate 3. *All the King's Men.* Taken from *Erwin Piscator: Das politische Theater*, courtesy of Officina Edizioni, Teatrino dei Fondi.

Plate 4. *The Flies*, with Piscator, Maria Ley-Piscator and ensemble including Judith Malina. Collection Alfred J. Balcombe, Institut für Theaterwissenschaft der Freien Universität Berlin. Copyright © Michael J. Balcombe.

Plate 5. Piscator outside the Workshop's summer theatre in Sayville, Long Island, with students including Marlon Brando, Rod Steiger and Bernie Schwartz (Tony Curtis). Taken from *Erwin Piscator: Das politische Theater*, courtesy of Officina Edizioni, Teatrino dei Fondi.

Plate 6. *Lysistrata* ensemble including Marlon Brando. Reproduced courtesy of Erwin Piscator Papers, Special Collections Research Center, Southern Illinois University Carbondale.

Plate 7. *Juno and the Paycock* with Judith Malina (far right), Gene Sacks and Anna Berger. Collection Alfred J. Balcombe, Institut für Theaterwissenschaft der Freien Universität Berlin. Copyright © Michael J. Balcombe.

Plate 8. Piscator with Maria Ley-Piscator, Saul Colin and Francis Adler. Reproduced courtesy of Erwin Piscator Papers, Special Collections Research Center, Southern Illinois University Carbondale.

Plate 9. Piscator with miniatures. Taken from *Erwin Piscator: Das politische Theater*, courtesy of Officina Edizioni, Teatrino dei Fondi.

Plate 10. Students with camera. Collection Alfred J. Balcombe, Institut für Theaterwissenschaft der Freien Universität Berlin. Copyright © Michael J. Balcombe.

Plate 11. Tony Curtis. Collection Alfred J. Balcombe, Institut für Theaterwissenschaft der Freien Universität Berlin. Copyright © Michael J. Balcombe.

Plate 12. Harry Belafonte. Collection Alfred J. Balcombe, Institut für Theaterwissenschaft der Freien Universität Berlin. Copyright © Michael J. Balcombe.

Plate 13. Outside The Dramatic Workshop entrance. Collection Alfred J. Balcombe, Institut für Theaterwissenschaft der Freien Universität Berlin. Copyright © Michael J. Balcombe.

Plate 14. Students outside The Dramatic Workshop entrance. Collection Alfred J. Balcombe, Institut für Theaterwissenschaft der Freien Universität Berlin. Copyright © Michael J. Balcombe.

Plate 15. Piscator standing under stage lights. Taken from *Erwin Piscator: Das politische Theater*, courtesy of Officina Edizioni, Teatrino dei Fondi.

Plate section II

Plates can be found between pp. 120–121.

Plate 16. Full repertory of plays produced at The Dramatic Workshop, 1940–52. Collection Alfred J. Balcombe, Institut für Theaterwissenschaft der Freien Universität Berlin. Copyright © Michael J. Balcombe.

Plate 17. Architect Joseph Urban's theater at The New School. Taken from *Erwin Piscator: Das politische Theater*, courtesy of Officina Edizioni, Teatrino dei Fondi.

Plate 18. McGrew mural in the Joseph Urban theatre. Collection Alfred J. Balcombe, Institut für Theaterwissenschaft der Freien Universität Berlin. Copyright © Michael J. Balcombe.

Plate 19. Piscator with Simone de Beauvoir and Saul Colin. Collection Alfred J. Balcombe, Institut für Theaterwissenschaft der Freien Universität Berlin. Copyright © Michael J. Balcombe.

Plate 20. Piscator with student. Collection Alfred J. Balcombe, Institut für Theaterwissenschaft der Freien Universität Berlin. Copyright © Michael J. Balcombe.

Plate 21. "The School that came to stay." Collection Alfred J. Balcombe, Institut für Theaterwissenschaft der Freien Universität Berlin. Copyright © Michael J. Balcombe.

Plate 22. Piscator's production of *Rasputin*, 1927. Taken from *Erwin Piscator: Das politische Theater*, courtesy of Officina Edizioni, Teatrino dei Fondi.

Plate 23. *Frankenstein*, The Living Theatre, 1967. Reproduced courtesy of The Living Theatre Archives.

Plate 24. *The Money Tower*, The Living Theatre, 1975. Reproduced courtesy of The Living Theatre Archives.

Plate 25. Piscator in jail, 1930. Taken from *Erwin Piscator: Das politische Theater*, courtesy of Officina Edizioni, Teatrino dei Fondi.

Plate 26. Judith Malina and Julian Beck in jail, 1971. Reproduced courtesy of The Living Theatre Archives.

Plate 27. Judith Malina and Maria Ley-Piscator teaching at The Dramatic Workshop II in 1990. Reproduced courtesy of The New School, New York.

Plate 28. *Eureka!*, The Living Theatre, 2008. Reproduced courtesy of The Living Theatre Archives.

Plate 29. Judith Malina, Brad Burgess and Tom Walker rehearsing *History of the World*, 2011. Tower designed by Eric Olson. Reproduced courtesy of Kennedy Yanko kennedyyankoart.com.

Plate 30. Judith Malina and Brad Burgess performing *Occupy Your World*, an expression of support for the Occupy movement of 2011. Reproduced courtesy of Cindy Ho.

Figures

Acknowledgments

With loving thanks to Garrick Beck, who worked long and hard to make this book happen.

Brad Burgess, who has guided me to keep to my best and highest standards in every phase of the work, and held my hand through thick and thin, and sacrificed much to help me in this book's creation.

Tom Walker, who, for the last forty years, has been unfailing in giving of his time and talents to my work onstage and off.

Mark Amitin, who has worked nobly for decades to make my work possible.

My beloved Hanon Reznikov, who worked with me on every page and paragraph of this book.

Jay Dobkin, who edited the entire manuscript and researched the details with his extraordinary intellectual gifts.

Richard Schechner, whose philosophy of the theatre has extended and fulfilled all my work.

My beloved Julian Beck, who first said that my Piscator notebook should become a book.

The entire Living Theatre company, whose patience has sustained me and whose fidelity to the theatre's work has inspired me.

Cristina Valenti and John Tytell, who chronicled my life and my work so that I could realize its patterns.

I would like to thank especially the following, who contributed enormous time, research and effort to discover and acquire the photographs in this notebook. In particular:

Michael J. Balcombe, Dagmar Walach; Dirk Szuzies, Karin Kaper, Joanie Fritz Zosike, the Institut für Teaterwissenschaft der Freien Universität Berlin and the Piscator Archives at the Akademie der Künste, in Berlin; Enrico Falaschi and Officina Edizioni, Teatrino dei Fondi in San Miniato, Italy; James Bantin, Suzanne Aldridge and the Piscator Collection, Morris Library, University of Illinois at Champagne, Illinois; Carmen Hendershott at The New School.

Foreword

RICHARD SCHECHNER

The thing about Judith Malina is that she is indefatigable, unstoppable, erupting with ideas. Malina is long-living, long-working; optimistic; and, by the second decade of the 21st century, girlish and old-womanish at the same time. She survives and she bubbles, both. Malina and Julian Beck founded the Living in New York in 1947 (yes, you heard me right). And as I write this in December 2011, the Living is still going strong. The Living is Malina but it is also in excess of Malina. The Living includes Malina's life partners poet-designer-actor Beck (d. 1985) and director-playwright Hanon Reznikov (d. 2008), who, after seeing *Paradise Now* at Yale in 1968, decided to join the Living (which he did in 1977). Today, Judith works closely with her and Julian's son Garrick and Hanon's former assistant Brad Burgess.

Over the 64 years of its existence, so many performers: Rufus Collins, Steven Ben Israel, Nona Howard, Cal Barber, Carl Einhorn, Diana Van Tosh, Mary Mary, Joseph Chaikin, Soraya Broukhim . . . oh, it is not my place here to list them *all* – the hundreds of performers. Or the writers whose plays and poems so affected the Living even as the Living took apart their texts to make something new: William Carlos Williams, Gertrude Stein, Jack Gelber, Kenneth H. Brown, Bertolt Brecht, Federico Garcia Lorca, Sophocles, Mary Shelley. And the participating audiences who, for a time, joined the Living on stages and then followed the Living into the streets.

No, to list them *all* would take up a big wall. And, anyway, the Living is not to be carved on any monument. The Living's flag is the black banner of anarchy, sometimes toned red with communism, puffed high by weed, twisted by acid; a neo-tribe shouting poetry, raging against the lunacies of authority, loving enemies, and friends too, to death, spitting scorn and then unexpectedly going soft and forgiving, embracing and inviting: "You, yes, YOU, come with us! Join us!" And many did.

Before there was the Living, there was Judith Malina the student of Erwin Piscator. Who was this Piscator and what did he teach Malina? A German by birth and language, Piscator also worked in the USSR and the USA. Today, Piscator is not so much remembered in his own right but as someone who influenced Bertolt Brecht. Brecht took the idea of "Epic Theatre" (*episches Theater*) from Piscator who had adapted it from the playwright Arnolt Bronnen, a friend of Brecht's. Epic theatre was a reaction against the bourgeois sentimentality of naturalism. This strong response against Stanislavsky – as expressed in the art of Vsevolod Meyerhold and Vladimir Mayakovsky – permeated the early years of the Russian Revolution. As John Fuegi put it: "Piscator demands [. . .] that the 'lies' of 'art' be replaced by the 'true' world of facts. The world out there will be brought into the theatre in all its 'epic breadth and fullness' and will be allowed to tell its own story. This story, rather obviously, will have profound political implications" (Fuegi 1972: 15). Piscator's productions at Berlin's Volksbühne treated "topical, historical, factual material [with] fluidity, simultaneity and cinematic cutting" (Willett 1960: 110). Piscator wanted the theatre to explode out of the theatre buildings into the streets; to take from real life and surge back into real life.

It was this theory and practice that Piscator brought with him to New York where he started The Dramatic Workshop in 1940. The Workshop's faculty included Maria Ley-Piscator (Erwin's wife), Lee Strasberg, Stella Adler, Herbert Berghof, and John Gassner. Among the students were Harry Belafonte, Marlon Brando, George Bartenieff, Rod Steiger, Walter Matthau, Tennessee Williams . . . and Judith Malina. Piscator's approach resonated with Malina. As she writes in her *Notebook*: "Monday, February 5, 1945. On my first day as a student of the theatre I had the rare experience of meeting a great man. When Erwin Piscator entered the room it was not the spontaneous applause of my fellow students alone that I felt, but the tangible presence of a personality. [. . .] He said that the great revolutions were often inspired by plays of high impact, like [Harriet Beecher Stowe's] *Uncle*

Tom's Cabin or [Gerhart] Hauptmann's *The Weavers*. His informality, combined with the fire and power of his ideas, led to him making the half-joking statement which I am tempted to use as my motto: 'The theatre is the most important thing, and anyone who does not realize this is stupid'" (Malina 2012: TK). Malina was 19 when she wrote these words, Piscator 52. Born in Kiel, Germany, Malina's family moved to New York in 1928 because her father, founder of New York's German Jewish Congregation, foresaw the horror that was to be Hitler's Reich.

Piscator, a communist, wrote *Das politische Theater* (*The Political Theatre*) in 1929, left Germany for the USSR in 1931, then came to New York in 1937. In 1951, with the rise of rabid anti-communism in the USA, Piscator returned to Germany. His most significant work during this period was his 1963 production at Berlin's Theater am Kurfürstendamm of Rolf Hochhuth's *The Deputy*, a work indicting Pope Pius XII for not taking any action in word or deed against the Holocaust. Piscator died in 1966.

Piscator hated bourgeois "decadence" and in the 1920s he staged fiercely pro-Soviet works. He proclaimed "Subordination of all artistic aims to the revolutionary goal" (Braun 1982: 146). As Julian Beck restated this axiom: "The actors at The Living Theatre are awkward, untutored, unconsciously defiant of the conventions. [. . .] To make something useful. Nothing else is interesting" (Beck 1972: Meditation 7, unpaginated). What Piscator taught – or, rather, to be more accurate, transmitted – to Judith Malina is the subject of the book you are about to read. I won't translate her felt experiences into scholarship, but of course insist that you find out for yourself. But I will say this: Malina (and Beck) reshaped Piscator's fervid communism into their own kind of leftward anarchism. Yes, Malina believes in and works to accomplish the "revolution," but that word in the Living's lexicon is not singular. It is a many-meaning metaphor generating an abundance of ideas and actions.

What Piscator's Workshop did to Malina was to awaken her so that she became capable of transforming herself and those who worked with her. "I entered The Dramatic Workshop fervent to be an actress and, after a few days of watching Piscator's work, I knew I wanted to do the more encompassing work that is called directing. Piscator looked at me coldly: He does not have a high regard for the staying power of women in the masculine professions. [. . .] I pleaded with him, swallowing my humiliation at his low opinion of my qualifications because of my sex, and he, somewhat reluctantly, allowed me to take the directing course" (Malina 1984: 3). Her work in Piscator's school, as Malina's *Notebook* amply demonstrates, encompassed a lot more than directing. She studied acting, voice, costume, make-up, design, dramaturgy, dance, theatre history and sociology, classical and contemporary drama – the panoply of "theatre arts." Of course, Piscator emphasized politics. As Malina writes in the *Notebook*: "In Theatre Research, Mr. Piscator spent the two hours talking about his 'political theatre.' It was one of the most inspiring lectures."

All this training, a detailed account of which Malina provides, led The Living Theatre not to become an ordinary theatre but something unique in American and, dare I say it, world theatre. Indeed, what is not predictable from the evidence of Malina's *Notebook* is what she and Beck, and their many colleagues, made The Living Theatre into. They internalized the fervid political dedication of Piscator and added – possibly more from Beck's input than Malina's – a highly poetic strain infused with an avant-garde painterly aesthetic. She a woman of the theatre, he a painter and poet. Julian and Judith's marriage was romantic and artistic; heterosexual, bisexual, gay: all-encompassing, holding in its embrace not only Hanon Reznikov (whom Judith married after Julian's death) but in a real sense the entirety of The Living Theatre tribe. The Living was singular for folding into its fiery political theatre elements of cubism, surrealism, Dada, proclaimed (not read silently) poetry and what was to become Happenings and then performance art. Maybe in our own post-postmodern epoch, it seems "ordinary" – but not at all so in 1940s–50s–60s New York. From 1964 to 1968, the Living went into exile. And even after their return to New York, the theatre remained peripatetic with outposts and members working in Brazil, Europe, India, and elsewhere. The Living aimed for a social revolution while enacting an artistic one.

Malina not only overcame Piscator's antipathy, but found her own voice – sometimes in opposition, sometimes in supplement, to that of her teacher. As she writes in the *Notebook*, "What mattered to Piscator was intensity without emotion in the communication. [. . .] But Piscator stopped at the glance, at the contact of the eyes. Why? Can't the actor speak directly to the spectator? And above all, why can't the spectator talk back, express herself, argue, shout . . . perform?" Then Malina grades her teacher: "Because Piscator, whose whole epicenter was the audience, also feared the audience."

Not so Malina. Fearless, she is.

References

Beck, Julian. 1972. *The Life of the Theater*. San Francisco: City Lights Books.

Braun, Edward. 1982. *The Director and the Stage: From Naturalism to Grotowski*. London: Methuen.

Fuegi, John. 1972. *The Essential Brecht*. Los Angeles: Hennesy and Ingalls.

Malina, Judith. 1984. *The Diaries of Judith Malina: 1947–1957*. New York: Grove Press.

Malina, Judith. 2012. *The Piscator Notebook*. London: Routledge.

Mitter, Shomit and Maria Shevtsova, editors. 2005. *Fifty Key Directors*. London: Routledge.

Willett, John. 1960. *The Theatre of Bertolt Brecht*. New York: New Directions.

part 1

Weimar to The Dramatic Workshop

Piscator is the greatest theatre man of our time, and possibly the greatest theatre man of all time. His love of experiment, his great scenic innovations, existed to serve humankind through all the means of the theatre.

Bertolt Brecht

1945 was a time of enormous political and cultural confusion. The post-war elation had died domestically and the upsurge of the 60's had not yet begun . . .

The little theatre movement of the Provincetown Playhouse was over and The Barter Theatre had lost some of its potency, though it still continues to inspire us. The Group Theatre, which had given us so much hope, degenerated into the more conventional Theatre Guild and, except for an all-too-rare new play by Eugene O'Neill, nothing was happening on the theatre scene.

Yet Erwin Piscator, though he carried the burden of much disappointment from his inability to find a place in the Broadway milieu – the rejection of Gilbert Miller who had promised him a Broadway production of his *War and Peace*, as well as his desire not to teach, but to produce plays – none of this discouraged his underlying belief in a theatre of meaning and political vigor. He fought for it, and he transmitted that vigor to his students.

He was not easy on the actor; his demands were high and for some unreachable. He wanted absolute attention, absolute concentration, but above all he asked the performer to change her focus. He called this Objective Acting, in which the object of the actor's focus is the spectator.

The actor speaks, stands in the lights, is the object of the audience's attention . . .

But the actor's work is to communicate with the audience. Traditionally, this would occur through her relationships to the other actors on stage – but in Piscator's and Brecht's Epic Theatre the fictional relationship between the character the actors are portraying is less real than the actual relationships between actor and audience members.

This required a special kind of playwright, and Brecht's Epic Theatre offers such a means.

But Piscator also produced the Classics. The examples of his Schiller play, *The Robbers*, and Sartre's *The Flies*, and a version of *Eumenidies*, are outstanding. Accompanied by an examination of the techniques he developed in such productions, he guided us to understanding the ways we could accomplish this essential shift, this initial shift of objective.

I started to keep a notebook on February 5, 1945, when I began my studies at Erwin Piscator's Dramatic Workshop at The New School for Social Research in New York. I was aware of, and even in awe of Piscator's reputation when I first came to the Workshop – and in a certain sense one could say that the encounter was predestined.

Personal History

My mother, Rosel Zamojre, was an idealistic young actress in the city of Kiel, a naval and submarine base in northern Germany. She was an admirer of Erwin Piscator, the revolutionary young director who was the bright hope of the avant-garde theatre of the Weimar Republic. Her ambition was to work with him when she finished school. She took part in Kieler theatricals, while she worked in the shop where my grandparents sold linens and lace. Her observant Jewish family must surely have disapproved of her theatrical aspirations.

But then she met Max Malina, an equally idealistic young rabbi, at that time serving unhappily as a chaplain in the German army. She fell in love . . . and he soon found a way to get out of the army.

It was in those days unthinkable that a woman could be both a rabbi's wife and an actress, so these two young people agreed that Rosel would give up her dream of the theatre, but that they would have a daughter who would become an actress; a surrogate, as it were, for Rosel's abandoned career.

I was born in Kiel, in June 1926, intended for a theatrical life – hopefully even in Piscator's theatre. Piscator was 33 years old when I was born, and was the director of the Volksbühne in Berlin. He had just opened Schiller's *Die Räuber*, and was rehearsing Ernst Toller's *Hoppla, wir leben*!

And it came to pass that Germany fell upon evil days, and my father, foreseeing the disaster approaching for the Jewish people, emigrated with my mother and me, in 1929, to New York City. There he founded The German Jewish Congregation, and devoted himself to making America's Jewish community aware of the growing threat in Germany.

Erwin Piscator: Germany to New York City

When Piscator left Germany in 1936, it was high time for a Communist revolutionary to leave. Though he was not Jewish, Thea Kirfel-Lenk, in her valuable book *Erwin Piscator im Exil in den USA* (Kirfel-Lenk 1984: 145) reproduces a document from the SS files of 1939 in which Piscator is designated as a Jew, despite it being well known that he was a descendant of Johannes Piscator, a Protestant theologian who translated the bible into German in 1600.

Piscator's history is one of heroic perseverance. He had been an apprentice actor in Munich's Hoftheater, but experienced a *crise de conscience* on the battlefield in Ypres, Belgium during the First World War. He was digging a trench, shells bursting all around him, surrounded by the wounded and the dead. A sergeant came by and noted the soldier's clumsiness with the shovel and asked him mockingly what he did for a living in civilian life. Young Erwin felt humiliated when he answered sheepishly, "I'm . . . an actor," and wondered why it made him ashamed.

He was determined thereafter to make the work of theatre meaningful work, to renounce the kind of theatre that made him feel disgraced to say the word "actor," to redeem the art from its degraded state. After the war he made the theatre his field of battle. In February 1942, Piscator remembered it this way in his essay on "The Theatre of the Future" in *Tomorrow Magazine*:

> War was hateful to me, so hateful that after the bitter debacle of 1918, I enlisted in the political struggle for permanent peace.

In 1919 Piscator participated in the formation of a small avant-garde theatre in Königsberg, called The Tribunal, which produced plays by Wedekind and Kaiser, and Strindberg's *Spook Sonata* in which Piscator played the young hero, Arkenholtz. Perhaps most significantly, it also produced *The Transfiguration* (*Die Wandlung*), a play of revolutionary pacifism that Ernst Toller had written in prison, after his experiences with the Soviet Republic of Bavaria, in whose brief but luminous story Toller was an active participant.

Germany was a political hotbed in 1919. The disaster of the First World War had set the stage for the uprising of the Spartacus League, the subsequent murders of Rosa Luxemburg and Karl Liebknecht, as well as the founding of the Soviet Republic of Bavaria by artists and intellectuals, soon followed by its bloody suppression. All this made for an atmosphere of revolutionary unrest that heightened the fervor of the times.

Leopold Jessner, who Piscator sometimes referred to as his teacher, was appointed head of the Prussian State Theatre. Dada flourished. Piscator organized several Dada events, as the Dadaists attempted "to put their nihilism to political use." In *The Theatre of Erwin Piscator* by John Willett, Willett quotes Piscator: "Dada saw where art without roots was leading, but Dada is not the answer." (Willett 1979: 47)

4

At The Dramatic Workshop, Piscator told the story of one of these Dada events, but I imagine that the details are apocryphal, because they sound almost too good to be true. Shown at a classy theatre with a well-dressed audience, the curtain opened on an empty stage, with large barrels piled high upstage. Then nothing happened. No actors, no music, nothing. After a time the audience grew restive, and began protesting, and shouting and berating the company as frauds, whereupon actors dressed as firemen barged onto the stage, and hosed down the audience with water. The insulted theatre-goers, seeing their wives' fine dresses drenched, rose up in anger and attacked the firemen, whereupon the barrels opened and 25 professional wrestlers emerged, and forced the audience back into their seats. Piscator told this story with gusto; perhaps it was one of those fantasies that artists like to conjure, even if they can't fulfill them, or perhaps something like this really happened. But hearing about it, in 1946, I know that visions of Paradise danced in my head.

In October of 1920 Piscator founded The Proletarian Theatre in Berlin, performing in various halls plays by Kaiser and Gorky and one by Upton Sinclair, in which Piscator appeared among the anonymous performers. Though modest in size and technical capacity, The Proletarian Theatre included such notables as John Heartfield, who projected maps and pho-tomontage onto the scenery, and Lazlo Moboly-Nagy, who worked with symbolic constructions. The Proletarian Theatre produced five plays, includ-ing the brutally titled *How Much Longer, You Whore of Bourgeois Justice?* Six months later the license of The Proletarian Theatre was revoked and it was closed, leaving behind plans for plays by Ivan Goll, as well as a produc-tion of Toller's *Masse-Mensch*, which the Volksbühne presented instead, without Piscator.

In 1924 Piscator created the *Revue Roter Rummel*, called RRR, for the Communist Party (KPD) election campaign of 1924–25. There were 14 scenes which were, according to Willett, "a model for the agit-prop move-ment." Scenes of decadent Berlin night life were interrupted by actors playing workers who came up onto the stage from the audience and proclaimed the Victory of the Proletariat, ending with a rousing chorus of *The Internationale*. The KPD lost the election by 1,000,000 votes.

Piscator, however, had discovered the flexibility of the revue form, whose short scenes could be altered or added to, night by night. In 1925 the KPD asked him for a pageant to open the party conference, for which he created *Trotz Alldem!* (*In Spite of Everything!*), with 24 scenes, numerous historical film sequences, and 200 performers. Only two performances were given, both to packed houses. Piscator wanted more performances but the party said no.

The spirit of experiment was alive everywhere. In Moscow, in 1922, Vsevolod Meyerhold produced the seminal constructivist play *Commelynck*, which launched his theory of biomechanics. In 1923, Meyerhold formed the agit-prop troupe the Blue Blouses, which traversed Russia in a riotously painted train, and taught biomechanical performance techniques to peasants and factory workers.

From 1924 to 1927 Piscator directed the Volksbühne in Berlin, opening with *Fahnen* (*Flags*), about the Chicago anarchists of 1886–87, and which its author, Alfred Paquet, subtitled "an Epic Drama." Piscator used a complicated divided set on a revolving stage with a treadmill street running through it, and images of the characters and documentary material projected on either side of the stage. A narrator spoke the prologue, and a balladeer commented in song. In this way Piscator intended "to connect the stage and the auditorium." He felt that he had succeeded in this. Piscator later wrote that

> The wall dividing stage from audience was swept away; the whole building a meeting hall. The audience drawn onto the stage.

It is strange that he said it so clearly, and described it so precisely, and yet he did not do it. He was speaking metaphorically when he said, "the wall dividing . . . was swept away." He continued to regard the division of the audience's and the actors' areas as sacrosanct. "The audience was drawn onto the stage," he wrote, but no audience members were actually encouraged to set foot on the stage. It was only a beginning.

Between 1924 and 1927 Piscator directed plays for the Volksbühne, each production experimenting with technical and cinematic forms and novel uses of screens and projectors, sometimes mixing or intercutting live actors and their screen images, sometimes playing two or three scenes simultaneously, but always reworking each play to emphasize its moral and political meaning. With *Gewitter über Gottland* (*Storm over Gottland*), which deals with the struggle between Hanseatic capitalists and a communistic league of revolutionaries, the management of the Volksbühne rejected him, saying, "This type of production is incompatible with the Volksbühne's principle of political neutrality." A great public controversy ensued, with hundreds of actors and thousands of Communists trying in vain to vindicate Piscator's position.

But Piscator was already preparing his own theatre, the Piscatorbühne, which he opened in 1927 on Nollendorfplatz in Berlin with Toller's *Hoppla, wir leben!* With *Hoppla*, he began to overturn all the conventions of staging. Its success lay in its fusing of staging innovations and political relevance. Traugott Müller's set was a four-story scaffolding built on a revolving stage. The play considers a cross-section of society, and this was literally rendered by the set. The different acting areas diagrammed the social order, the actors representing social classes.

He followed this success, which ran for two months, with another overwhelmingly technical production, *Rasputin, the Romanovs, the War and the People that Rose Up Against Them*, adapted from Tolstoy by the Dramaturgical Collective of the Piscatorbühne, who added the characters of Lenin, Trotsky and the emperors of Germany and Austria. Müller's set consisted of a huge hemisphere, covered with silver fabric, symbolizing the world, which rotated on a revolving stage. This globe had doors which opened to reveal various settings, from the Tsar's headquarters to Rasputin's room, while documentary films of history and of recent events were projected both onto the globe and onto the backdrop. The ex-Kaiser, Wilhelm, sued Piscator for defamation and the character had to be cut from the play. Piscator had the text of the court order read out instead. For Piscator, this was proof of the relevance and immediacy of the play.

The third important play of the Piscatorbühne was *The Good Soldier Schweik*, adapted from Max Brod by Piscator, Gasbarra and Brecht. A simpler set consisted of two treadmills that allowed Schweik to pursue his endless march to war without moving from the spot. Each treadmill was 17.5 meters long, and weighed 5000 kg. In performance they made a terrible noise and the actors had to shout to be heard over them. But they made it possible for Schweik to travel all around the world while milestones, scenery, and even pursuing armies passed him by. Piscator called on the great political painter and graphic artist George Grosz to create the figures, soldiers, hanged-men and snarling dogs that Schweik encounters. These images were interlaced with cinematic images, of Prague, of war, and of corpses. Piscator added a new ending, a scene in heaven where God is tried for his crimes. A parade of 20 mutilated war victims marches past God. Some of these, it is said, included actual veterans.

The first Piscatorbühne opened in September 1927, and went bankrupt the following June. But oh, what a wealth of historical productions it created! The second Piscatorbühne was also a financial disaster, but managed to produce *The Merchant of Berlin*, a four-hour play about the Jews of Germany, for which Moholy-Nagy built a set of intricate mechanical bridges and platforms that could be raised or lowered, as well as signs, symbols and traffic lights. There was also an overwhelming soundtrack of bells, whistles and the roar of traffic.

When the second Piscatorbühne failed, Piscator formed the Piscator Collective, which created *The Kaiser's Coolies*, a play about an uprising in the navy, with a set representing a cross-section of a battleship anchored in Kiel. It was the fourth of his productions to end with the audience joining the actors in singing *The Internationale*.

The third Piscatorbühne opened with a play developed by the Collective, Crede's *Paragraph 218*, on the theme of abortion. The performance included the appearance of a real-life doctor or hospital administrator, making a speech about the subject. The audience was asked to vote, by a show of hands, on the abolition of the statute. It was the first time, wrote a reviewer of the production, "that the end of a play turned into a public meeting." If so, it is indeed a milestone.

The last production of the Piscatorbühne was Fredrich Wolf's *Tai Yang Awakens*. It was written as a counter-play to Klabund's *Circle of Chalk*, which Wolf found "over-sweet"; in his early drafts Wolf had even called his heroine "Hi Tang," as Klabund had called her. Tai Yang is a textile worker who organizes her fellow-workers to strike. The play was done without the elaborate scenery of Piscator's recent productions. The play begins with the entrance of the actors from the street, talking about politics and then putting on their costumes and make-up onstage. At the end, one of the actors, in street clothes, explains the relevance of the play to the situation of Germany in 1931. Ten years later Piscator directed Klabund's *Circle of Chalk* in English at The Dramatic Workshop where, in 1945, I played the role of a Teahouse Girl.

After *Tai Yang Awakens* and the collapse of the third Piscatorbühne, Piscator did not direct another play until he came to the United States in 1941, though he was never inactive during that time, exploring other outlets for his art.

In 1931 the situation in Germany was worsening every day. Piscator had already been briefly arrested on tax charges at the beginning of the year.

Fredrich Wolf was arrested for breach of the abortion laws, and the police banned agit-prop performances.

Dozens of German theatre workers went to Russia at this time, attracted by socialist ideals. Piscator was invited to Moscow to direct a film based on Anna Seghers' novel *The Revolt of the Fishermen of Santa Barbara*. Willett describes it as the story of "a lone agitator's arrival in a semi-mythical fishing village, and his desperate, almost fatalistic leadership of a broken strike." Originally the plan was for two versions to be produced, one in German, with Lotte Lenya, and the other in Russian. But although they actually imported a cast from Germany, after several months of delays, the German version was abandoned.

The film took two years to complete. It was beset by numerous difficulties. According to Maria Ley-Piscator, because of a dearth of nails to complete the construction of the set, Piscator feared further delays in the shooting. So he himself went out and brought back the needed nails to finish the work. However, he was accused of buying them on the black market, which was considered a serious economic crime. I doubt that Maria was right in saying, "That's why he was thrown out of Russia," but in her old age, that's how she chose to remember it.

Piscator was not "thrown out" of the Soviet Union just as his film opened on October 5, 1934. Rather, he became an active member of The Revolutionary Writers Union (MORT) and was elected its president in 1935. Bernhard Reich wrote in *Im Wettlauf mit der Zeit* that "Unfortunately Piscator used all his energy and imagination to set up the organization and get it running, with the result that as an artist he stagnated." (Reich 1970)

Willett points out that by the time *The Fishermen* opened, the German market was closed to it, and the Russian audience was tiring of revolutionary films with their emphasis on "the fate of the masses." In "Basic Principles of a Theory of Sociological Drama", Piscator wrote: "It is no longer the private, personal fate of the individual, but the times and the fate of the masses that are the heroic factors in the new drama." (Piscator 1929, reprinted in translation in Drain 1995)

Piscator wasn't satisfied with the film, but already had plans for half a dozen others. He wanted to work on a Schweik film with Brecht, though that plan, like his plan to film *War and Peace*, eventually fell through.

Piscator never directed another film, nor did he ever direct a play in the Soviet Union.

Piscator was never without grandiose ambitions, and even as the cultural scene in the Soviet Union began to harden and move from its creative phase into its dictatorial phase, he was at work on great plans. He wanted to create a German-language experimental theatre in the city of Engels, in the German-speaking Volga Republic, using all the best anti-Nazi talents – Granach, Neher and Helene Weigel among them. Piscator also lured 20 young German actors to Engels, then sent them to the Maly Theatre in Moscow for two months of study. But when he heard them two months later, he fired the lot of them. The project was further delayed by contract problems, by housing problems, by malaria . . .

Piscator left Russia in July for a trip to Paris, expecting to return in the autumn. On October 3rd, Bernhard Reich telegraphed him a two-word warning: *Don't Return* (*Nicht Abreisen*). MORT, the author's union, had been dissolved, Granach was arrested in Kiev and Carola Neher had also been arrested, later to die in a prison camp. The purges were just beginning.

Piscator never returned to Russia. As for the Volga Republic, it was dissolved and the entire German population was deported during the Second World War.

For almost three years, Piscator lived in Paris without directing any plays. He began work on an adaptation of Tolstoy's *War and Peace*, though it was never produced there. He made dozens of plans and schemes for productions, films and touring companies, including an attempt to persuade Max Reinhardt to work on a grand peace festival at Versailles. For this he went to visit Reinhardt in Salzburg where he met Maria Ley, an Austrian dancer who was working on the choreography for Reinhardt's *Midsummer Night's Dream*. On April 17th, 1937, they married.

The actor Leonard Steckel wrote of this period of Piscator's life that "Piscator has wasted some of his best years by not having the modesty and the guts to start from scratch, but wanting to work on a lavish scale right away" (Willett 1979: 194). He considered Denmark, where the Brechts had gone, and even Germany, where to Piscator's horror, Gordon Craig told him he would be well-received by Goebbels. He considered Barcelona, which was ready to welcome him. He outlined plans for Mexico, Stockholm and Copenhagen.

In the end it was Gilbert Miller's promise of a Broadway production of *War and Peace* that convinced the Piscators to come to New York. Helen Hayes and Paul Muni were considering the lead roles, and Miller wanted Laurence Olivier for Prince Andrei. The Piscators sailed for New

York on Christmas Eve and arrived on New Year's Day, 1939. They arrived in a fanfare of publicity, and settled into the Hotel Pierre, one of the city's most elegant and most expensive, for which Piscator was bitterly criticized by the communists in Europe and their fellow travelers in the United States.

Piscator was counting on Gilbert Miller's promise of a production of *War and Peace*. Since Gilbert Miller was one of Broadway's most successful producers, Piscator and Maria Ley had high hopes. But then Miller rejected the project, saying that the script was inadequate. A long struggle began then, to rewrite, to find collaborators and to find another producer.

The whole weight of Broadway, with its relentlessly conventional standards and its commitment to popular success, confronted Piscator. His motives were entirely different, as were his standards. Only years later at his Studio Theatre at The New School could he produce his *War and Peace*. He never really found his own theatre in New York. He never directed a major commercial play, though there were several feeble efforts in that direction. He never partook of the fleshpots of Broadway. Not that he didn't try.

The Founding of The Dramatic Workshop, 1940

Thwarted by Broadway, Piscator founded The Dramatic Workshop at The New School for Social Research. When The New School itself was founded in 1933, it was created to be an academic haven for the many scholars who were forced to leave Europe because of the grip of fascism. It was in fact known as "The University in Exile."

When, six years later, Dr. Alvin Johnson opened the doors of The New School to a theatre department, Piscator at first resisted. He wanted to direct his plays. He had never wanted to be a teacher. And though he had a great gift for transmitting ideas, and taught his classes and seminars with evident passion, teaching was always for him what he later called "an interim achievement." Yet he was persuaded, and in January 1940 he opened The Dramatic Workshop.

Piscator's Workshop was animated by the vision that possessed him all his life, since that day in the trenches of Ypres where he found his calling. Maria Piscator quotes him on the opening of the Workshop:

"Not art," said Piscator, "but life. From its very beginning here at the Workshop, let it be life! The here and now. Art is man's ambition to create beyond reality. What is needed now is reality. Reality, the Sphinx of all Sphinxes, the riddle of all riddles. But every new beginning . . . is it not a riddle?"

(Ley-Piscator 1967: 105)

The Studio Theatre

Piscator needed a theatre in which to work and he needed to work with the best, that is, with experienced actors, and so nine months later, The Studio Theatre was created within the context of The Dramatic Workshop. The plan was to create a repertory theatre, casting older, professional actors in the leading roles, with the Workshop students in the supporting roles, as well as running lights and props and building sets. It was a perfect plan allowing the students to work with experienced actors while continuing their classwork and technical education. At The Studio Theatre, Piscator produced some of the most significant work of his American exile: *King Lear* with Sam Jaffe, Klabund's *Circle of Chalk* with Dolly Haas, *Nathan the Wise* with Herbert Berghof, and finally, the long-awaited *War and Peace*.

But the power of the Broadway establishment is not easily overcome. The modest success of The Studio Theatre attracted the attention of the unions. At first only Actors' Equity insisted that the union actors be paid Equity scale. Piscator raised the money to pay them. But then, the technicians' unions demanded that the work on lights and props and costumes, which the students were doing as part of their training, would have to be unionized.

This is not economically possible in a small theatre, as the thorny history of the Off-Broadway theatre movement demonstrates.

Piscator's Studio Theatre was in this way, as in many other respects, a forerunner of, as well as an inspiration to, the whole Off-Broadway movement. Off-Broadway was never an effort to produce Broadway plays more cheaply, but rather an attempt to create a whole other kind of theatre that Broadway never wanted any part of and had openly rejected. The Studio Theatre set the standard for experimental theatrical forms in the context of the highest art. And it still serves us as an example of freedom from the high costs of theatrical production, through the inventiveness of the artist to create great effects without great budgets.

Since the closing of The Studio Theatre in 1944, the Off-Broadway theatres have put up a valiant struggle to convince the unions to allow Off-Broadway to survive; that is, to allow experimental theatre, art theatre, and political theatre to survive by creating contracts that make small, non-institutional theatres fiscally possible. Progress has been made, but there is still much to do. Piscator's Studio Theatre showed us the way.

The Teachers at Piscator's School

Piscator was able to assemble a fine roster of teachers! It is no coincidence that theatre training in America from the 1960's through to the new millennium has been dominated by three gifted teachers who taught at The Dramatic Workshop: Herbert Berghof, Stella Adler and Lee Strasberg. Each later opened their own school, and between them they have shaped the craft of a whole generation of actors.

Margrit Wyler

Margrit Wyler, a ravishingly handsome and insightful actress, had been a leading lady in Vienna at the Deutsches Volkstheater and at the Schauspielhaus in Zurich. Her course was intended to teach us scene-work from texts, and this she did with patience and skill, but above all she taught us to humanize our characterizations and our approach to a role, and to appreciate the dignity of our place in the world and the theatre. What did I learn from Margrit Wyler? That in the male-dominated theatre there are only two roles for women: the Mother and the Whore. Most actresses play either one or the other all their lives, but Wyler taught her students that *we* can play either, because like every woman we have both within ourselves.

Raikin Ben-Ari

Raikin Ben-Ari was a great acting teacher who had worked with Stanislavsky and later with Vakhtangov, Meyerhold and Reinhardt. He was the author of a prize-winning book on the Habima. He taught us improvisation and the exercises of Stanislavsky, and elements of Vakhtangov's magic realism. He taught us the high value of practical experience in our acting. What did I learn from Raikin Ben-Ari? That the stage is not a mirror but a magnifying glass, and that I could overcome my Jewish inhibition about making the sign of the cross on stage because, as an actor, "there is no facet of human nature alien to myself."

Chouteau Dyer

Chouteau Dyer was at first a student of Piscator's and later became his assistant and assistant director. Chouteau was one of those brilliant minds that geniuses like Piscator need around them. A gifted director and an amazing person, I learned from her the substance of the director's work, of which Piscator taught the spirit and the meaning. I remember her sitting in the little Italian restaurant across the street from the theatre where the students hung out, a production schedule spread out in front of her, surrounded by students, moving her pencil over the lists and calendars, assigning the work for *Twelfth Night* with alacrity. She knew each scene. She knew who and what was needed where. She understood the play in terms of its most concrete manifestations. She understood the idea, the *director's idea* in terms of props, backstage placements, and cues.

A flood of comprehension swept over me. I wanted to do *that*! To have the whole play in my consciousness, to be aware of the profoundest interpretation in terms of the smallest prop . . . Chouteau pointed at each of us. She pointed at me and said, "Props . . . Malina, you'll be at the backstage left prop table." I wanted to do that. I wanted to be a director. What did I learn from Chouteau Dyer? That I wanted to be a director.

Leo Kerz

Leo Kerz was a graduate of Piscator's Academy in Berlin. Before coming to America he had an outstanding career as a set designer for the Royal Academy in Amsterdam and with The Joos Ballet in The Hague. At the Workshop he designed the remarkable shadow-play *Twelfth Night* set, with projections reflecting the play's playful mysticism. He later designed several Broadway plays, most notably Ionesco's *Rhinoceros*, and in the 60's, Piscator's production of Hochhuth's *The Deputy* in Berlin. At the Workshop he taught Stage Make-up, Costume and Set Design. He was reserved with us, as if he didn't really want to teach, because he felt his place was as a designer. He was a thinker and imbued the practice of stagecraft with ideas. What did I learn from Leo Kerz? That in modern theatre the setting is as important as the text and the actor. And that black is a color never to be used in theatrical make-up.

He married Louise Kerz, who curated his works after his death, and who later in life became the wife of Al Hirschfeld, the quintessential theatre caricaturist. In the last years of Maria Ley-Piscator's life, Louise remained her close friend during trying times, and was present at Madame Piscator's 100th birthday celebration.

Paul Zucker

Paul Zucker was a brilliant analyst of art and sociology. He had taught in Berlin and later at The Cooper Union, and was the author of many scholarly books, among them *Space and Architecture in Painting of the Florentine Quattrocento*, *Stage Decoration During the Classical Period* and *The Development of the City*. He taught with gusto and rare energy two courses in which he presented us with a well-developed philosophy of art. He expected that we could comprehend his nuanced account of the development of the three kingdoms of Egyptian art, or the qualities that differentiate the Baroque from the Rococo. Dr. Zucker taught Styles Through the Ages, a comprehensive history of Western art, illustrated with hundreds of slides, in each of which he found the key to some step in the development of theatre. He also led a remarkable course called History and Sociology of the Theatre, with charts and diagrams to explain the relationships between audiences, performers and the state of the world. What did I learn from Paul Zucker? That no one can influence their culture as much as their culture has influenced them.

Gloria Montemuro

Gloria Montemuro taught voice and speech at the Workshop. She was the source of much distress for me, as my school notes amply illustrate. With the moderation of retrospect, I realize that my resistance to her exercises was foolish and infantile. On the other hand, what I was resisting was the standardization of speech, a kind of theatrical vocal quality that I do reject. Of course, I should have learned first and rejected later what I did not want to use. Years later, under the name of Gloria Monty, she became successful as the director of the television series *General Hospital*. What did I learn from Gloria Montemuro? That the breath comes from the diaphragm and that I must learn to control it.

Alexander Ince

Alexander Ince taught a course called Current Broadway Plays. In Europe he had produced American plays like *Abie's Irish Rose* and *The Trial of Mary Dugan* and published several stage magazines. In America he worked for Paramount and MGM and Gilbert Miller. Piscator often pointed out that he was important for us, because those of us who rejected the Broadway theatre had better know something about it. During his teaching years at the Workshop he produced several Broadway plays, none of which were successful. What did I learn from Alexander Ince? That though theatre is a great art, it's a rotten business.

Hans Sondheimer

Hans Sondheimer taught us Stagecraft. At the Bavarian State Theatre in Munich he had worked as an assistant to Adolf Linnebach, the lighting genius, whose projection boxes still bear his name. In the United States he lit Robert Edmond Jones' set for *The Passion of St. Matthew* at the Metropolitan Opera. At The Dramatic Workshop he lit *Nathan the Wise*, *Winter Soldiers*, and *War and Peace*. He was The Dramatic Workshop's technical director and he taught me how to use a jigsaw. What else did I learn from Hans Sondheimer? How to drive a three-penny nail through a half-inch plank in three strokes.

Henry Wendriner

There were two significant staff members who complemented the teaching staff, both of them fervent admirers of Piscator's work – Eleanor Fitzgerald (see Part 3) and Henry Wendriner. Wendriner was a mainstay of Piscator's staff, and his was the fiscal and administrative burden. Piscator was in financial difficulties all his life, always in debt, always on the brink of economic disaster. Nevertheless he had often been given important theatres to work in, except in the United States, where he could find no support for the Total Theatre plan that he and Walter Gropius designed, and where he settled for the "interim achievement" of The Dramatic Workshop.

There it was Henry Wendriner's job to shield Piscator from all problems of money, but Piscator's needs were always grandiose. The Epic Theatre requires a big stage and costly stage machinery. The New School was limited in its stage space, but Henry Wendriner eked every possible budget advantage out of them, including running up debts which they had to shoulder for years after The Dramatic Workshop was no longer located there. Years later when I taught classes on Piscator at The New School, I still heard complaints from the associate dean, Lewis Falb, about the debts that Piscator, through Wendriner, had piled up. Wendriner also taught a class called Theatre Management from which I profited much. He covered everything from the cost of paper towels to the secret of distributing the sale of seats in such a way that an audience of ten looks like a half-full house.

Wendriner, a short, stocky, amiable bald man, was enamored of all the actresses in the school. He asked me to translate some of the romantic and erotic poems that he wrote in praise of Priscilla Draghi, who was playing Hi Tang in *The Circle of Chalk*, and Elaine Stritch, who was playing Feste in *Twelfth Night*, all the while pursuing me, among several others. Bea Arthur, some 60 years later, recalled Wendriner's harassment as the one dark spot in the Paradise of her student years. I took it lightly, and laughed when I rejected him, and he asked me if it was because I loved another.

"I love Mr. Piscator," I answered impertinently. "Ach, ja!" he exclaimed. "We are all supposed to be in love with Mr. Piscator!" And so it was. Piscator was our idol.

The Students

George Bartenieff

"He couldn't suffer fools, not even for one second," says George Bartenieff, recalling both Piscator's high standards and his impatience with those who could not meet them. Bartenieff is one of the most noteworthy alumni of The Dramatic Workshop.

In 1945 Maria Ley-Piscator quickly recognized young Bartenieff's abilities and cast him in the title roles of two plays in her Junior Dramatic Workshop: *Pinocchio*, in which he played the puppet-boy with an innocence and immediacy of presence that he never lost (I played the wicked Cat) and *The Prince Who Learned Everything out of Books*, a fable in which George again challenged the decadent intellectual establishment with his incorruptible child's purity. I played the Ugly Sister, and fellow student Bernie Schwartz (Tony Curtis) played the Dionysian tempter, a reflection of Piscator's first role in Strindberg's *Spook Sonata*, with its theme of the rejection of the old corruption by idealistic youth. The young Bartenieff grasped Piscator's meaning.

The son of dancers and performers, George was brought up in an artistic milieu, and he recalls that his father wanted him to take Diaghilev as his artistic role-model. Though he was born too late to have seen him, from the tales his father told him, and from photographs, he became and remains his idol. When I spoke to him recently, he said, "That was how I came to seek such a high level of imagination, and found it in Piscator. I remember his production of *All the King's Men* . . . When I saw the set! A tower atop which Huey Long sat at a desk with a telephone, dominating everything and everyone. That set was as organic as the body of the actor; it projected visually, architecturally, and theatrically, the core of the play's meaning."

In the 1960's Bartenieff worked with The Living Theatre. In *The Brig* he gave an unforgettable performance as the most vulnerable of the prisoners, eventually driven to breakdown by a bullying guard. Years later, in Karen Malpede's delicate *Us*, he played husband and father with electrifying insight.

In 1970 he founded, together with Crystal Field, the Theater for the New City, a bulwark of the Off-Broadway movement, eventually providing five venues (in one building) for a wide range of experimental work, as well as initiating an annual Street Theatre Festival to speak to and for the community. In the years when The Living Theatre had no space of its own in New York, Theater for the New City presented The Living Theatre's productions of Michael McClure's *VKTMS*, Malpede's *Us*, a revival of the 1964 collective creation *Mysteries and Smaller Pieces*, and three plays by Hanon Reznikov: *The Rules of Civility and Decent Behavior in Company and in Conversation*, *Capital Changes*, and *Anarchia*.

Today, under Crystal Field's direction, the TNC continues to be an important landmark of avant-garde theatre. Piscator would be proud to see his work taking root in this way.

Bartenieff has joined with Malpede, a writer whose anti-war activism has often ennobled her work, to create a series of important works of political theatre – most notably, his internationally-acclaimed portrayal of Victor Klemperer, who kept a sensitive and politically-aware diary throughout his struggle for survival during the Nazi years.

Piscator didn't fail to point out that the great actors of his time, like Olivier, had always used the techniques that he described as Objective Acting. And I know of no better example of it than Bartenieff's exquisite narrative style in the Klemperer play *I Will Bear Witness*. His attention to the audience's presence was as great a piece of Objective Acting as our Stanislavsky-drenched time allows.

I asked Bartenieff how Piscator had treated him personally: "Well, I was just a child, so he treated me . . . well, you know . . . more like a dog."

And yet, when he considers Piscator's place in the history of modern theatre, he does not hesitate to say, "He is one of the heroes of the avant-garde. He is the father of everything we do in the theatre today. It is he who has inspired the modern, political use of street theatre. He created a style that was organic."

Anna Berger

Anna Berger is one of the most persistently creative actors to come out of The Dramatic Workshop. She came to the Workshop as I did, on a scholarship, and like me, both adored and came into conflict with our beloved teacher. As a youngster, she did a show which a wealthy theatre-lover saw, and he offered her a scholarship to any school at the theatre of her choosing. She chose the Neighborhood Playhouse, but the director there scorned her. "Do you realize how many really beautiful girls walk through that door every day?" he asked her.

She returned home in tears, but her mother insisted that she not be so brusquely discouraged. Someone suggested Piscator's school. Piscator said she must audition, and she said she didn't have anything prepared, but that there was a cockroach dance that she could perform. So she danced her cockroach dance for him and at the end he asked, "Is this theatre?" "Yes," she replied, "it is." And he smiled and said, "Yes, it is!" She shared many classes with me, and we performed together in *The Aristocrats* and other March of Drama plays.

When she graduated from the Workshop she worked with On-Stage and The Interplayers at the Cherry Lane Theatre – two companies formed by Workshop students that performed Lorca and Sartre and Auden and Isherwood's *The Dog Beneath the Skin* – even before she made an admirable career for herself on Broadway and in Hollywood.

I asked her recently what Piscator meant to her. We met in March 2004 in the Westside Diner in Hell's Kitchen in New York. She had just finished a rehearsal of her one-woman show *Absolutely Anna* at The Actor's Studio.

"He was my God!" she exclaimed. "But what did you learn from him?" Her brilliant comedienne's eyes twinkled mischievously: "That 'Go-eeth' is pronounced 'Goer-ter'." But then she grew serious:

> Piscator had a vision of what the theatre should be. He taught us to be brave, to be daring. "Go out and change the face of life," he said. "Do plays that excite and stimulate and that improve the world."

I find it significant that the politically-aware young artists working with Piscator in New York did not feel his potent political influence. I believe it was part of the strategy of the Cold War to blur the boundaries between the "subversive" (as in, "un-American activities") and the progressive, which the Roosevelt administration once represented. Erwin Piscator was canny and wise enough to escape from the American witch-hunt, as well as the Nazis and the Stalinists. But what it cost him was this: the clear comprehension of the nature of his political commitment by his best students. Perhaps it was a wise choice on his part; he had witnessed the massacres of German artists by the Nazis, and was horrified by the murder of Meyerhold in 1940, in a Moscow prison. He had good reason to be cautious. At the Workshop he certainly never referred to himself as a "communist," but always as an "anti-fascist."

Though Berger modestly claims not to understand what Piscator meant by Epic Theatre and asked me, in fact, to write down a "precise definition" of it for her, everything she says and does reveals a deeper understanding of the idea than such a definition can render.

Sylvia Miles

Sylvia Miles is a unique performer on the modern stage and screen, inventor of a personal and bold style that has made her a diva.

She says of Piscator that "Having this Prussian teacher was the best thing that ever happened to me. He was philosophically important to me because he was a true artist. The discipline that he instilled in me became part and parcel of my bones."

Miles' creation of a dazzling persona, so unlike any other, draws its strength from this early experience.

Coming to Piscator on the recommendation of a friend, she was "Stupified with awe" as soon as she confronted him. As we all were.

She likes to imitate his accented language when she tells the story of her audition:

> "So, you have done some theatre?"
> "Yes . . ."
> "So . . . and what plays have you done?"
> "*Hamlet.*"
> "Aha! And what role did you play in *Hamlet*?"
> "Hamlet."
> "And where did you play this *Hamlet*?"
> "In Washington Irving High School."
> "Ah so! Vell, let us hear . . ."

And in a voice that is inimitable, though myriad performers have tried to imitate it, she cried out: "O, that this too too solid flesh would melt/ Thaw, and resolve itself into a dew . . ."

"Ja, ja!" cried Piscator, interrupting her, "You can do it."

She recalls that she was given many understudy roles at the Workshop, but that she always remained an obedient and willing student. "When I was told to understudy, I always learned the roles even though I only sometimes got to play them. When I was told to do props I did props."

"Piscator," she says, "taught me 'result direction'." Which, she claims, has helped her in working with many diverse directors in her long and successful career. I wasn't familiar with the term and asked her what "result direction" was:

It means he didn't speak psychologically, and he didn't speak of motivation. He told me what he wanted – and then sometimes he showed me exactly what he wanted – and I did exactly that. He meant for the actor to find her own justification.

Piscator believed that the role of the director should not be to "teach acting" to the performer during rehearsals, but rather to convey to the actor his deeper understanding of the play, the scenes, the character, and the important "director's idea" of the meaning of the play.

The critic may disparage Piscator's refusal to play psychologist to the actor during rehearsals as a lack of attention to the actor's craft. But the actor could feel it as a mark of respect that her analysis, her comprehension of the character, and her justification, even though they may have derived from the director's "result direction," remained her own valuable contribution to the work.

Like many of Piscator's Workshop students Miles was not really aware of his politics.

I never knew he was a communist – or was he a socialist? – until long after I graduated. I mean, he never spoke about it. I didn't even realize that he was a Christian. You see I thought of him as a refugee, and so I imagined he was Jewish . . .

Even the students who were politically aware were hardly able to imagine the caution with which someone who had so narrowly escaped the murderous repression of the fascists, was inhibited from free expression, in a potentially hostile environment in which the coming of McCarthy and HUAC loomed.

Marlon Brando

Though few now remember Piscator's work, he imbued his students with a sense of social responsibility, even when they were not fully aware of his politics, nor of the nature of his commitment.

When I recently spoke to former students such as Sylvia, Anna and George, nearly 40 years after his death, none of them realized that he was a communist. Nor that though he hid his true feelings, out of justifiable fear, he never deviated from the profound social commitment which he found in the early ideals of communism, before the abuses of power set in.

One of those that I did not reach was Piscator's most illustrious pupil, Marlon Brando, who Piscator had expelled from the Workshop just before I got there.

Peter Manso's book *Brando: The Biography* devotes 22 pages to Brando at The Dramatic Workshop. Manso gives us a curious, insightful view of The Dramatic Workshop in the season before my arrival. He seems more concerned with Brando's sexual escapades than with his studies or his development as an actor. He shows us Piscator's school on a cruder level than Piscator would ever have wished, and even now I hesitate to bring up the full, lively vulgarity of it. Manso quotes Walter Matthau, one of the more erudite of the Workshop's famous alumni, as mocking it as "The Neurotic Workshop of Sexual Research" where "people want to become actors because they want to get fucked from here to China." I must add that I did not find this to be so; that with the exception of Wendriner's notorious and much derided skirt-chasing, I found only a normal, quite wholesome adolescent sexuality among my classmates. But of course, that was the season *after* Marlon was expelled.

Brando was a rebellious youth, happy to thwart his teachers, or anyone who impinged on the free expression of his childish impulses. And he did more than thwart them, not only with his impish ways, but with the extraordinary force of his talent as an actor. Though Brando and his fellow musketeers (the other two were Darren Dublin and Carlo Fiori) were surely "in pursuit of the girls," as soon as he did his first March of Drama performances everyone was in awe of his easy grace and his depth.

His success at the Workshop was most striking in the dual role of the Teacher and Jesus in Hauptmann's *Hannele's Way to Heaven*. One of the students, Mae Cooper, remembers the general astonishment: "It was like the dawn of something great. It was like, suddenly you woke up and your idiot child was playing Mozart."

It was Stella Adler who singled him out and worked hard with him. But as Manso reports, "From the beginning there was a rivalry between Stella Adler and Erwin Piscator. A fundamental philosophical difference arose as well. What Adler was looking for among her young actors, were observers, sympathetic students of human behavior, while Piscator saw actors as the servants of their director, and the director himself at the beck and call of the playwright."

I don't agree with Manso's characterization of Piscator's intentions, but the description of the rivalry seems accurate. Manso continues: "Adler was, in fact, running her own institution within The Dramatic Workshop – an isolated acting class" – as indeed Piscator put it indignantly, in the course of one of their fights. Many of the students were torn. There was Stella, teaching downstairs in the basement, screaming, "Don't act! Stop acting!" at the slightest sign of theatricality. While Piscator was upstairs on the main stage, shouting, "Be big! Bigger!" when someone failed to project.

What Marlon Brando absorbed from Piscator's classes was a sense of the responsibility of theatre work, and throughout his career he chose to make films about the social ethic.

In the archives of the Akademie der Künste, among Piscator's papers, is a scrawled note in Piscator's hand, "I will write to Brando," and the following draft:

My dear Marlon,

I know you are capable of anything you want to do and I have seen many students but very few so gifted . . . I'm not afraid you will rebuke me, as you childishly did all the time . . . You may do so, but I write this as the man who recognizes that you can play every classical hero and villain from Romeo to Hamlet to Richard III to Mephistopheles. As much as I admire your early success, I am afraid of it. You told me that you learned nothing at The Dramatic Workshop and I was crushed. But I want to address the real artist in you – that one is with me.

In his great personification of the Godfather, and that film's focus on the tragic visitation of the sins of fathers upon the lives of their sons, one is reminded again of Piscator's early production of Strindberg's *Spook Sonata*, in which the ghosts attempt to corrupt the youth. For every artist there are certain basic themes to which he returns again and again. In Strindberg's play the youth resists the temptation, whereas in *The Godfather*, politically a more pessimistic work, the son (Al Pacino), who has tried to resist the corruption, is drawn into it in an orgy of bloodshed.

In *Last Tango in Paris*, Brando portrayed the power games that underlie sexual relations, drawing on the understanding of power relations he learned from Piscator.

In the astonishing *Apocalypse Now*, the heart of darkness extends the corruption to war. The young hero, played by Martin Sheen (who, during the picture's shoot, organized the Filipino workers on the set in their demands for better treatment), violently encounters this corruption in the person of Brando, who, with all his bravura ("Bigger! Bigger!" cried E.P.), shows us the raw face of wickedness.

Brando's lifelong struggle on behalf of the rights of American Indians was part of his defiance of authority as a student, which resolved itself in a lifetime of making movies that challenge and defy the social order.

Bea Arthur

Bea Arthur, famous for her acerbic portrayal of Dorothy Zbornak on television's long-running *Golden Girls*, smiled and shook her head when she spoke of Piscator. I visited her in Los Angeles in April 2006, as *The Golden Girls* continued to appear daily in syndicated reruns. She sat by her pool and vividly remembered her days at The Dramatic Workshop.

"When I first got there I couldn't act my way out of a paper bag, but Piscator was impressed by my tallness. He cast me in those classical roles because I was so tall." She has always thought of her commanding stature as a flaw, a disadvantage. I assured her that it was because Piscator recognized her obvious talent and her unique character that he cast her in "those classical roles." "No," she said, "Piscator tore into me. 'You are too grand,' he said, 'too dominant, too forceful'."

He scolded her. But really this is why Piscator cast a young and inexperienced actress in *The Flies* in the role of Clytemnestra, replacing the venerable Frances Adler: because he saw that she was "grand, dominant and forceful." Piscator was a man of contradictions, scolding her for what he also admired in her. Or was that part of his didactic method?

At the Workshop I had thought that Bea would become the great classical actress of our time, the Duse who would play Medea, Jocasta, Electra and Lady Macbeth, but she chose a different path. She chose comedy as her preferred form. "I'll tell you how it happened," she said to me. "I was playing Lucy in *Threepenny Opera*. One night when I thought I was doing a miserable job, suddenly I spoke a line and I heard a laugh in the audience. It was so elating that I knew then and there that this was what I wanted to do. To get that laugh, to get that direct response from the audience."

This awareness of the audience, this need for the audience, is it not that to which Piscator wanted the Objective Actor to commit? Perhaps the audible laughter of the audience makes it easier in comedy. When playing tragedy, my mother said she counted the handkerchiefs.

Having chosen comedy as her preferred form, Bea chose television as her medium. As the housewife Maude, or as the substitute teacher, Dorothy, in each episode she treats with wit and keen political insight some of the most important social issues of our time: racism, abortion and drugs, for instance as when Maude outrages her black cleaning woman by trying to buy marijuana from her. And in all of the episodes of *The Golden Girls* the ageism of a culture that despises old women is shown to be a phenomenon that can be resisted.

She had many affectionate memories of our fellow students – of the mischievous cleverness of Walter Matthau, the impish charm of Bernie Schwartz (later, Tony Curtis), the trenchant presence of Rod Steiger; of how Arla Gild could make you laugh and cry at the same time, or how Al Armstrong amused her, or how Harry Belafonte boasted of his sexual conquests at the Footlight Pizzeria across the street.

She raised her arms as if to express the expansive spirit of that time. "I never felt any restraint. Everything was always so poetical and so political, because at bottom there was always the meaning of the play, and the joy of it . . ."

But among these exuberant memories she recalled with horror Wendriner's sexual pursuit of her. I told her that she took him too seriously. He was just a frustrated older man who enjoyed chasing after young women who rejected him. But there she was, a woman near 80, still disturbed by a sexual harassment that took place 60 years ago. That this, too, was political was probably not evident to Piscator. He knew about it. We all knew about it. But it didn't seem important because we didn't yet know it was political.

Howard Friedman

Howard Friedman is a philosopher. He was the most assiduous of my fellow students and was my very special friend. He came to Piscator because he was in search of excellence. Not for his theatre, but for his genius. Like Piscator, Howard Friedman was a classicist, in that they both understood the necessity of using the historical foundations of art and science as the *materia prima* of the avant-garde. Both knew that the new work must be built upon the rules of the old. Howard taught me the fundamental principles of higher mathematics and showed me that the arts and sciences are linked in a deeper way than I ever suspected. Howard is today the Executive Director of IPPNO: International Philosophers for Peace. Piscator would be proud of this student.

I recently asked Howard about his perspective on Piscator's work and here is what he wrote:

Piscator was one of the outstanding luminaries of western theatre. The productions he conceived and directed were unflagging in their suspense, power and originality. Combining the terse theatricality of the work of Orson Welles with the visual intensity of a film by Eisenstein, his work surged with a flow of prodigious, pulsing energy.

Like a Beethoven of the stage, Piscator broke the customary bonds of his medium. Particularly striking was his use of unconventional lighting (with back-lit images projected on screens that were part of the set), rotating stages which became part of the action, and a blurring of the distinction between actor and audience. These were the obvious hallmark features of a typical Piscator staging.

But in considering the range of theatrical styles and subject matter embodied in his productions, I became aware that they also shared a far less obvious feature: somehow Piscator had put his own stamp also upon the manner in which his actors spoke, moved and interacted with each other. The characters they played and the world they inhabited had become Piscator's.

But no description of his work can overlook his views concerning the purpose of theatre. It was Marx who said that philosophers in the past had interpreted the world but the point now is to change it – and I believe that Piscator took Marx's statement as a fundamental precept, applicable not only to philosophers but to his own work in theatre. Thus the role of a director should no longer be merely to provide a credible chunk of life for the audience to view, rather theatre must also change the audience's view of the world – and in so doing initiate a change for a better one. For Piscator, this meant to use the full resources of theatre to instill a vision in his audience of a world free of the savage economic and social dissonances all too present then and now.

This may sound inspiring but perhaps also dreadfully pedantic. Yet Piscator's art was to avoid the customary rhetoric of the revolution and to present instead a world in which deep questions arise that can only be answered by rejecting that world. For instance, in his production of Eugene O'Neill's *Mourning Becomes Electra*, we inevitably become involved with the enormous sorrow of Electra and we ask ourselves the question, "Why should she suffer so much?" The text of the play itself provides no satisfactory reply. But Piscator's productions do offer hints of an answer which, when we reflect upon the subject, suddenly becomes clear as the midday sun. An Electra suffers specifically because she is a member of an elite class in a world order that is fundamentally unjust and which – for its success – systematically treats others inhumanely! Thus the successful ways of a corrupt society make living in such a society itself the source of inescapable sorrow. In this way, Piscator takes the text of a traditional middle-class play and uses it to pose the dilemma: "Suffer or change the world order." So by indirection, he points out the answer: "Change the world order!"

This is indeed an unusual form of theatre. For this conclusion comes to the spectator only well after the performance is over. But should we not expect the unusual in the work of a genius?

Piscator's Students

Beyond the academic air that flowed through Joseph Urban's building and the scholarship that flourished there, there was the student body, and it had a life of its own. Even as we attended the lectures of W.H. Auden, and Hannah Arendt and Karen Horney – since our being part of the larger institution gave us the privilege of attending all the major lecture series – we were somehow schoolchildren too, and an energy flowed though us, that led us to form natural affinity groups. The circle of friends I belonged to was small and eclectic. We thought ourselves the be-all and the end-all, the best and the blest . . .

"Let us all don togas and tunics and eschew the ugly fashions of our time!" cried Ben Moore, a blond beauty who was already, in 1946, working in experimental films with his mentor, the poet Willard Maas. And Brandt Kingsley, an outrageous actor, a star of our inner circle, responded, "And we'll go barefoot when it's warm, and wear huge capes when it's cold!"

28

"And we'll dance in the streets!" called out Lola Ross. We felt ourselves capable of changing the world. But of course, we never did wear the classical costumes, though I did affect a cape for a time, but it was only one of hundreds of fantasies we shared of something inexplicable, something new that we felt was on its way – and we were its harbingers.

We should have been more attentive to Piscator, for he talked of this over and over, but we were young and wanted to make our own revolution, and not the historical revolution of which Piscator spoke. We began brewing the fervor of the 60's right there, behind the striped metal doors of the 12th Street building, with Piscator there to guide the movement he had spawned along the wild path of revolution.

Just as Piscator never carried out his vision of a truly participatory audience, we were not yet ready for revolutionary action . . . There was something towards which we were moving, though the time was not yet ripe. We were moving towards the spirit of '68, still 20 years ahead of us, just as the socialist revolutions of which Piscator spoke were 20 years behind us. Piscator didn't live to see the Total Theatre of '68, but he cooked it up.

Lola Ross was my closest friend and confidante at the Workshop. She was a strong-willed character who had a deep and unshakable belief in herself. We shared mischievous laughter, and liked to compare the attractions of the young men, as we confided in one another our plans for the future. Her devotion to the theatre remained steadfast. Piscator gave all of us this sense of mission. And though Lola didn't work in the theatre for a number of years while she raised two sons, as soon as they were grown she came back to The Living Theatre where she managed the box office while performing in several productions at our Third Street Theatre. Her performance of the put-upon matriarch of an aristocratic household in *German Requiem*, Eric Bentley's version of Kleist's *Familie Schroffenstein* was particularly memorable. She held herself with royal disdain, and played her belief in herself to great comic effect.

My other close friend was Steffi Blank, a profoundly serious young woman, a woman of ideas and of very controlled feelings. She was grounded in the classics, and accepted Piscator's innovative theatre as a mere historical phase in the smooth course of the theatre's historical development. We worked on many scenes together, and her careful analysis proved a boon to me in learning an intelligent approach to a text. She will always be one of my wise women.

Harald Brixel was an Austrian actor who aspired to be an opera director. He came to The Dramatic Workshop to learn the director's art when he was already 30 years old. We believed that we were enacting a Wagnerian romance, even as we studied the great lyric operas together in Herbert Herzfeld's class on opera composition . . . that is until I learned that he had a wife and family in Sweden. I wrote a libretto for Dr. Herzfeld's class about Cassandra and her abandonment by Apollo. Harald directed Wolf-Ferrari's opera *The Secret of Suzanna* at the Workshop, on which I worked as assistant director, and through which I gained experience in the exquisite exigencies of tempo that opera demands, which has informed all my theatre work since. Harald left America to work at the Salzburg Opera.

It was Harald who gave me three blank notebooks when he left America, suggesting that I keep a diary, which I began on my 21st birthday in 1947, and which has given me a sense of order and form to my life, ever since. A diary for which my Notebook was the prototype, in many respects.

Recalling my friends at the Workshop, I realize that I think mostly of what I learned from them, for we were surely a part of each other's education. And this, too, derives from Piscator's dedication to the collective process.

Not everyone among the student body shared our vision. At the end of the war, the G.I. Bill of Rights and Vocational Training assured all those who had served in the United States armed forces the privileges of education, and The Dramatic Workshop experienced a sudden influx of new students. Some of these were wonderful actors, like Harry Belafonte and Walter Matthau, who clearly grasped Piscator's meaning, but many chose a theatre school because it seemed to them a less burdensome choice than academic studies. Why not become an actor? That might be fun.

But Piscator's school turned out not to be such an easy choice, and some of the ex-G.I.s became discouraged.

Thus the school was divided between those of us who were passionate about the art and politics, and others who came along for the ride. But the gift, that inexplicable talent that makes us say, "Ah!" could appear anywhere unexpectedly, and amaze us.

The number of alumni who became prominent in theatre, film and television is extraordinary and suggests a wider diffusion of Piscator's influence than is generally recognized.

Marlon Brando, the legend among them; Harry Belafonte, whose films have always been heavy with social content and social criticism, and who became a leading anti-war activist during the Iraq War; Rod Steiger, Walter Matthau, Harry Guardino, Jerry Stiller, Ben Gazzara (recipient of the 18th annual Erwin Piscator Award in 1995), Jack Garfein, Gene Saks and Louis Guss. Elaine Stritch, who speaks of Piscator in her Broadway solo show; Bea Arthur, who also talks about the Workshop in her solo performance; Sylvia Miles, inventor of a bold camp style. Vinette Carroll, Michael Gazzo – who played the Paycock in O'Casey's *Juno and the Paycock* at the Workshop, and went on to become a successful Broadway playwright with *The Man with the Golden Arm* – and Tony Curtis, who became as famous as anybody.

And then there is Tennessee Williams, who took the playwriting course, and wrote to Piscator asking for a job, to which Piscator replied: "I think it more important for you to be perfectly free to write your plays." Tennessee vainly hoped that the Workshop would produce his first play *Battle of the Angels* which was subsequently done at The Theatre Guild, some time before his meteoric success.

It was an extraordinary group of cohorts and together we got more out of drama school than anyone I can imagine.

My Personal Struggle to Enter The Dramatic Workshop

I entered The Dramatic Workshop five years after it was created . . .

1945 was the year the Second World War ended. The dreadful ordeal that had drained everyone's energy and filled us with fears was over. It was a time when fear gave way to hope, and to a rhetoric of optimism . . . and a poetry of optimism.

It wasn't easy for me to afford The Dramatic Workshop. My father's death from leukemia in 1940 had left me and my mother penniless, and tuition was $1000. I applied for and was eventually given a scholarship to cover half of it, and had to earn $500 to cover the other half.

I worked at two jobs. I had a day-time job at Consolidated Laundries, where I did the worst work – opening the bags and counting the dirty wash and dealing with all the other filth people stuff into their laundry bags. And I took a night-time job as waitress, singer and hat-check girl in Valeska Gert's Beggar Bar.

Valeska Gert

Valeska Gert was the innovative *Grotesk-Tänzerin* of Berlin's avant-garde in the 1920's, and an inspiration to the expressionists. She often boasted that it was from her gestures that Mayakovsky derived the style of his constructivist theatre.

She, too, had fled the cultural darkness of fascism. In a cellar on the corner of Morton and Bleecker Streets, in the very heart of Greenwich Village, she created a cabaret in a tiny cellar, painted black, with the ambience of a Berliner *Kneipe* of the 20's, but without a liquor license. Valeska, who had famously played the role of Polly Peachum in G.W. Pabst's film of Brecht's *Threepenny Opera*, named her cabaret The Beggar Bar. Here she performed an extraordinary repertoire of solo satires in the grotesque style that she called *Irregularity* (*Unregelmässigkeit*).

Lunar Bowels: An Audition Piece

While I worked at two jobs I was also preparing my scholarship audition for the Workshop. Influenced by Valeska's performances I created a dance drama, enacting my poem "Lunar Bowels," about a voyage to the moon, or the risks of venturing into the great unknown. It was a very physical performance.

I was to perform it first for Maria Ley-Piscator, who received me in a blue velvet gown in her blue, mirrored office. It was Madame's blue period. Maria Piscator was always called Madame at the school. It was an honorific in deference to her European roots. She had been a leading ballerina in her youth, and had lived a full, adventurous life, the subject of several biographies and autobiographies. Madame lived a long time, and when she was 100 years old she was still speaking of establishing Dramatic Workshop II, a plan never fulfilled, but ever a part of her relentless ambition to fulfill Piscator's dream.

I came to her with great trepidation, but she responded favorably to my surreal piece. I leaped about the blue office shamelessly, as only an 18-year-old would dare to, with as much bizarre vocalization as I could borrow from Valeska Gert's shrieks and whispers, along with the memory of a scratchy record my mother loved to play of her favorite actor, Alexander Moissi. I cried out:

"My foot upon the moon,
My foot upon the slippery moon . . ."
[and I slid across her blue carpet till I struck a mirrored wall]
"Ungravitated

Dance

and

Leap

A hundred feet!"
[and it seemed a hundred feet as I jumped as high as I could and landed
    face down on the blue carpet until . . .]
"My body (bones alone left now)
Rattles in the moon
Like dice in a Big Hand."
[and I flung myself, shaken by spasms, around the blue office]

Madame approved my unlikely audition and authorized me to perform it
again for Piscator the following week.

But that week there happened to be a crisis at Valeska Gert's Beggar
Bar. It was suddenly closed by the authorities for being a cabaret without a
liquor license. Valeska served an eggnog concoction that was sold, bottled,
in grocery stores, and had a slight taint ("for flavor") of alcohol. My friend
and fellow waiter, who went by the stage name of Françoise La Soeur, and
was in fact the person who had first brought me to Valeska's, was arrested
for serving the eggnog. I vehemently urged Valeska to pay his bail bond,
since none of us, including Valeska, had any idea that we were doing anything illegal, and she reluctantly agreed to bail him out of jail.

And then La Soeur vanished forever from New York City and Valeska
was stuck with his full bail, usually ten times the amount of the bond. All
this happened the week of my audition with Piscator, when I was terrified
of meeting the great man after years of hearing his praises sung.

And now . . . at last . . . I held my breath as the door to Piscator's office
opened and . . .

Suddenly it was Valeska Gert who came out of the door, Piscator behind
her. And seeing me, she shrieked in her wildest grotesque voice: "There
she is! *She* is the one! *She* made me pay the bail! *She* made me lose all
my money! This is all her fault!"

Apparently Valeska had gone to Piscator to ask for some financial help
during the La Soeur crisis, and by the looks of it he had refused her . . . I
feared it was the end of all my hopes.

In his cold, dignified manner, he ushered me into his office, ignoring the shouts of Valeska . . . I was shaken . . .

Piscator's office was quite the opposite of Madame's romantic room. It was book-filled and paper-strewn, and behind his desk was a large map of the theatre of war. He had placed colored pins to denote the battlefields, marked the front lines of the Allies and the Axis, designated the bombed cities, indicated the retreats and advances . . .

How beautiful he was! His noble, silver head, like the idealized sculpture of a Roman emperor: proud, authoritative, patriarchal, wise.

This was the office of a political man. Nothing here was theatrical; dramatic, yes, but only in the sense that war is dramatic. In front of his Spartan desk I danced out my moon poem. It seemed much less outrageous following Valeska's hysterical outburst. Piscator was pleased and I won my scholarship to The Dramatic Workshop.

Plate 1 Piscator in tweed jacket.

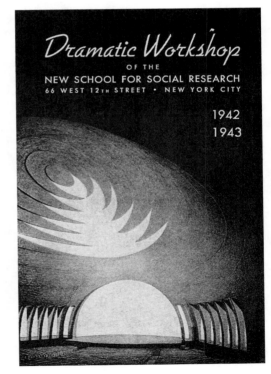

Plate 2 1942 Dramatic Workshop program cover.

Plate 3
All the King's Men.

Plate 4 *The Flies*, with Piscator, Maria Ley-Piscator and ensemble including Judith Malina.

Plate 5 Piscator outside the Workshop's summer theatre in Sayville, Long Island, with students including Marlon Brando, Rod Steiger and Bernie Schwartz (Tony Curtis).

Plate 6 *Lysistrata* ensemble including Marlon Brando.

Plate 9 Piscator with miniatures.

Plate 10 Students with camera.

Plate 11 Tony Curtis.

Plate 12 Harry Belafonte.

Plate 13 Outside the Dramatic Workshop entrance.

Plate 14 Students outside the Dramatic Workshop entrance.

Plate 15 Piscator standing under stage lights.

part 2

The Notebook

The classes at which these notes were taken were focused on the training that Erwin Piscator and his teachers were able to convey, which meant that it spanned the enormous gaps between the methods of Stella Adler, Lee Strasberg, Raikin Ben-Ari, Herbert Bergof, Maria Ley-Piscator, and Piscator himself.

These classes did not represent a method or a "school," but strengthened the actor, not only in body and voice, but in the deepest attitude of his or her artistic self, her commitment, her larger vision, her sensibility. This strength could then be applied in the one hundred thousand ways of the artist – each one unique – but trained to offer their unique input to the collective work.

Each of us knew that what we were learning was not only the fulfillment of our potential. It was also the way that this fulfillment could – indeed must – fulfill the needs and largest capacities of the whole company, of the play, and of the audience, which was our motive for doing the play.

Monday, February 5, 1945

On my first day as a student of the theatre I had the rare experience of meeting a great man. When Erwin Piscator entered the room it was not the spontaneous applause of my fellow students alone that I felt, but the tangible presence of a personality. He welcomed us with an informal introductory speech about the artistic and political power of the theatre. His love for the art came across to me in the form of a high constructive enthusiasm, and I assume it was the same for those around me. He said that the great revolutions were often inspired by plays of high impact, like *Uncle Tom's Cabin* or Hauptmann's *The Weavers*. His informality, combined with the fire and power of his ideas, led to him making the half-joking statement which I am tempted to use as my motto: "The theatre is the most important thing, and anyone who does not realize this is stupid."

After this and other speeches by our teachers-to-be, we all had lunch together as an opportunity to make acquaintance, since Mr. Piscator emphasizes the importance of actors knowing each other well in order to create harmoniously. At the dinner, several of the older students made impromptu speeches and even did little imitations and skits. It was not the quality of these but the straightforward, facing-the-audience atmosphere that I noted. A certain poise, a preparedness, has come to these young people through their training that seems truly remarkable to one as stage-frightened as myself.

Afternoon brought my first class, a stage make-up class about using the right materials and tools. Our teacher, Leo Kerz, is a quiet, intelligent young man whom I fear will be quite hard to know. A benign, knowing dignity puts up a teacher–pupil barrier here. I shall try to overcome it. In the short lecture, the teacher stressed the necessity of the actor's skill in the uses of make-up on stage, which are three: 1) the preservation of one's own features and personality which the artificial conditions and lighting of the stage alter considerably and blur still more, 2) characterization, which involves actual facial changes or particular accentuation and 3) stylization for certain types of plays.

Our second class was called Current Broadway Plays. We are supposed to be the enemies of the commercial theatre, but no one spoke of it as critically as I thought they should. Broadway, its lack of standards, of artistic integrity, of theatre in Mr. Piscator's sense of the word, was not under discussion. Mr. Piscator believes that it is important that we understand what the other side is doing. The teacher, Alexander Ince, himself a Broadway producer, gave us some insights into the difficulties of obtaining movie rights, and the division of money whose source is such a transaction, which seemed more like the Broadway small talk to which I was accustomed when I was making the rounds. It did not surprise me when he said his office was in the Sardi's Building.

After this discussion some of the older students read, quite cold, the script of a new play, and an interesting one, concerning a woman of five facets – the poetic one, the mother, the bitch, the drudge, and the club woman. All were admirably played by young girls who entered into the spirit of their parts and the play immediately, and fitted their characterizations to the role. Virginia Baker as the bitch was especially effective and, though overplaying it, still managed the subtlety of the nuances.

This class was followed by a class in stagecraft, a completely new facet of the theatre for me. Though I have always been awed by its complexities, I had never before thought of mastering it. The class started in the last semester and we entered in the middle of the course, but the material was so well explained by the teacher, Mr. Hans Sondheimer, that I followed easily. The class was on stage curtains, a subject not fully covered in two hours. I have been aware of curtains, but never of the intricacies connected with them. Technically, I have never been highly accomplished, but I have great respect for the importance of this course, the importance of a sailor knowing his ship, an actor knowing his stage.

At our last class of the day I was already a bit tired, for our work day involved 12 full hours and by 8:30 I was bewildered by so many new ideas and people.

But the last class was Mr. Piscator's directing class and I am ardent to take what I can of Mr. Piscator's ideas and make them my own. He spoke of the creativity of the director's role, of its recognition in Hollywood, though not at all in such companies as the Comédie Française or the Metropolitan Opera. He compares the theatrical director with the musical conductor and the director's book with the score. Then he spoke at length of the importance of the director's book. The first version of the director's book, he suggested, should be in the form of a novel: a story of environment and actions and thoughts on the play. And the second version should be a mechanical book of directions, that should later become the stage manager's book. Mr. Piscator then asked the class what would be their first step in staging a play. One student caused laughter with his answer,

"Read the play," but Mr. Piscator agreed with him, pointing out that most directors do not read plays correctly.

He even went so far as to tell of his own experience in misjudging a play which he finally realized was meritorious only after reading it ten times. Here a student interposed that when he read a play he knew it was either good or bad, and when it did not appeal to him he did not even finish reading it. Mr. Piscator said that this was a perfect example of a lack of the ability to read a play. We then discussed the proper attitude toward a new play from the director's point of view. After reading a play, we should attempt to assimilate it and feel it from the inside; then we must visualize certain scenes, and let certain characters take shape, till finally we come to the analysis of plot and character, breaking down the play into its elements. With this class our day ended. The fullest day of my life, confirming the general impression that "The theatre is the most important thing."

Tuesday, February 6, 1945

My first class was Mr. Piscator's Theatre Research, the aim of which is to establish a philosophy of the theatre. Actually a class in criticism, Mr. Piscator explained that criticism is a noble art practiced by Aristotle and Lessing and not the ignoble thing practiced by the newspaper reviewers of our day. Criticism is not merely positive or negative judgment as expressed yesterday by the young man who "either liked a play or didn't like a play on first reading or seeing it, and that's all there is to it," but something far more objective. To criticize we must first learn to think dialectically, we must learn Hegelian thinking. For we are all prejudiced, whether by wealth or poverty, or our bourgeois heritage – whether by culture, or by being part of a minority or part of a majority. The influence of our environment is present and shows itself in our judgment. It is only when we can sever our prejudices "and thus our beliefs from our judgment that, we are criticizing justly."

He went on to speak of what constitutes the theatre, saying that the audience is an integral part of the play. Here Piscator breaks with Stanislavsky. For Piscator feels that the audience should not just be taken into consideration by the actor, but actually be made the confidante of the actor, whereas Stanislavsky's method is a way of entering into the part and forgetting the audience. Mr. Piscator feels that the ideal theatre would be one in which the play took place before an audience seated at little desks, who were permitted to interrupt to ask for the repetition of a word, or ask the meaning of a phrase at will. I would not like to act in Mr. Piscator's ideal theatre. Perhaps in two years I shall feel differently.

Mr. Piscator does not admit "outside effects" which he classes as entertainment. Here he criticized the Broadway theatre saying it worked entirely for outside effects, until it now has become a superficial style. He ended the lecture by declaring that religion, which once unified human life and gave us higher-than-materialistic ideals, is losing its power more and more as a community bond. Here art enters, and here theatre enters, to give the strength and beauty to our world that religion gave to the medieval world.

My second class was a March of Drama class in which the older students discussed *Nathan the Wise* for a future production. In the reading Miss Virginia Baker once again showed herself a master of her art.

Then, before a solemn assembly of Mr. and Mrs. Piscator, Mr. Raikin Ben-Ari, Miss Chouteau Dyer, and the other teachers, Mr. Piscator called on us to repeat our auditions. He said it was a good way for the old students to get acquainted with the new class. Repeat my audition?! And in the presence of my new schoolmates! I was terrified again. Still, I thought it would be fun to show off my bizarre, expressionist piece in contrast to their conventional auditions. I admired their monologues from O'Neill, Arthur Miller and Chekhov. There were two exceptional performances – an emotional scene by a young lady named Arla Gild, and a fine reading of Edmond's "bastard speech" from *King Lear*.

Then it was my turn. Mr. Piscator had warned the other students not to "perform" so much, so I started with slight misgivings, but then I threw my body gingerly across the room and slid my foot along the polished floor of the dance studio and cried out sharp and hard,

"My foot upon the moon . . ."

And falling forward, I enacted the claustrophobic nightmare with voice and body.

After each audition, Mr. Piscator challenged the student. His questions were brusque: "Why do you want to be an actor?"

"What have you got to say, that you want to stand up and make everyone listen to you?"

"What do you think you can accomplish with your work?"

"What are your politics?" He was bold and asked outright. He told us in his teacherly, directorial manner: "You have no right to stand up in front of the public, to stand in the center, to stand in the light and demand their attention because you speak so well, or because you look so beautiful, or because you move so gracefully, or because you can make them laugh, or make them cry. You can only demand their attention if you have something that you are burning to communicate." Since my scene was one of the last, I had time to prepare my response to Mr. Piscator's challenges.

"I am a pacifist!" I said, feeling sure that this would answer all Piscator's demands. "So am I," he answered, rather dismissively. "But what kind of pacifism do you imagine in a world at war? What kind of society can you suggest that would be a peaceful society? How would you regulate life, food, work and water in a pacifist world?"

I was startled. "I . . . don't know . . ." I said, feeling as humbled as Piscator once did in the trenches at Ypres, when he said he was an actor . . .

"This is what I have to study," I said, brazening it out.

And so I will, along with my study of the dramatic arts, study the answers to Mr. Piscator's questions.

Mr. Piscator said he liked my poem, which he applauded, though he did not comment further.

We then met a group of actors from The Hedgerow Theatre, including their inspired director, Mr. Jasper Deeter. He founded the Hedgerow in 1923, making it the oldest repertory company in the United States. The Hedgerow is a "little theatre" group, but Mr. Piscator says, the "little" theatres here should be called the "great" theatres and the Broadway theatres should be called the "little" theatres. The Hedgerow then is a "great" theatre, with high idealistic standards from which, according to the introduction their representative gives, they do not stray. It has been in existence for 20 years, never a financial or critical success, but always an integral group, living together and working in complete unity. An admirable enterprise, if their productions are on as high a level as their standards.

Our last class of the day was Stage Design with Mr. Leo Kerz. He said that one of the great errors of the theatre was "judging new methods by old standards." Justifying the inclusion of a stage design course in an acting course, Mr. Kerz attempted to show that the difference between the old and the new drama is that the old consisted of action and character, whereas the new is compounded of action, character and setting. Setting including the sense of time, environment, the influence of the period, political and other factors. The where and why must be shown by "circumstantial evidence." A Greek or Shakespearean play can be done in modern clothes. Hamlet and Juliet can be given contemporary significance, but you cannot do *Awake and Sing* or *Street Scene* in classical costumes. The modern theatre has added a visual dimension to our auditory art.

Stage Design had its origin in the same impulse that changed the actor from a masked, stilted orator to a real person living through real experiences on the stage. Here a discussion ensued on the merits and demerits of Wilde, Shaw and Shakespeare, and the difference between good plays and good literature, which was found to be considerable.

Wednesday, February 7, 1945

My first class was in Dance Movement with Maria Ley-Piscator. She begins with breathing. She asked us to chase our breath to our spine and our sides, all of which was a little beyond my understanding. The *barre* work, *pliés* from positions 1, 2, 3, 5 and some foot movements, were simple enough and wonderfully stimulating. Madame Piscator explained the importance of dance movement for the stage, of relaxation as taught in modern dance, and control as taught in ballet, both of which are necessary to the actor – so that we shall make use of both. She showed how tension was displayed in raised shoulders and how lowering the shoulders was a good method of overcoming tenseness on the stage. Demonstrating the differences between an inside movement and an outside movement, she showed us how the latter grows up and out against gravity. A person should grow out of their hips freely and elastically like a flower from its cup, and not "sit in their bodies" as in old age. The energy center is in the solar plexus, the center of our body, and not our hips or arms or hands, and all movements should begin there (shades of Isadora Duncan). We ended the class with some arm movements and bending exercises. All of which was enough to give me a pleasant, though painful stiffness. She explains her points clearly, and I think I shall advance well in this class.

We then had an orientation class in Pantomime, in which Mr. Ben-Ari asked for improvisations. Mr. Ben-Ari, formerly of Moscow and the Habima, and still a great worshipper of Stanislavsky, explained the meaning of sense memory. He asked the girls to enter a room from a storm, to warm themselves and take their coats off. At first none of us did well. Mr. Ben-Ari's suggestions helped us to become more realistic – how to remember the cold, to allow ourselves to really feel it . . .

Mr. Piscator had asked that the new acting students not take the directing course without having had former directing experience. Stubborn and over-ambitious as usual, I went to his office to ask to be permitted to take the directing class. Piscator looked at me coldly. He does not have a high regard for the staying power of women in "the masculine professions". I pleaded with him, swallowing my humiliation at his low opinion of my qualifications because of my gender, as well at his low regard for actresses, and he somewhat reluctantly allowed me to take the directing course. His reluctance to admit me to his course means that I must work all the harder, catch up on the reading, and at the same time, keep a high standard in my acting work. But it also assures me that I will be able to study not only acting, but stage design, theatre management, lighting, and above all, take invaluable directing classes with Piscator.

Chouteau Dyer, Mr. Piscator's assistant, took the aspiring directors to a conference room where we were all – myself most of all – frightened at the prospect of entering an advanced class in the middle of the term. Directing students are asked to actually plan and execute a production for the Friday March of Drama. The standard of those productions which I have seen thus far is well above my ability but it may be that, when I get over the awe of it, I too shall reach that point of daring to direct a production.

After class I bought the book, *Fundamentals of Play Directing* by Alexander Dean, which is used in Mr. Piscator's class. There is so much to read, even to catch up with the class.

At 8:30 I entered Dr. Paul Zucker's class on Styles Through the Ages. I had been forewarned that Dr. Zucker was "the most learned man in the whole world," and his class made me regret the grain of salt with which I had taken that statement. Dr. Zucker did not speak about the theatre, but it is wonderful that The Dramatic Workshop had the insight to ask drama students to take a course by an historian of the arts to study periods rather than productions and personalities. Starting the new semester with the Renaissance, Dr. Zucker explained that the Renaissance form of expression was painting, just as in Elizabethan times it was drama, in Roman times, architecture, and in modern times, the novel. Raphael and Da Vinci were most expressive of Renaissance style, though a man can be great in his time without being of his time. Brahms wrote in the 19th century, but his music expressed the style of Brahms and not of the 19th century. Mozart, who wrote in the 18th century, expresses the style of his century perfectly and reflects it in his music.

Dr. Zucker then presented slides. He began with a primitive Byzantine mosaic of *The Last Supper*, and showed how the times and styles influenced the development of this theme, leading to the epitome of achievement in Da Vinci's masterpiece. He showed us anatomical and architectural and scientific studies by this versatile genius of the Renaissance. Then he showed us Raphael's Madonnas, from the very earthy mother of *Madonna of the Chair* to the exalted *Sistine Madonna*. An interesting example of Renaissance style was shown in Raphael's *Betrothal of the Virgin*, and a painting of the same name by Raphael's teacher, Perugino. The ideal building of the Renaissance forms the background of both these pictures. This ideal building was constructed so as to appear equal from any side and from any entry. Doors and arches were built symmetrically. This lecture with slides was the last class of the day.

Thursday, February 8, 1945

My first class this morning was a voice class with a young woman, Miss Gloria Montemuro. After listening to the speech of several students, Miss Montemuro discussed with each his or her individual speech problems. She told me that I needed a great deal of work in breath control, of which I am, of course, aware, but she also asked me to put more voice behind my final "m's" and "n's" to prevent nasalizing. I see no point to this whatever in my case. Then she said that I over-aspirate my vowels in words like "stop." I don't want to differ with my teachers, especially in fields they know best, but the sheer ugliness of drawing out an "m" or "n" and the undervaluation of a final aspirate are not, to my mind, desirable speech characteristics. Meanwhile, I must content myself with chasing my breath about my insides. It seems I have been breathing like a fool all my life, and now must breathe with my diaphragm (located where I always thought my stomach was), instead of just taking in air at random, unintelligently. During the rest of the class I was desperately trying to read the second half of *Faust*, which I must finish by Friday for my March of Drama class.

My next class was an orientation class in which we chose our technical courses. I asked to take Stage Design and Costume Design – hoping my experience in designing jewelry may prove helpful when applied to theatre. During the interviews of the students I read some *Faust*.

Then we heard another lecture by the brilliant Dr. Zucker. This course is called History and Sociology of the Theatre. The first lecture was on the ancient theatre. Dr. Zucker explained that the Greek Drama began in magic cults and religious rites. There were gods who needed to be placated, and the chorus moving about in front of the temple was intended to pacify the gods. Eventually, a dialogue between a protagonist and a Choragos was introduced. The protagonist was a questioner who carried on a dialogue with the chorus. This was the first actor.

The second actor was not present until much later, at the time of Aeschylus (525–456 B.C.E.), and the third actor was introduced by Sophocles. Dr. Zucker showed how those who created the very means of the theatre reached poetic heights never surpassed by any playwright in later times.

Dr. Zucker then showed slides of the development of the Greek amphitheatre, from a semi-circle in front of a Dionysian temple to the ornate Roman two-story columned theatre, like the one at Orange in France. He also showed us masks from both the tragedies and the satires, with their unique megaphone mouthpieces. The Greeks, whose theatre sprung up, original, uninfluenced and unadulterated, reached a technical perfection that is superior in its way to ours.

Our last class of the day was Costume Design, with Mr. Kerz. He will trace the history of costume, starting with Egypt. We discussed the difference between costume and clothing. Costume is the decorative endeavor in dress. He pointed out the lack of utility in our contemporary clothing. This was highly contested, but of course, it is true. It is precisely the point of Ad Reinhardt's current exhibit at the Museum of Modern Art, "Are Clothes Modern?" Clothes, even today, are governed by convention, taboo, and primitive urges. Mr. Kerz asked us to read something on Egyptian civilization so that we may correlate it with his next lecture.

Friday, February 9, 1945

This morning we had our first acting class with Mr. Ben-Ari. Stanislavsky's books, *My Life in Art* and *An Actor Prepares* didn't seem to me to be the

203 HISTORY AND SOCIOLOGY OF THE THEATRE

15 weeks, fall and spring. Tuesdays 8.30–10.15 P.M. $20.00   Paul Zucker
Illustrated by lantern slides

THE ELEMENTS   (Fall term, beginning October 8)

The stage of today is viewed as the most recent step in a historical development, and the aim of the course is to find the most appropriate and effective
means of expression for our own day. With this in mind, the sociology of the
audience in various periods is analyzed, its influence on the theatre set up,
types of actor, form of the stage, scenic techniques etc., showing how each
age found its own scenic expression in terms of contemporary culture.

I **The Actor 1.** Psychology, physique, character, their influence on the
concept of the role and the interpretation of the play.

II **The Actor 2.** Basic types, artistic limits: casting. The various possibilities of expression. Individual actor and ensemble play.

III **The Audience 1.** Sociological differences and the variety of theoretical
interests, common reactions.

IV **The Audience 2.** In various historical periods: their influence on the
form of dramatic literature.

V **Sociology of the American Theatre today.** Broadway, community,
college theatre, summer stock. Experimental theatre. Box office, entertainment, literature.

VI **Artistic means of the stage through the ages:** word, gesture,
setting.

VII **Styles of Representation 1.** Realism and Naturalism.

VIII **Styles of Representation 2.** Symbolism, various aspects of stylization, abstraction, condensation, their technical means.

IX **Function of color and light:** realistic and symbolical meaning.
Psychology of perception.

X **Form and space on the stage.** Perspective, dimension, scale. Levels.

XI **Costume and setting.** Archaeological faithfulness vs. artistic truth.

XII **Tools of the stage.** Props, scenery, wings, backdrop, the closed wall,
turntable, treadmill, projections.

XIII **Theatre and movie 1.** Differences of art forms and of perception.

XIV **Theatre and movie 2.** Difference of artistic means.

XV **Conclusions.**

HISTORY OF THE THEATRE   (Spring term, beginning February 4)

I   **The roots.** Children's play, disguise, the mask. Ceremonial. Magic and the Mime.

II   **Greek theatre.** Dialogue and function of the chorus. The form of the stage. The beginning of dramaturgy.

III **Roman theatre.** The machinery. Pantomimes.

IV   **Mysteries and Passion Plays.** Miracles and Moralities of the Middle Ages. The liturgical origin.

V   **The theatre of the Renaissance.** Intermezzi and trionfi.

VI   **The Commedia dell'Arte.** Farce. Eternal types; costumes.

VII **The Shakespearean stage and the stage of the Restoration.** Inigo Jones.

VIII **Opera, its history and aesthetics.** Specific needs of the opera stage, based on the integration of action, music and set.

IX   **Dance and ballet.** Their specific art forms.

X   **The Baroque theatre on the international scene.** Illusion and machinery. **The great stage designers.** From Furttenbach to the Bibienas. The influence of the theatre of the Jesuits.

XI   **The theatre of the 19th century.** Classicism and Romanticism. The academic style. The "Meininger." The beginnings of Naturalism.

XII **Naturalism and the history of the naturalistic theatre.** From 1890 through today.

XIII **The revolution of the modern stage,** through Gordon Craig and Adolphe Appia.

XIV **The experimental theatre of today.** Influence of the Russian stage.

XV   **The Epic Theatre.** Erwin Piscator.

Figure 1 Lecture Program for History and Sociology of the Theatre, Fall term and Spring term, taught by Paul Zucker.

beacon lights of acting when I read them three years ago. But Mr. Ben-Ari's application of Stanislavsky's principles is a fascinating and instructive experiment. Mr. Ben-Ari asked us to talk about our acting problems, and offered us hope that none of them are insurmountable. He then asked Barbara Sisson to read us an article from *Theatre Workshop* magazine by the great Italian actor, Tomasso Salvini, entitled "Studying My Art."

46

Salvini wrote that he began by studying the classics, from which he learned style and poetic grandeur, and gained an acquaintance with the great figures of all ages. He also studied love and hate, desire and vengeance, kindness, cruelty and all the other human passions, good and evil, and learned to note and to remember the manners, movements and expressions connected with each. He studied people and history so that he could, when called upon, create a fictional character or play an historical figure, giving each a distinct personality. The article ended ". . . and then study and study, always study." This, Mr. Ben-Ari said, should serve us as an actor's bible.

We discussed justification, taking the art of listening as an example. The wide-eyed cocking of the head is not necessary, to genuinely listen is far more effective. In real life, we look without seeing and listen without hearing. We were asked to be very still and listen. When, somewhere in another room, a tapping sounded, no one could count the number of taps accurately. Then Mr. Ben-Ari asked us to speak and listen simultaneously. Since we were concentrating on listening, we all spoke slowly and in low tones. But when Mr. Ben-Ari told us that in the next room our dear friends and teachers lay dead, our quiet speech took on a meaning and our listening became real. This is what he calls "motivation."

In a lesson on observation, we each described an object we saw on stage without looking at it. Mr. Ben-Ari explained that these physical descriptions would be very different if the object had a personal meaning. If, for instance, the table we were describing had a murderer's gun on it, or if we were trying to buy it or to sell it . . . Here again, motivation supplies meaning to our words or actions. When we illustrate them in these exercises, the ideas of Constantin Stanislavsky are stupendous.

Our next class was an acting class with a *charmante* European actress, Miss Margrit Wyler, who has played both classics and roles that feature her very evident sex appeal. Whereas Mr. Ben-Ari teaches improvisation, Miss Wyler will teach us acting from scripts. Today she asked us to repeat our auditions, which she criticized and improved markedly. She teaches less from the theoretical side and more from the actor's experience. She asked me not to repeat my audition as she said it was rather "polished," but next lesson I will probably get a chance to read. I am sure I shall learn much from this vivacious lady.

The afternoon session of The March of Drama was the final rehearsal of *Faust*. I said that I had read the play (though that was years ago), and

Miss Dyer asked me to retell the story. I was not doing too badly with my memory, when Mr. Piscator entered, and I suddenly regretted that I had not finished rereading the play. He did not interrupt me, so that in front of Piscator, who had acted in and directed *Faust*, and who knew it practically by heart, I had to tell the story that I had not read in years. That I got away with it I must consider the height of successful bluffing. But I shall read it tonight and tomorrow, so as to never have to face such a situation again.

Esther Nighbert then told us about the production of *Faust* which she directed for tonight's March of Drama. She presented heaven with Eugene Van Grona playing an endearing Mephisto, and then the pact scene with Bob Carricart, a young but energetic Faust. The Garden scene had a vaudeville version of Mephistopheles to which Mr. Piscator objected, and in spite of the good performance by the girl who played Martha, Mr. Piscator asked that the scene be omitted this evening. Then, as Esther Nighbert put it, going from the ridiculous to the sublime, the Dungeon scene, with Virginia Baker as the unfortunate Gretchen. She and Bob Carricart did the grim scene with dash and power. The scene between Mephisto and the young student was presented as an allegory of The Dramatic Workshop. The student, like myself, "wants to specialize in everything."

In the evening, Mr. Gassner's lecture on Goethe and the Romantic movement showed how it corresponded in time with the revolutionary movements, and was a phase of these movements. The Romantics were interested in the individual, in the unlimited horizons of mankind, and man's scope. Also, in the form of the writing, the Romantic wants complete freedom. In *Faust*, Goethe fulfilled both of these Romantic ideals, although he denied that he belonged to the Romantic movement, preferring the classical style to Romanticism. His *Faust* is the story of man's ascent to grandeur, his search and striving and his successful attainment of spiritual happiness – "to see a free people, upon a free soil" – which is the epitome of the revolutionist aspiration. In form as well, *Faust* is rambling, free of the unities of time, place and action. The performance was prefaced by Miss Dyer's reading of a short essay of Goethe's on dilettantism. Now to prepare a critique of the performances for the Theatre Research class on Tuesday morning.

Tuesday, February 13, 1945

Directors' Council, with many fears that I shall not be able to accomplish what is asked of me. I am given two positions. I assist the Stage Manager in *Nathan the Wise* and assist on costumes in Molière's *Imaginary Invalid*.

My next class was in Theatre Research, with *Cher Maître* again. Discussing the last production, *The Vultures* by Henri Becque, all the actors stated that they did not like the play. Mr. Piscator said this was foolishness. Charles Zimmermann played the chief Vulture, M. Tessier. He said he disliked the part at first, and could not find a way to play it. Then he decided to walk through it to see whether it could be approached physically. He found himself in a hunched position. In that attitude, he realized the whole being of M. Tessier and from this core created the role, quite successfully. Mr. Piscator said that here is an example of finding a role through posture, which he normally considered a superficial element. Elaine Stritch, who played the Mother, said that she liked neither the part nor the play. Priscilla Draghi, who was very convincing as Blanche, said that Blanche's attitude was hard for a modern girl to believe.

A discussion ensued in which the men felt that a girl would behave in this fashion, and the girls protested that a modern girl would either fight or give up the young man of her own free will. Louis Guss, who played the Father, said that he could not feel any intimate family relation with the rest of the cast. Another student told a relevant story concerning the Group Theatre. Once Morris Carnovsky could not feel that the cast was his family until it occurred to him that he had acted with this same group for years, and they *were* his family! Louis could have assumed the same attitude. He also mentioned that he did not feel at home on the set, whereas in *Hannele's Way to Heaven*, he had. Mr. Piscator asked if he remembered how he achieved this feeling. Louis explained that he walked on the set alone among the props, until he believed it.

A student then read his critique of *Faust*, noteworthy for its clarity and also its complications. The student spoke of Goethe intelligently, but perhaps too intellectually. He was hypercritical of the production, which he felt should never have been attempted, but which I thought was excellent, given the limitations of a school production. He found Eugene's Mephistopheles reminiscent of a French barber. A much more favorable critique was read by David, who has worked here longer and knows the school better. After these bursts of analytical expression, I hesitated to give my essay to Mr. Piscator, who said that he would have liked me to read it.

After lunch, we had a March of Drama class, which consisted of a rehearsal for our performances. Some readings from *Nathan the Wise* were done beautifully by Louis Guss as Nathan, Virginia Baker as Recha, Esther Nighbert as Daya, and, in especially fine voice, Jimmy Walsh as the Templar. Miss Dyer spoke of Racine's *Phèdre* and recommended our reading it in French if we could. The Workshop had done *Phèdre* a few years ago, and the actors had listened to a record of Sarah Bernhardt reading the long speech in the first act. At first, it sounded like nothing but a most unhappy chicken, but after perhaps 20 hearings and reading along with her, one stopped hearing the interference of the scratchy recording as one became accustomed to the gliding, classical rhythm and the beauty of Sarah Bernhardt's rendition became clear. Miss Dyer explained that the untranslatable music of the French words should force us to read the speech aloud, and then we could ignore our bad French just as we learned to ignore the poor technical quality of the record.

The class that followed was Stage Design. Mr. Kerz said that the designer must consider the audience, but that actors never understand what it is that affects them or how. The impression they get from a set is either "nice" or "not nice" without even considering the technical means or difficulties of achieving an effect.

Victor Hugo said that there are three types of people who go to the theatre: the thinkers, who want characterization; the women, who want passion; and the mob, which wants action. Mr. Kerz believes that a modern audience does not go to the theatre to see a play but to be emotionally moved. In reading a novel or looking at a painting you are alone and your reaction is an individual reaction; in the theatre, not being alone, we laugh and cry because others do. If all the individuals in the audience saw the play alone they would not laugh, whereas, as part of an audience, they do. The critic, who makes first nights a torment for the players, is so exasperating for this reason: he keeps himself apart from the audience and will not render his judgment in terms of the mass spirit. Shakespeare kept all this in mind in his plays, for even in an intellectual characterization like *Hamlet* he catered to the pit with fights and poisoned daggers.

At the end of the class, Mr. Kerz listed three types of drama. In the mid-17th century, the drama of rhetoric; in the 18th century, the drama of convention (still in existence in plays like those of Noël Coward); and in the 19th and 20th centuries, the drama of illusion, of which all our Broadway plays are examples, *hélas*!

Wednesday, February 14, 1945

An early Voice class at ten o'clock – still not the sort of thing that wakes me up. Miss Montemuro further explained the technical parts of speech, giving our speech-making organs long names, and again made us breathe in the middle of where I always thought my stomach was, but which is, in fact, my diaphragm. Having practiced, I am now able to expand it when I inhale, although it makes me very dizzy to try. We all said 1–2–3–4–5 and breathed. I hope that the point of all this will become clear to me soon. We also did some exercises for the development of our speech organs, which consisted mostly of arm movements. Here we ended the class, and tomorrow again! But if I practice it and note some improvement, perhaps I will not be so unhappy about it.

Madame Piscator could not be at her dance class and Eugene Van Grona taught in her absence. Eugene (with whom I promptly fell in love) emphasized movements that we can use on the stage. After some relaxation exercises, he taught us the two rest positions. Rest position one, being slightly forward in tendency; rest position two, somewhat back. Utilizing these two positions in a series of movements, we developed them into a smooth and gracious walk. We walked to the music first in humility and then with authority and arrogance. Eugene showed us how we must bring out the important points for the gesture to carry across footlights. As I walked I began to understand how I should do it, but was still inhibited.

Then we practiced a deep, low bow and a complete faint, which I did not even dare attempt. The first step in learning this is to overcome the fear of falling, which sounds simpler than it is. Grace Huffman volunteered to faint for us. While graceful, her falling slowly sideways and letting her head drop down was not quite realistic. Eugene demonstrated very vividly that the actual reaction before falling is a backward movement of the head. He gave us each a more or less gentle jolt behind the knees, and we noticed that the reaction of our head dropping backwards was completely instinctive.

Since he is directing a Molière play at the moment, Eugene gave us an example of how period and costuming determine movement. We then repeated some of the exercises, imagining ourselves to be wearing corsets from slightly below the waist to the bust. We performed them once again as though they were ballet movements, without the use of the waist and hips. Then Eugene returned to the topic of *The Vultures*. Grace, Priscilla and Elaine had all moved in long, modern strides, utterly impossible in the bustled dress of the period. It was a fine class and we all hope Eugene will have a chance to go on with us.

In Miss Wyler's class we worked on the last scene of *St. Joan* by Bernard Shaw. Reading through it we tried to analyze it and get it right. Rotating the parts to give everyone a chance at reading, we barely got through the third speech. Her words "perpetual imprisonment" are spoken after Joan, who was been promised her life in return for a confession, is told that her life will be spared though she will be imprisoned for life. It seems to me a moment of incredulous realization, slowly said and awful. But Miss Wyler, on the assumption that Joan is a soldier, criticized me for what she terms "baby talk," though I am sure that Elizabeth Bergner, my model for the role, said it in very youthful tones and I feel her interpretation nearest to mine. Though of course I shall try to do it Miss Wyler's way, even though I do not agree with it completely. Although almost all the girls tried the scene; none, including myself, gave anything approaching an adequate rendition. The long speech that follows will probably be easier than the words "perpetual imprisonment." This scene, or rather, these lines, took up all of a two-hour lesson. How long does the direction of a whole play take?

Before my next class, I went to Barnes and Noble to buy Mr. Gassner's *Masters of the Drama*, on which his lecture series is based. It gives an amazingly concise description of what seems to me every play ever written.

Then Dr. Zucker's Styles Through the Ages lecture, which covered the second part of the Renaissance. Concerned mainly with Raphael and Michelangelo, the lecture was lost on me because I had a headache. The slides left only the impression that Michelangelo looks bad on slides.

The gist of the lecture was the transition to the baroque. In comparative slides, Dr. Zucker showed us the same subjects by Michelangelo and later sculptors who leaned toward the baroque, where no two lines move in a parallel direction. A fascinating piece is the *Pietà*. In actuality, the Christ figure would completely cover the Mary figure, so Michelangelo made the Christ figure 3/4 the size of Mary. The scaling is completely unnoticeable and extremely effective.

The De Medici tomb figures, especially the *Night and Day*, are majestic. Michelangelo often made portrait statues that did not resemble their subjects physically, but were symbolic of the subject's character. So the famous Moses with the tablets is actually a portrait of Pope Julius!

The composition of the Sistine Chapel ceiling is too crowded and the beauty of the individual figures is lost. Dr. Zucker tells of his first visit there and his terrible disillusion at the sight of the benches below, filled with all types and ages of Anglo-Saxons peering at the ceiling with binoculars, reducing the entire experience to an absurdity. The Roman example of the ideal round Renaissance building was another disappointment to Dr. Zucker, and from the slide it was obvious why he said it looked like a "trolley car waiting station."

Dr. Zucker showed us the floor plans of St. Paul's Cathedral and its well-known dome. Two portraits of two popes done by Raphael at different times gave me pause. The first is of Pope Julius, an angelic, spiritual old man with a simple hand gesture, framed on either side by his chair. The other pope was a younger man showing a vulgarity of feature, while the others in the picture and the heavy stone walls behind him display a materialistic link to worldliness. The question arose as to how much of the difference was in the popes, and how much in Raphael's painting.

Thursday, February 15, 1945

Beginning with a voice class and finally some vocal exercises. The first, merely "dot-bad-bad-bad" was an exercise in differentiating our "t's" and "d's" and, for me, to prevent over-aspiration. "Double, double, toil and trouble" served the same purpose and I encountered the problem of saying "tchrouble" (roughly like that) and, according to Miss Montemuro, I need to develop a more agile tongue. "Boomelay, Boomelay, Boomelay, Boom," the chorus of Vachel Lindsay's "The Congo" was good for vowel practice. As for my breathing, I was complimented for showing improvement, and assured Miss Montemuro that I had practiced. March of Drama meant chorus rehearsal, and I, with my light voice speak slow sing-song lines from Racine's *Esther*, lines that have an intrinsic beauty but which require a certain grandeur of speech unattainable in this group. Miss Montemuro, however, was nice to me, which makes me very happy.

History and Sociology of the Theatre followed, with a lecture on the theatre in the middle ages. Between the year 600 and the year 1000, all the theatres in England were closed. It was thought in the middle ages that the year 1000 would complete the history of the world, and this led to extreme displays of piety, but when the end did not come, the stringent laws were relaxed and the theatres started anew. The first plays were done in the church in front of the altar, and generally portrayed the nativity at Christmas, the crucifixion on Good Friday and the Easter resurrection. The actors were monks and priests. Later, bible plays were given in the marketplaces of some cities. It was here that the "mansions" stage started with rows of "houses" representing Rome, Jerusalem and Heaven and the Jaws of the Monster representing Hell. This was the beginning of the passion play, which is still performed in Oberammergau. The casting of these plays, the most famous of which was in Valencia, was done by the guilds, so that the shepherds were played by wool merchants, and so on. The choicest role was the devil, played by the most talented and ambitious actor; the one who would, in modern times, become a professional actor.

Dr. Zucker also showed us medieval pictures depicting the lack of artifice in the movement of the times, the walking with linked hands, the fine groupings, all of which are ignored on the stage when we attempt to portray the period. On the other hand, the Moscow Art Theatre did it wonderfully. One begins to regard the Moscow Theatre almost with the feeling one has towards the good cousin, about whom one constantly hears the reproach, "Look how nicely she does it, why can't *you* be as good at it as that?"

Costume Design turns to Egypt's ancient attire (one surely gets about in history in this school). I have gone to the Metropolitan Museum of Art, where the predominance of mummies so overwhelmed the living Egyptian pictures as to make a study of Egyptian life impossible. Mr. Kerz explained that death and the embalming of the dead was the most important function of Egyptian life. Their habits of cleanliness were admirable and their clothes . . . well! The workers wore merely a short apron-like cloth wrapped around their loins. These were always in brightly dyed colors, except for the slaves who always wore blue. Clothes denoted rank, and protection was a very minor consideration, when considered at all. Priests wore white, but could not enter a temple with any kind of material made from an animal. Animal forms (in headgear, for instance) were, however, imitated. Women wore skirts with belts below the breast and above the hips. An ornamental collar was worn but the breasts were uncovered. Jewelry and elaborate hats were very common in Egypt.

Friday, February 16, 1945

Miss Montemuro was not present at voice class, so Eugene, the illustrious member of our class, led us in some breathing and relaxation exercises. Then came many syllable phrases, "Tu, tow, toe, tae, toi." Not difficult to say but hard to remember. We then read tongue-twisting sentences like "I am the very model of a modern major general." Repetitions of this and similar poetry. A resumé of speech classes is difficult because the work is all practice and no theory.

To start the Acting class, Mr. Ben-Ari told us the difference between the imitator and the artist. The imitator is the mechanical actor who uses neither soul nor imagination. His performance may be flawless but, being completely cerebral, will lack the inner feeling which is what carries across the footlights. He went on to some exercises, the first of which was the entrance of a mother into her child's room, covering the sleeping child and leaving again. A chair served as a crib. Steffie Blank made the first attempt, Alice Blue the second. Alice did almost the same thing that Steffie did, yet somehow we could not "see" the baby in Alice's performance. We next worked on finding a needle we had dropped. All of us on stage sought the needle and, at a signal, froze in our poses, showing a picture of ourselves in this act. It was more difficult to seek the needle than I would have thought. Ethel complained that it was impossible without more motivation. She was thereupon asked to take the stage. Mr. Ben-Ari told her about her date and her only pair of stockings and the run and the lone needle in the house which she had just lost. She looked for it but without conviction. Mr. Ben-Ari then helped her look for the needle, demonstrating that he seemed to really need the needle.

In another exercise, Eleanor Epstein received a letter from a soldier. With no prop to use she seemed only to glance at it, not really to read it. Mr. Ben-Ari then read an invisible letter for us, and as we followed his eyes we saw him read it line by line. To do this an actor must mentally fill in the words of the letter just as he would mentally hear the answers in a phone conversation.

In our final exercise, Charlie Coleman entered Helen Braille's room and said, "Hello . . . don't you remember me?" "No, I'm afraid I don't."

Helen didn't seem to be trying to remember, though Charles made an effort to remind her of the time they worked together in The Dramatic Workshop. Mr. Ben-Ari showed us how this same scene could be done as tragedy or as comedy. In tragedy the concentration is more intense. It is more important to remember. Not to be recognized by someone whom you remember is sad, while in comedy the eventual recognition is boisterous. "Oh yes, of course I remember, you're . . . no . . ." (with a sudden drop of tempo), "You're not him." Mr. Ben-Ari said that the line dividing comedy and tragedy is infinitesimal. He quoted a burlesque of Hamlet as done by Vakhtangoff. The stage was carpeted, there was a fold in the carpet, and before the grand soliloquy, the actor's foot hit the fold. By letting it pass and going on with the speech the moment is forgotten. But Vakhtangoff slipped, and turned full around to stare at the carpet, and then turned back and began, "To be or not to be." Mr. Ben-Ari's demonstration of this breach in concentration made us all laugh.

Miss Wyler's acting class gave us some opportunity for improvisation that was all the more difficult for being done in ensemble. Taking as a framework Thornton Wilder's *The Happy Journey from Trenton to Camden*, we read through the first page of the script and then, building the scene, went on in our own words. Mr. Wilder's one-act play was made even more fantastic by Alice's inspired addition of the Cat as a character. All the parts were alternated, male or female interchangeably, the largest role being that of Mom. Each Mom was completely different. Cherie raised the social standing of the family. Steffie gave it warmth. Charles', oddly enough, was the best Mom, as his was the most imaginative. As we went on, each actor created business which became cumulative, making the scene more complex.

March of Drama consisted of a chorus rehearsal for tonight's reading with Mr. Berghof. I, with my light voice (dammit!), and they with their darker tones. Choral reading presents terrific difficulties. We are asked to chant less and bring more emotion to it. I want to emphasize, pause, regulate my rendition, but if the others interpret differently, I become either too fast or too slow, too soft or too loud, and so I am inhibited. The words of the chorus in *Esther* are splendid but the girls tend to chant; the other "light" voices, Ethel and Alice, use sing-song voices, breaking the reading down to line by line.

At the *Nathan the Wise* reading, Mr. Gassner's lecture was on Lessing and The Enlightenment, "the age of reason," the time of the rationalists, and cited the great clear thinkers of the time, from the Encyclopaedists to Jefferson and Tom Paine. Lessing, he said, showed great audacity in conceiving of a Jew as the hero. In Mr. Gassner's opinion, *Nathan the Wise* is not a plea for tolerance but a plea for a natural religion. I beg to differ.

Mr. Berghof's Nathan was so wise, so Semitic, so humorous as to elude description. The deliberateness of the pace was of interest. The Jew was asked a difficult question unexpectedly, and he did not have the answer ready. He stopped to think, then the ring story occurred to him, and he stopped to think again how to tell it. He considered his ideas. He was speaking to the powerful Saladin and carefully weighed his words. The performance had a clarity and a logic that sent a feeling of its importance through the audience. Jimmy Walsh, with a fine strong voice, was an authoritative Saladin, in contrast to the thoughtful Nathan.

Monday, February 19, 1945

Dancing. Eugene teaching. After relaxation exercises we treated dance movements as acting problems. The first resembling a yawn with a sit or low bend and then a stretch; not too much imagination was used. However, Eugene amazed me with the variations he could put into such a movement. Most of us did not understand how to tell a simple story in movement. I made hardly any effort in that direction. Then each pupil danced across the floor in a waltz rhythm, "1–2–3 turn 1–2–3 run off." We had a letter, an invitation to a ball from "our soldier" and danced in anticipation. The interpretation ranged from Arla Gild's dreamy vision of waltzing with him, to the gay and romping joy of others. In one of these "step problems" I composed a sort of hide-and-seek game, running the first four steps wary of pursuit, then turning in search of my pursuer, seeing him, then running off quickly. But alas, Eugene said that he didn't understand my story. It had seemed so clear, but I still lack the power to project.

In the next problem, the same girl was unhappy because the letter said that her soldier's furlough had been canceled. Here we were even less successful. We didn't know how to turn unhappily. Eugene solved it with a slow twist, rather than a turn. The point of these problems was to fit our ideas to movements to the music, and be defined by it as it sets our tempo. My steps hindered me terribly, which Eugene blames on my "not knowing how to waltz," although I have always managed on the dance floor.

Next a Make-up class. It seems that my work here will be to forget everything that I know. We are working now with straight make-up, which consists of a base, rouge, powder, eyeshadow, enlarging the eyes, shaping of the eyebrows, and lipstick. All of which is quite all right, except that these versions of Mata Hari's eyes are most unpleasant to me. Esther Nighbert, taking over the beginner's class, shows us a heavy line on the upper eyelid against which I protested until she said, "But the bright lights," only to have Mr. Kerz tell me that my eyes would look like burnt-out holes. "*Doch mit recht*" – so they should.

Current Plays followed and a discussion of *Hope for the Best*, the play we saw Thursday night. A return to Broadway for Mr. Franchot Tone of Hollywood was a dismal disappointment to all. Mr. Tone's subtle sex appeal was completely lost in a pointless play which, if we count its slim premise as a plot, is based on a false argument. The writing was pitiful. The story: a young columnist, who writes human interest stories, and who possesses more charm than intelligence, decides to "do something important" and resolves to write about politics. His intelligent fascistic Republican sweetheart wishes to stop him, while a young factory worker encourages him. His simple-minded ideas are concretely displayed by a rather childish (but well played) Russian who makes insipid "drama-grams." He writes about politics, gets the sweet gal, curtain.

The class shared my negative opinion. An argument came up when a student said that it was worth his 70¢ but that he would have felt cheated if he had paid $4.50 for his seat. We argued that this was a purely commercial standpoint and had nothing whatever to do with theatre. Mr. Ince, being a producer, of course, asked, "Well, isn't theatre commercial?" The debate became too heated and was suspended. The motto, "We hate commercial theatre" seems applicable to the general opinion. It had one or two defenders though, who thought the play better than some musicals. My only regret is that Franchot Tone, who professes to love the theatre far more than Hollywood, and who was a member of the historical Group Theatre, and to whom this play meant so much, seems to be failing. He needs direction, which he did not have, and projection, which the prox-imity of the movie camera has made him forswear. Moral: "Don't go to Hollywood – you may never come back."

Directing Class in the evening with *Cher Maître*. Estelle Press was given the problem of dramatic emphasis in stage composition, and using actors as dramatic elements she placed them. Mr. Piscator's patience is immense.

He can sit in a classroom while Miss Dyer draws a diagram showing stage right, left and center, and upstage and downstage. Estelle then placed students facing front, one quarter left and right. Half left and right or profile, three quarter and full back, these are body positions and though elementary, the terminology is important. Emphasis can be achieved by placing the actor to be emphasized in a contrasting body position to the other actors. Or one can achieve emphasis by placing an actor in a different plane or area. The most important area and plane meeting-point is center-stage, but in the case of one actor being separate from the others, he will be emphasized even if he is upstage to either side. Differences in level, entrance, position, attitude all lend emphasis.

Naturally, in these exercises, when we are trying to determine which actor is emphasized, we disregard height, color of clothes, etc., though in staging a scene all these factors would be considered. Mr. Piscator created several stage pictures, shifting emphasis in each composition. These exercises were followed by the ever-recurring *Vultures*, from which scenes were presented for classroom discussion. The scenes done were Tessier and Marie's encounter with the family, the scene between Blanche and Madame Sans Gene, and the fourth act family scene. There's a considerable difference in my perception given that I know the actors. I see them as actors and less as the people they portray. Eugene, who made a convincing Bordon, now seemed miscast, his own personality overshadowing that of the character. Charles Zimmerman's Tessier held up well and Harriet Charney *is* Madame Sans Gene.

Tuesday, February 20, 1945

Directors' Council. More discussion of the intricacies of organization in which I am fortunately not involved. Program conflict. Barbara Sisson had an argument with Mr. Piscator, and such overwhelming confusion seems really insurmountable. I wonder at the success of any production. For Tuesday I am to prepare to cast a scene from Jonson's *Bartholomew Fair*.

The Theatre Research class completed its discussion of *Faust*, carried over from last week. It was an individual character analysis in which such amazing facts came out, as that Robert Carricart, the student playing Faust, did not know that Faust had been rejuvenated between the study scene and the dungeon scene. It seems he had not read the play. I'm sure

Mr. Piscator did not expect any of the students to really do any part of the play correctly, not to say artistically, but nevertheless he criticized each one individually. In speaking of Eugene's Mephisto, he said that Mephisto is another part of *Faust*, not a stranger but a facet, and an intelligent facet of the same man. The dialogues between Faust and Mephisto should have the tempo of a man's struggle with a part of himself. He quoted the "spirit that denies" speech, "*Ich bin der Geist der stets Verneint*," with such color and tonal animation that those who could not understand the German were just as impressed as I, who felt in awe as if I were in a holy temple.

We then went on to Lessing and as I had anticipated, Mr. Piscator asked me to read my critique. I did so very self-consciously. A mixture of run-on sentences composed with an adolescent disregard for grammar, word order or punctuation and highly personal constructions with complex forms (like this). It was more difficult to read than to write. As for content, my biographical and research work was all right but my criticism of the performance was pitiful. I have not the heart to deride, a necessary attribute of the critic. I cannot find fault with honest efforts and when I can I make too many profuse excuses for my criticism. With *Nathan*, of course, I found no fault, and it seemed rather empty to say so. In speaking of the individual roles, my criticism became a mere matter of adjective hunting (a literary crime). My critique was both approved and hotly debated, as most papers are. I am frightfully afraid of being challenged, but that uncertainty will pass.

The March of Drama is in two parts today. A discussion of Racine, and then a rehearsal for the chorus. The sound of the chorus is lovely, although one day we had 20 voices and the next day, six, and in any case, my voice does not blend in evenly. Besides which I have a cold.

Mr. Kerz in Stage Design spoke of the development of the stage setting from its earliest use. In pre-Restoration days when all the theatres in England were closed, plays continued to be presented in salons and ballrooms for the amusement of the aristocracy. It was here that Davenant first used settings instead of ornamental backdrops for his musical plays. It was almost at the same time that women began to take part in stage plays. From here on the development of staging followed naturally, though very slowly. Settings require a curtain for changes. Then came footlights (much later). When footlights were gas, the actors had to approach the audience and stand downstage near the footlights to be seen. This brought about the "apron stage" which is still used in vaudeville, musicals and in some dramas, *hélas!* This century brought about the curse of the box set from which designers, actors and audience cannot or will not escape, which seems ridiculous now that our technical possibilities are tremendous. It was the invention of the electric light that made the modern stage possible and that, it is to be hoped, will make the future stage intelligent.

Mr. Kerz gave us what he termed a "simple problem." He drew a picture of a series of walls to give the impression of a depth of 45 feet at the farthest upstage point, though the stage on which it was to be used was only 15 feet deep. To diagram the floor plan of this set was the problem. One student who had done some staging did it easily. I had some difficulty till I approached it as a drawing problem. If I can draw it flat, giving the illusion, then I can build it flat; or if not flat, going no deeper than 15 feet, and create the illusion by having the flats become shorter, as they are further from the audience.

Wednesday, February 21, 1945

A voice class. We said, "The pendulum ticks and tocks, dissecting time, casting piece after piece into the abyss, lost forever." Miss Montemuro wants slurred words ("blended," she calls it) with such word combinations as "lost forever."

Then a marvelous Dance class with Madame Piscator, with lots of *barre* work, though some of it is rather painful. I took the advanced class which was earlier so as to have time for my rehearsal for *Esther*'s chorus. The work was so much more tiring but then again so much more challenging. Another rehearsal, and if I do not manage to cure my cold by tomorrow I fear for the performance.

In Miss Wyler's acting class, we returned to the problem of *Saint Joan*. We sat in a circle around the dance studio. We were to be the jury, in order to participate in the scene as performers, not as audience. The inquisitor sat in the center of the circle with Joan. To bring the situation closer to us, we transposed it to a Nazi trial with Joan as a party member on trial for treason, so that the sentence – instead of reading, "We declare thee by this act set free from the danger of excommunication in which thou stoodest . . . but since thou hast sinned most presumptuously against God and the Holy Church, etc. . . . . thou art to be confined to the end of thy earthly days in perpetual imprisonment" – was changed to: "Since you have confessed, we are glad to tell you that you will not be forced to give up your membership in the National Socialist Party, but since you are a dangerous person we will have to confine you to a concentration camp for the rest of your life." Several students played both parts. Somehow no one succeeded with St. Joan. Steffie could not address the jury freely. She claims that her difficulty in emotional scenes is due to the fact that in a crisis she is always completely quiet, turning inwards and displaying nothing at all. She realizes that this is the antithesis of acting, but I recognize the problem of expressing what is contrary to one's nature. But then again, "*Humani nihil a me alienum puto*" ("There is no facet of human nature alien to myself" – Terence, *Heauton Timorumenos*). A motto I have written decoratively on the cover page of this notebook.

Fortunately, I express myself very much outwardly. I made an attempt at the scene but was criticized for my "stylized acting," since naturalness was our aim. I was natural enough until I came to the reminiscences of my country life, of "roads in sunlight." Then they said I had a "professional smile." Arla, always a successful improviser, made a fine inquisitor, starting the proceedings with the court standing and a "Heil Hitler," which immediately included us all in the action.

Miss Wyler wanted my St. Joan to be more dramatic, because no one except Charles had succeeded in making the scene dynamic. Therefore, we changed the time and place and had St. Joan already in prison (behind the piano) with the guard passing in front of her cell, telling her to keep quiet and that she should be grateful that they saved her life, while she protests that death would be better than a life in prison. Without realizing it, I applied Stanislavsky. Into my mind came the violent impression of the Danville, Virginia jail where I had spent a frightened and miserable night in November 1944, when the police arrested me and my girlfriend, Mariya Lubliner, when we were hitchhiking. Charles, playing the guard, approached. Then suddenly I said (perhaps half aloud), "Danville," and it was night, and from across the square the neon hotel lights lit up and the prison bars and the humid metal sweated cold. My hands struck them. I shouted. Someone hateful called for quiet, and I screamed and pounded the bars with my fists. I spoke of freedom and roads and people and cells and felt my hairline damp and my hands wet, when I stopped with relief to find myself in a classroom, free, playing a scene about Joan of Arc. I was always skeptical about the story in *An Actor Prepares* in which a young girl amazed Stanislavsky with her weeping over a dead baby, until he learns that she has recently lost her child, but I find it quite plausible after this experience.

Cherie followed me in this exercise. Miss Wyler told her to suddenly see a rat cross the floor of the cell. The disgust set off the whole horror of the situation. After much trouble she saw the rat but her speech was still too poetic. She spoke of red soil through her fingers and the line of the rain or some such thing, too similar to my smiling reminiscences in the courtroom scene. Miss Wyler told us that we all had the tendency to poeticize too much. She wanted reality, even brutality if necessary. She showed us the shout of despair that she wanted, and said, "In scenes of passion, be free, and do not be afraid of making ugly sounds."

For my Styles Through the Ages class, my friend Adolph Giehoff, a surrealist painter, visited the school, as I thought it worthwhile for him to hear a lecture by Dr. Zucker, who spoke today about the Venetian school of painting, beginning with an introduction to Venice and its history. Venice suffered greatly because of Rome. Its people were on a completely different level and its painting showed this. The Venetian merchants appreciated richness in painting. They also promulgated the technique of easel painting, because the merchants and rich bourgeoisie wanted to buy paintings suitable for their homes. Yet the Venetians for all their commerce and traffic, were a naïve people in the sense that they were not striving for an intellectual art but for a beautiful and pleasing art.

Dr. Zucker explained that the climate in a city built in a lagoon would be humid, and haze and coloring would tend to give an impressionist style to the paintings, and also foster an interest in light and shadow, unlike the sunlit world of the Romans. There were slides of paintings by the brothers Bellini – Jacopo, Gentile and Giovanni (whom I had always thought of as one man, *the* Bellini) – of which I particularly remember one by Gentile Bellini, depicting the martyrdom of a saint, a smooth body, not really pierced by arrows, showing no pain whatsoever, and a background of diverse subjects seemingly disconnected from the main picture. We looked at some details, including the balconies of the surrounding houses with rich Venetian tapestries, a mother and child, and a sleeping soldier painted with his feet toward the spectator, lying on the ground in foreshortened perspective. Dr. Zucker showed us several portions of Carpaccio's mural of St. Ursula and told us her story. A young lady of royalty, she was to marry an English king who fell in love with her portrait. She protested, saying she would rather become a martyr than marry, so she gathered 10,000 other virgins and they made pilgrimages, converting people *en route*. In Cologne she was killed by the Huns, along with the other 10,000 virgins. One room pictures all her adventures in a sumptuous, narrative mural. We also saw paintings by Giorgione, Titian and Tintoretto. A comparison of nudes by various artists showed the development towards the baroque, with the twisted corkscrew torso movement and the increase in the sensual. The two most beautiful pictures were of the child Mary ascending the steps of the temple to be presented to the High Priest. The earlier work, which at first appeared exciting, seemed dull and flat when compared to the same subject done later with the baroque variations of planes, lines and levels.

Thursday, February 22, 1945

George Washington's Birthday. No classes, but rehearsal for Racine. I have a terrible cold. I have no idea how I shall manage tomorrow. The sing-song is not yet gone, and only one more rehearsal. Today we had our first rehearsal with the entire cast and the play seems much more finished than our part of it. Jimmy Walsh is powerful and exciting. They all have a fine tempo while we, the chorus, lag miserably, and I especially. Well, tomorrow.

Friday, February 23, 1945

Racine's *Esther*. Nervousness, which often plays too important a part in my appearance on the stage, was diminished here since the part was done in a chorus. The play was successful, but my role in it is a horrid failure. As "unimportant" as a chorus part may be, my individual effort should be as great as the leading actor's.

It is, of course, simple enough to pass my shortcomings off on the splitting headache and the clogging cough, and by rationalizing, I might do so. Starting well (except for the cold), I spoke accurately enough but was not for one moment anywhere near "belief" in the story or the speeches. I attempted every plausible, and some implausible methods of concentration, but the more I tried, the harder I was thinking of thinking and the less I was being a Jewess freed from slavery.

Finally, in a part carried by three light voices, I stopped. I stopped not because of the cold, headache or other inconveniences, but on account of my old enemy, the fear of breaking up.

There was no reason for laughing, I saw nothing that was humorous, and I do not laugh so very easily. My sense of humor is rather hard to arouse, yet on stage, I am impelled to laugh. I hate myself for it, yet I am impelled to laugh. I almost cry over it at times, and yet I am impelled to laugh. So strong is the desire to laugh that I cannot enter a stage without thinking, "I will not laugh." Immediately I think, "No, don't laugh, don't even think about laughing," and there we are. If I could find a solution to this, it would be the most decisive thing I could learn. Perhaps Stanislavsky or some method of overcoming fear of the audience might help me get rid of this impulse which I cannot explain.

Monday, March 5, 1945

I spent the morning in the 42nd Street Library trying to find two letters for Mr. Piscator, and had the library staff helping me, though no one succeeded in finding either Romain Rolland's letter to Tolstoy or Rolland's letter to Gerhardt Hauptmann, which Mr. Piscator wanted for a Romain Rolland Memorial that he is organizing for The New School. Mr. Freedley, head of the drama department, who is always helpful, was not there. I had to cope with the impatient library staff. Now for my dancing class.

Madame Piscator could not come to class and Eugene was still tired from last evening's production of *The Imaginary Invalid* so Alice Blue, one of the students who has studied ballet, did *barre* work with us, some *pliés*, and then some pseudo-tightrope walking across the floor, which looks easier than it is. The object was to be as daring as possible and think of amusing or dangerous exploits to perform atop the rope. But most, like myself, were scarcely able to cross without falling. Then we carried the circus idea further and in a final exercise to circus music, we were the most splendid lions defying and obeying our keeper. Arla Gild and I engaged in a terrific battle that Ringling's would pay thousands for (if we were lions).

A make-up class. Barbara Sisson and I attempted middle-age make-up. We tried to get the effect with only two slight shadows from nose to mouth and slight shadows for sagging under the eyes, since the make-up was not for a very old person but for a woman about 42 and rather well-preserved. The result, with Barbara using brown liner and myself using grey liner was that, as Mr. Kerz put it, she looked "as though she had missed a few hour's sleep," and I looked "degenerate, haggard and emaciated," which was perfectly true. Barbara's face retained her freshness and her youth, while I looked like a very sloppy prostitute of indefinite age. I shall try it with brown liner next week.

In Current Plays we read further in *Margret*, the girl with five distinct personalities. Last week the authors of the play, Sterling North and Yasha Frank, were in class and we read for them. I read the role of The Drudge. The authors were impressed with Virginia's rendition of The Bitch, which she does to perfection.

But today we read among ourselves, and I took the part of The Clubwoman, and could not quite give it the sense of "lording it" that Harriet Charney had. I read a little too clipped and hard. It is rather a difficult part for me but . . . *Humani nihil a me alienum puto*.

In my evening directing class, Mr. Piscator discussed and illustrated counterfocus. Counterfocus is emphasis achieved indirectly through an emphasized figure. In other words, x, y and z are looking at A, but A is looking at B. B is emphasized more by x–y–z's indirect focus than by A alone. We illustrated this with several examples from Alexander Dean. We then did a scene from the archives, that is, from recent March of Drama productions, choosing Strindberg's *Bridal Crown*. I saw Virginia Baker do it before I came to school, and have since considered her Kirsti as the finest thing that I saw in The Dramatic Workshop. Tonight, instead of being overwhelmed I was analytical. Virginia's reading of the lines was technically perfect and her pauses and stresses were probably as well planned (I could feel the planning) as in the earlier production.

The *Bridal Crown* is the story of Kirsti, a peasant girl who loves a miller's son and in secret bears his child. The bridal crown that Kirsti aspires to wear on her wedding day is a symbol of virginity and so she kills her child. She is tormented by this, and the story of her final redemption seems to me to make this the most gentle, the most ethereal play I have ever seen. Yet tonight I was not carried away by its spirit. More than anything, the importance of lights is borne in upon me in such a reading, for the lighting had added an aura of mysticism to the play which, when uniformly lit, became too earthy.

Tuesday, March 6, 1945

In Directors' Council this morning, Mr. Piscator gave us one of his inimitable speeches on the theatre and acting. It started with a letter from Edna Edison, a student who opposed many school policies and wanted to discontinue classes. She complained of having to attend *The Imaginary Invalid* rehearsals and learn the role of Angelique, which she was not given the opportunity to play, and she did not think it was right to rehearse so long for nothing, and to come to rehearsals to wait for two hours until she had something to do. It was essentially the same complaint that Barbara Sisson made when she refused all production work, and wanted only to attend classes.

Mr. Piscator referred us to the example of the Russian theatre and of Stanislavsky's methods of rehearsing a play. Once, Stanislavsky rehearsed a play for four years before deciding against presenting it. Patient work was not in vain because of what was gained in rehearsals.

In the name of discipline it was decided to divide the school among the directing students, letting each take two to four acting students and become their delegate, commissar, or spokesman, and to serve as a clearing-house for their complaints, comments and conflicts. I am timid enough about my own progress without having to be responsible for others, but even as a newcomer I was assigned to Ethel Shephard and a brand new arrival, Anita Fortus. I shall do what I can, though the task seems beyond my capacity.

In the Theatre Research class, Mr. Piscator continued his discourse on acting. He described the high purpose of rehearsal because it is then that an actor finds the "creative moment." It is for this moment that an actor lives, for only in this moment is he an artist, a creator. Mr. Piscator cannot teach us to find this creative moment, but he can teach us to listen for it and to recognize it. We must "listen to hear the grass grow," as Piscator put it. It is difficult to be prepared to perceive such moments, and Stanislavsky cannot help us, for this is something which is deeper than even the penetrating Stanislavsky can reach. As young actors we must first find our means of expression, we must learn to breathe and move, and do many simply mechanical things. We cannot hope to be creative in a classical role while we are still concerned with language and meter.

When Piscator studied to be an actor he was first taught rhetoric. He told us how, when he was young, he wanted sheer classical beauty in all things. Like my mother, he admired Alexander Moissi, the great German classicist with his gentle, sweet, perfect voice, who played Max Reinhardt's Everyman. I recall that when I was 10 years old and was certainly not a judge of acting, my mother played me a record of Moissi reading a fairy tale, *Die Princessin mit der Erbse* (*The Princess and the Pea*). His rendition made a vivid impression on me. I remember saying to my mother how strange it was that when he spoke of the little princess being out in the cold and the rain and said, "*und der Wind hat geblasen*" ("and the wind was blowing"), I really felt the wind blew in his voice, as though it really blew then and there.

Piscator told us how he aspired to speak like Moissi. After a performance, Piscator (the boy) went home and tried to do exactly the same thing. He, too, wanted the classicist's perfection of voice and gesture. After seeing Moissi's *Hamlet*, he spent hours trying to say (and here he demonstrated), "*Sein oder nicht Sein, daß ist hier die Frage.*" He spoke in the aspirated syllables and used the long vowel sounds that Mother used, which she also acquired from her idol Moissi, whom she never ceased emulating.

Piscator ceased emulating Moissi after the war. For in the war he was awakened to all the problems of humanity, and society became a factor in art and not a factor outside of art. He could no longer tolerate the beautiful escapism of the ivory tower theatre. He fought against the classics, against Reinhardt. He invented Epic Theatre with its sociological and political implications. This was one of many theatrical revolutions. He told us of Meyerhold's biomechanical revolution and the unemotional theatre. Naturally this was a failure, since it was based on a false premise.

He concluded with more words on acting, on the importance of technique, and of attacking a role from all angles. He drew a parallel between the actor and the painter. The painter decides on a subject or a certain composition and then before painting it, he sketches it, over and over, as in a rehearsal, before he is ready to call the painting finished. He cited Picasso's *Guernica*, for which Picasso did so many sketches. The detail of one of the horse's heads which, in the final painting, is an abstraction of suffering, was worked on in many different ways. I have seen these sketches and it is obvious that neither the realistic heads nor the indecipherable shorthand drafts were Picasso's goal. His craftsmanship in realistic drawings prepares him for the perfection of the abstract masterpieces.

We then read some of the class critiques of *The Imaginary Invalid*. I was not asked to read mine, which I had written only that morning. Virginia Baker played Toinette, the saucy, impertinent maid, with verve and energy. Eugene Van Grona as the invalid Argan blustered and shouted and moaned alternately, wailed sickly, and scampered gaily. I could no more think of the crazy old man on stage as the charming, graceful dancer of our classes, than I could imagine the bullying, loud Toinette as Faust's tragic Gretchen. Caroline Townley played the hypocritical wife with finish and style. Gerence was indeed the ingenue, with a sweetness to match the name of Angelique. Hal Tulchin had the Molière sense of *joie de vivre* with lots of clever dance movements. Gene Benton was all pomp, and Darren Dublin played in falsetto with terrific comical results. The acting was exaggerated and done almost with a snicker. Pupils from the Children's Workshop were used to excellent effect as a chorus of doctors. The settings – which the class disliked – were expressionistic, though the furniture was of the period. Make-up included putty noses of improbable shapes and sizes. I liked the concept of the production, although most of my opinions were contradicted either by other students or by Piscator. Fortunately, I was not required to express these unpopular sentiments.

Today The March of Drama consisted of readings from the Elizabethans: *Volpone*, it seems, is as vulgar as *Bartholomew Fair*, which in my critique last week, I characterized as a cheap vaudeville show. The "robust Elizabethans" do not appeal to me. Steffi Blank did a scene from Webster's *The Duchess of Malfi*. She read the Duchess in the gory murder scene. Eugene read the killer and I read an angel's voice, part of an attempt to frighten the Duchess. It went quite well. Gloria Cacarro then did a reading from Molière's *The Doctor in Spite of Himself*. She endowed the shrewish wife with all the quick-witted humor of the lines. Charles Zimmerman was a gentle wood-chopper. The immense difference between two farcical scenes, one by an Elizabethan, the other by a writer of the court of Louis XIV, makes one shudder at England's late acquisition of refinement. As we are now approaching Shakespeare, everyone will attempt to read a favorite passage from the Bard. Steffi and I are collaborating on *The Tempest*, she as Prospero, I as Ariel. Such a lovely part, if only I could give it that spritely quality. She has played Prospero in England and can direct me somewhat.

A Stage Design class, in which Mr. Kerz explained intensive and extensive drama and presentational and representational theatre. The representational drama (insofar as I understand it) attempts to convince the audience of the reality of the play – though it is not necessarily realistic – whereas presentational drama admits that the play is a play and that the actor is an actor and not the character he is playing. A nightclub comedian or M.C. is the most common modern vestige of presentational acting, while most of the legitimate theatre is representational. Our theatre today is also intensive drama; that is, it shows one small segment, or slice of life, magnified and concentrated. It does not concern itself with the outside world or other aspects of the problem but only with this room, these people, and this immediate time. Extensive theatre concerns life itself. It takes a broader view of the world, and the plot is affected by it, as it affects the plot. It unifies the various aspects in order to show us the environs of the situation. The theatre today has reached a dead end in representational intensive drama. To go on with it after it has reached its peak is to stagnate or, worse, to be reactionary, therefore the theatre of the future must be new, must seek a change. It may be in some form of expressionistic theatre or Epic Theatre (the highest form of extensive drama) but a new theatre will come after this war and this new theatre is ours.

Wednesday, March 7, 1945

A voice class. I dislike these foolish exercises. I shall not go into detail but rather go on to my dancing class. Our *barre* exercises become more exciting and harder, yet easier, each week. The fundamentals of choreography have always eluded me, but with concentration I can now master most steps. It takes several times the mental effort to control my body than to do any mental gymnastics. When I finally mastered a simple step it took so much effort that Madame Piscator remarked that "it is certainly not necessary for anyone who can write poetry to stand and move so." I tried to get it right and only wish we had more dancing classes.

Then an acting class with Margrit Wyler. We read the scene from *Candida* between Lexy Mills and Miss Prossy. I was asked to read Miss Prossy. Miss Wyler said that I maintained my own identity and neglected Miss Prossy. Evelyn read Lexy Mills. Miss Wyler asked us to speak on an emotional subject. Evelyn retold – in the first person – the story of the birth scene in *A Tree Grows in Brooklyn*. Then I told (with modifications) the story of Françoise La Soeur and Valeska Gert. The ardor with which I had asked the bondsman and the judge for help, only two weeks ago, was gone completely, and only the righteous indignation of a meddler was left. Miss Wyler said that I showed the aroused emotion but not once my heart. Again, I broke up laughing and felt more miserable than ever about it. Miss Wyler asked me to imagine that the man in question was my husband, and although it seemed absurd to think of myself as La Soeur's wife, *there is no facet of human nature alien to myself.* I explained my problem to Miss Wyler, who says that if I concentrate, I could not possibly be distracted enough to laugh. I'm afraid she is wrong. I wish there was someone who could help me.

A Styles Through the Ages class on German art of the 15th to 16th Century. Dr. Zucker disputes the name "German Renaissance." German art in 1500 was still artistically in the middle ages. From Gothic architecture and other medieval forms, it leapt into the baroque in the late 17th century, never really developing the style of the Renaissance. Yet Dürer and Holbein were of that time, and theirs are among the most masterly works of art.

In the slides we saw a medieval statue of Eve by Riemenschneider, her face very young, very gentle and very German. Then some Cranachs – an Adam and Eve, a Martin Luther, and a Holy Family against a fairy tale background. Cranach's *Adam and Eve* was described by Dr. Zucker as being "just one big embarrassment" contrasted with Dürer's copper engraving of Adam and Eve, decorative, sedate, and intelligent. In another Flemish Adam and Eve, life and movement overflowed. The *Isenheimer Altar of Grünewald*, with its many details, was truly astonishing. A self-portrait of Dürer done at the age of 12 was a miracle of craftsmanship with no trace of immaturity. In his mature portraits – we saw images of his mother and of an old man – Dürer's brutal frankness spared no one. Another painting, *The Young Jesus*, caricatured the elders of the Temple. Dr. Zucker ended the class with some of Holbein's royal paintings, the lovely *Prince of Wales* and the austere *Jane Seymour*. The sumptuous painting of Henry himself, with its disproportionate shoulders, reveals the boorish, voluptuous fool that he was, over-adorned and disgusting.

Thursday, March 8, 1945

My voice class today proved too much for me and my resentment has reached an uncontrollable point. I realize that Gloria Montemuro has helped me as far as voice production goes, but that does not make up for the self-consciousness I feel during class. I spoke to her afterwards. I told her quite frankly that I was unhappy in her classes. I explained my speech background. She tried to be sympathetic but did not really understand. We came to no conclusion, but at least she knows my attitude and my reasons. I cannot judge the effect until my next speech class.

My History and Sociology class, now that we are done with the history part of it, has become even more interesting. For now we are dealing with the psychological aspect of the theatre, and more particularly, with the audience's psychology. In asking for a definition of psychology, we arrived at the subject of definitions in general, and reached a conclusion about what a good definition is. We defined psychology as the science dealing with the faculty of perception and of the human mind's reaction to this perception, as well as with the processes of the emotions, the intellect, physical motion and willpower. Dr. Zucker then divided the five, or rather six senses into those affecting the theatre (sight, hearing, and touch – as in costumes), and those not of the theatre (smell and taste). The "sixth sense" – definitely part of the theatre – Dr. Zucker defined as the "indefinable factor" of personality or personal magnetism, call it what you will. It is completely apart from beauty and intellect. Some may call it charm, yet it is not always a positive quality, for it encompasses Hitler as well as Sinatra, Roosevelt and Rudolf Valentino. But the sixth sense is not in our own control, whereas we can work with the other faculties.

The senses of sight and hearing should concern us most. The majority of audiences are visual, not auditory in orientation. We proved this in class by taking an ordinary word and letting someone say the first thing that came to their mind. With words like a parade where association of sight or sound is possible, the answers given were more often of a visual than an auditory nature. Dr. Zucker then told us of a theatrical law which holds good for no other art and in no other case: the importance of an active or an auditory ending. In other words, the curtain should fall on a piece of business, or a sound, like bells or an explosion – anything but dialogue. For the intellectual content must be sealed by a physical effect. As examples, he mentioned the weather vane in *St. Joan* and the sunlight in the windows in *Ghosts*. The climactic bell chimes in *A Bell for Adano* are a contemporary example. Achieving this is as often the director's job as the writer's. I think that almost all the plays I have seen end with action rather than dialogue, even if it is the lovers' final embrace. Dr. Zucker explained the slowness of audience reactions, and that the audience must be fore-warned of everything that comes later. A clue to every action must precede that action.

The audience frequently takes a few moments to laugh at a comic line. The actor must wait for the laugh. If he goes on talking, he will lose the comic effect of the laugh line and the sense of the one following it. Or he can freeze, but the wisest thing he can do is to fill in with a piece of incon-spicuous business or a gesture. The other actor on the stage has a greater problem. When he hears the humorous line to which he is supposed to react, he has two possibilities. He can either aid the audience in speeding up the laugh by laughing himself immediately, in which case his laughter is in danger of distracting the audience from the original line. But if he does not laugh, there is the danger of a silence and an empty pause. For an actor cannot move between the lines and the laugh. It is clear now why Piscator requires students to study psychology in their second year.

Next, a class in costume design, with a lecture on Roman costume. Rules and regulations concerning clothing were strict and complex. Social position was indicated by clothing, as is true less and less today. Prisoners wore trousers like "the trousered barbarians" of other nations, which, to the Romans, was a sign of subjugation. The toga was worn only a short time and then only by the patricians to distinguish them from the ple-beians. Among varieties of togas, there were differences showing rank. The shape of the toga is disputed, but the way it was worn is known.

Mr. Kerz gave us complete directions for putting on a toga. Whether diamond shaped or semicircular, the cloth is known to be 18 inches wide. One end of its length was thrown over the left shoulder to the floor. The rest, taken across the front under the right arm, is wrapped girdle-wise across the belly, then wrapped across the back and tied to the wrist. Pulling the toga out bag-wise in front forms a receptacle called an "asinus." Back drapery was sometimes used as a hood for rain or as a sign of mourning.

The tunic, as in Greece, was worn underneath the toga. Eventually, the plebeians wore togas of grey or brown cotton, but never, as the patricians later did, of silk from the Orient. Black togas were for mourning. Caesar and conquering generals wore purple togas. Priests, boys under 14 years of age, and magistrates wore the toga pretext, which was white with a purple border, as a sign of purity and character. Knights wore alternating wide and narrow stripes of purple.

About 200 B.C.E., elaborately embroidered tunics replaced togas. Plebeians wore the palladium (named for Pallas Athena) from Greece. Women wore a form of the Ionic tunic. Headdresses and coiffures were even more foolish than ours.

Friday, March 9, 1945

Unhappy at missing acting classes, I was assigned to "tour" with the Molière. The tour took us all the way to Brooklyn, to P.S. 221, and any classes that I missed were well-sacrificed, for I learned a great deal. We overcame such practical difficulties as a girls' dressing room with one mirror, one light and no tables. My job became more one of wardrobe mistress than costume supervisor, and my odd jobs were innumerable. The script, having been adapted for children, turned Beline into a witch, and put Toinette into direct contact with the children. Toinette incorporated the speeches of the absent Beralde and Cléante. I cued Virginia as she put her greasepaint on, and found that she knew hardly any of the lines, but had complete self-confidence in her inventiveness and faith in her ability to improvise.

Standing backstage, I viewed an amazing spectacle. Told that the audience would consist of children, we expected a group about 12 years old. Instead, there appeared little wobbling ones of eight to ten, at most. Well, no sooner had the *Imaginary Invalid*, Argan, begun to speak, than the children started to think of other things. But our actors really went overboard. Virginia beat Eugene and threw him down. Eugene screamed himself hoarse and chased Caroline Townley (Beline) around the auditorium. And in the general bedlam, Darren Dublin, as Thomas Diaforus, broke up the actors – in every cast, there is a practical joker to take advantage of the bedlam. The fact that the play was presented at all, and that it was able to gain the children's attention, is more than could have been expected, although the presentation would have made Molière revolve in his grave at an amazing speed.

The second performance was given to a slightly older and less noisy audience, who at least followed the play. In the earlier show, when Darren spoke his long speeches, the meaning was so obviously lost that he turned to Eugene and said quite loudly, "It stinks." Even this went unnoticed by the audience. And yet this second audience followed most of what was

74

going on and enjoyed it. Afterwards, the cast had a taste of fame when hundreds of children besieged them for autographs. We struck the set and rode home. I felt that this was a tremendous lesson in feeling free and uninhibited on the stage. Even the slightest fear makes it more difficult to improvise in chaotic situations.

Today The March of Drama dealt with the later Elizabethans. Mr. Gassner spoke of Webster, Jonson, Dekker, Ford, and the subject of the night's demonstration, Phillip Massinger. They "embraced culture in a kind of bear hug." They loved humanity and caricatured it bitterly. The demonstration was from Massinger's *A New Way to Pay Old Debts*. Eleanor Epstein was a gentle Margret, Gene Benton was a rather good Overreach, but Louis Guss, as Greedy, outdid himself. In the end, when the food-loving Greedy is told that he may not eat, his expression changes slowly with the realization, and the disappointment is made visual by a klieg light which changes from red to orange to yellow to a deep green.

Sunday, March 11, 1945

A Sunday evening program in the Urban Auditorium at school in memory of Romain Rolland. I was able to attend as an usherette. Piscator, who admires Rolland especially for his book *The People's Theatre* assembled a wonderful group of speakers. Barrett H. Clark, who has translated much of Rolland, spoke of Rolland as his teacher in Paris. Of all the descriptions of Rolland during the evening, his portrait of the gentle teacher, with his love of music and his unworldliness, touched me most, perhaps because I saw Jean-Christophe in him. Fredrika Zweig read an excerpt from her husband Stefan Zweig's biography of Rolland, a stereotyped description of a small, quiet man with flashing eyes. Henri Torres, a French newspaper editor, then spoke in French, and from what I understood he reminded everyone that fascists are not good and that we all hate them and that Rolland hated them. But he said it so beautifully, the rhythm of his speech, the effective pauses, the tonality, and even the gestures were so charming, that the audience was spellbound. André Spire, a French poet with white hair and a little white beard, read a letter from Rolland in an admirable manner. Fritz von Unruh, the poet, spoke in English. I don't know his poetry, nor his expression in his own language, but his speech was terrifically bad. "Romain Rolland," he said too loudly, "we have to look to you, Romain Rolland! You are our inspiration!" etc. Then, as a personal tribute, Bronislav Huberman and Bruno Walter played Beethoven's *Kreutzer Sonata* splendidly. I sat next to Eugene Van Grona ("Music I heard with you was more than music"). Stella Adler, fine voiced and stately, read a passage from *The People's Theatre* in which Rolland says that there cannot be an "art" theatre as distinguished from a people's theatre, and that the people's theatre must be of, as well as for, the people. Jean-Benoît Lévy's French was beyond me, and Jules Romain, whose writing I respect, did not impress me. A scene from Rolland's play *The Wolves* was read by the magnificent Mr. Berghof, the less magnificent Philip Houston, and the boys of the Workshop. The writing was on an intellectual plane, a wonderful lecture, but poor theatre.

Monday, March 12, 1945

A dance class with Eugene Van Grona. After some exercises, he went on to the principles of walking, walking in the dance. He showed us how to motivate our walking from a particular place. The upper chest in a line from under the shoulders, but above the breast, can direct our forward line, as well as show the mood of that movement. If we let this spot pull us forward as by a magnet, remembering to leave our shoulders down, we assume an authoritative walk, clean and fresh. This is a spirited and vital way of walking. If, on the other hand, we react and contract the chest, our whole body seems sunken and humble and negative.

We tried two exercises. First, we walked across the room haughtily, aggressively, and even tyrannically. In doing this, I thought of O'Neill's *Lazarus Laughed* and the line, "Hail, Caligula, Emperor of Rome" as I walked. Next we were to walk humbly, and here I made a connection in my mind with a picture that Dr. Zucker had shown us of Mary as a child going to receive the High Priest's blessing. We made further experiments: a dry, business-like gait, dull and unsensual. I tried this for the class, and though I could not find out where my characterization lay, those who watched felt that it was in my shoulders. To gain this feeling, we tried the opposite, the poetic, and then the sensual figure. The sensual figure, especially the woman, walks mostly from the hips, moving from the waist down, her body following. After this, we tried the dry character with tight hips, moving with shoulders forward and leading with his upper body, and there we had the character perfectly. We ended this class with some fencing movement which, although I fear I failed at it, was dazzlingly done by the teacher.

Make-up class. Continuing from last week's attempt at early middle age, we went ahead to later middle age. Where last week's make-up had made me look like a very ill old prostitute, this week the class asked who had disinterred me. It seems hard for a teacher to realize that in a face as narrow and sallow as mine, the faintest shadow will stand out as a big indentation. The heavy line, therefore, takes my whole face in with it until there is nothing left but a hollow mask. Nevertheless, I am learning the rudiments of make-up.

In Current Plays, the class discussed *Jacobowsky and the Colonel*, which I thought was the best comedy I have seen on Broadway, although the class as a whole did not like it. Perhaps the European, Semitic flavor was closer to me.

In directing class, we discussed offstage emphasis, which puzzled some of the students, though Mr. Piscator made it quite plain. He got on to the stage and spoke to someone, then called to another person below, "Hello, Oscar, come on. You coming?" The manner in which he did it was so funny that the class dissolved in hilarity for the entire session and no concentration was achieved. Even Chouteau Dyer was uncontrollable and left in order that Piscator could continue the lesson. This, at any rate, made the idea of offstage emphasis clear. We then worked on building an entrance.

Last Friday's March of Drama reading was then discussed. Hal Tulchin had directed it and Gene Benton told us how Hal struggled to help the cast with some of the more obscure passages. The lines from *A New Way to Pay Old Debts* that caused the trouble were those in which Overreach praises his daughter's appearance and says that her feet, too, must be well-dressed, for they draw as much attention as the face. We spent the rest of the hour paraphrasing these words.

Tuesday, March 13, 1945

In Directors' Council, we again discussed discipline: if a student is unwilling to do technical work, they may not participate in the acting work at school. All of which may be very important, but Mr. Piscator has so much to give us that it is frustrating to spend an hour listening to him scold Sidney Schwartz.

Theatre Research was a continuation of the scolding, but on a larger scale. It seems that no one in school had written their critique of *A New Way to Pay Old Debts* except for me. After he concluded the scolding, Mr. Piscator asked me to read my critique and made me wish that I had not written it only this morning without having reread it. I felt frightened, so naturally I laughed. Mr. Piscator doesn't know about my weakness yet, and I blamed the play's humor, which this time I got away with, the critique being judged satisfactory.

Our March of Drama class was made up of readings from Shakespeare. Steffi Blank and I were called on first and did our scene from *The Tempest*. She did Prospero emphatically, while I, as Ariel, worked to achieve a certain lightness. The class naturally drew comparisons with Zorina's and Arnold Moss' performances in the same roles on Broadway. As Zorina is a dancer and not an actress at all, the comparison was favorable. I was said to have "felt it," which was not really true. I "felt" the poetry, I felt the beauty of what I was saying, but the meaning, although clear, did not express itself emotionally. Harriet Charney read the Shrew, from *Taming*. She did well with the shrewishness. Eleanor Epstein read an intelligent Lady Macbeth, almost too beautifully, and with fine *crescendi* as she reached toward the climax. But no matter how well she did it, she does not yet have the emotional maturity to convey the character.

In our Stage Design class, we addressed some further perspective problems, after a short review of extensive and intensive methods. Starting with the simplest and most frequent, if the most uninteresting design, we discussed the box set and solved some of the problems it presents. First we considered the elements of a stage and its measurement. This includes the proscenium measurements in the average Broadway theatre, which are 36′ to 40′ wide, 16′ to 18′ high and 30′ to 34′ deep. The "teaser" and "tormentor" frame the top and sides of the set respectively, while the "border" and "legs" are drapes serving a similar purpose, and are sometimes called "the false proscenium." We spoke about the cyclorama and the ground row, which is necessary to hide the bottom of the cyclorama. A common mistake in lighting is the lighting of an outdoor scene from above. The lightest part of the sky should be that nearest the horizon, as in painting.

Wednesday, March 14, 1945

An unfortunate Voice class. My discussion with Miss Montemuro has not only not helped, but actually hurt.

Dance class with Madame Piscator. *Barre* work and some dancing to strange music, Oriental, Russian, and *bolero*. Being very tired, I derived very little from it but deeper tiredness.

An acting class. Cherie Ross read the part of Martha from *Bury the Dead*, my favorite drama of a few years ago. She read sensibly and smoothly. Miss Wyler tried to have her express the feelings of Martha, whose husband is dead – because he saw no reason for the war or for his death, he stands up with five other dead soldiers and refuses to be buried. The soldiers' wives, mothers, and sweethearts plead with them not to upset the placid ways of custom. Martha is not really sorry that her husband is dead, as she has lived a poverty-stricken life which she blames on his lack of ambition and ability. Miss Wyler wanted Cherie to feel this lonely poor life, but came to the conclusion that she was too young to understand it. But I think it was rather her lack of understanding of poverty, for if I could convince her of anything on the stage, it would be the stifling feeling of being poor, just as I was able to capture the feeling of imprisonment.

Then I read an unprepared speech. Miss Wyler chose Martha's love speech from *The Children's Hour*. My reading, she said, was intelligent, but too beautiful. I strive for beauty in word and phrase, to a point where my reading becomes almost stylized. I tried the speech again but it was still on that level, which detracts from naturalistic acting. By now, I was familiar with the content of the speech and Miss Wyler asked me to give its essence without looking at the book but directly at her. I spoke more haltingly, but, as Miss Wyler had hoped, less beautifully. She said that I was not very convincing, that is, I did not convince her that I loved her. Reading from a paper I feel completely free to say anything, but speaking directly to another person, I feel the hesitation of embarrassment. A little experience will doubtless cure me of that.

Steffi then read the "We will not suffer any more" speech of Karen in *The Children's Hour* and somehow seemed at odds with the text. Alice very sweetly read Alice from *You Can't Take It With You*. As I needed the unbeautiful speech for comedy (I had told Miss Wyler of my inability to act comedy, although I don't think I lack a sense of humor), she asked me to read Grandpa's speech to the rich man from the same play and I did it properly, but any humor apart from that already in the lines themselves was lacking.

In a Styles Through the Ages class on Spanish painting, Dr. Zucker described Spain as a land of extremes. The Inquisition, he said, was the cruelest of historical phenomena. He spoke of Spanish poverty – the poorest in the middle ages – and Spanish wealth transcending that of any other nobility. This duality is mirrored in the painting of the time, for it is rich in contrast and color. Spanish Renaissance painting is also rich in contrast. Abrupt lines and strong variations in light and shade predominate, with an almost Russian love of strong color.

The first slide was of a cathedral portal carved with a scene of hell, portraying the most sadism per square inch imaginable. Then a painting of Christ in a most terrific agony. Three high churchmen by three painters: one by Titian, Velázquez's Pope, and El Greco's Cardinal. We see some magnificent El Grecos, showing how his art developed: *Christ and the Money Changers*, and then the same subject, painted 20 years later with loose brush strokes and freely rendered figures, and the use of translucent oil paint. Then his *Repentant Peter* and the menacing storm over Toledo. Velázquez followed, with an ugly historical picture of the conquerors of Bredo. A dwarf of the Spanish court with the saddest face showed us the tragedy of finding him comical, bringing to mind Oscar Wilde's *Birthday of the Infanta* with its sad dwarf. *Las Meniñas*, Dr. Zucker explained, was a trick picture. The mirrored king and queen in the background and the daring representation of the artist himself, half hidden by his own canvas, are bold innovations.

Then, *quelle surprise*, a Venus by Velázquez, the only thin Venus I have ever seen, dark and fragile, and I was very glad that even at the time that Rubens flaunted his large ladies, a Venus who was slender could be painted. Dr. Zucker showed a Titian Venus for contrast. Murillo with his Christmas cards followed, but found no sympathy from me. Some Goya portraits and drawings (none as sublime as his war drawings) ended the class.

Thursday, March 15, 1945

A voice class. Then the most fascinating History and Sociology class. Dr. Zucker discussed the psychology of the audience, first identifying seven classes. All these were worked out in group discussion, and we found reasons for all our classifications. The first and highest class, the most appreciative audience, is the intellectual class, "the receptive society." Society, Dr. Zucker points out, might seem an undemocratic way of designating the wealthiest class, but the well-educated, well-traveled man who has not spent his life working, is apt to be intelligent. Provided, of course, that he be receptive (i.e., not a dope). Next on the scale is the professional – the lawyer, doctor, etc. Then, in order: the upper middle class businessman, the dependent white collar worker (the librarian, the teacher), the blue collar worker, the lower-paid white collar worker (the stenographer), and last of all, the matinee audience.

He then classified the type of theatre that each audience prefers. The first two classes, intellectual and professional, prefer the literary theatre and the comedy of manners (Noël Coward), and for the tired businessman, musical comedy. The dependent white collar worker prefers sugar-coated realism, or the normal fare of Broadway such as *The Voice of the Turtle*.

PSYCHOLOGY OF THE AUDIENCE

CLASS	PREFERENCE	PERCEPTION	NY%	TUCSON%
INTELLECTUALS AND RECEPTIVE SOCIETY	LITERARY THEATRE	INTELLECTUAL-VISUAL/AUDITORY	20%	10%
PROFESSIONALS	LITERARY THEATRE	INTELLECTUAL	20%	20%
UPPER MIDDLE CLASS	LITERARY THEATRE/COMEDY OF MANNERS/MUSICAL COMEDY	VISUAL/INTELLECTUAL-AUDITORY	40%	60%
DEPENDENT WHITE COLLAR WORKERS	SUGAR-COATED REALISM	INTELLECTUAL	8%	10%
WORKERS	ALL OF ABOVE & POLITICAL THEATRE	VISUAL-INTELLECTUAL/AUDITORY	10%	–
LOWER WHITE COLLAR WORKERS	MUSICALS/FARCE	AUDITORY	2%	–
MATINEE AUDIENCE	SENTIMENTAL PLAYS	VISUAL	2%	–

Figure 2 Paul Zucker's "Psychology of the Audience" chart.

The blue collar worker enjoys all of the above, preferring the political theatre, which speaks directly to him. Lower-paid white collar workers like musicals, while the matinee audience is all for sweet sentiment. We decided that only the first two classes and the last two really want to go to the theatre.

In New York City, the composition of the audience is probably 20% from the first two classes, 40% upper middle class, 10% workers, 20% matinee audience, with 10% white collar workers. In a rural community, Tucson, for example, you would find 10% intellectuals, 20% professionals, 60% upper middle class, 10% dependent white collar workers, and only sometimes a stray individual from the other classes. Food for thought when we next play Tucson.

Dr. Zucker made a second chart showing the sociological differences and common reactions of the modern audience, and the variety of theatrical interests, depending on the respective social stratum.

Audience taste is influenced by three factors:

A: Plays dealing with something within their range.
B. Seeing things known to them through reading or education.
C. Snobbism.

Farmhands Unemployed Shiftless	NP + incidental	Westerns and mysteries
Lower Middle Class	NP + pulp magazines	Western + mysteries + love stories
White Collar Worker	NP + romantic novel + middle class magazine	Musical + love story + political
Secure Upper Middle Class	NP + romantic novel + middle class magazine	Musical + love story + political with emphasis on entertainment
Professional Intellectual	NP + literature (*New Yorker Magazine*)	Musical, love story, political, documentary & comedy of manners
Society	NP + literature + romantic best seller	Musical, love story, political, comedy of manners with emphasis on entertainment

Figure 3 Paul Zucker's second sociological chart.

A class in costume design: France became the center of the fashion world in 55 B.C.E. when Caesar crossed the Alps, and it has remained so till the present day. During the dark ages, fashion changed slowly because of the difficulty and expense of making garments. The fashion center was Marseille, later changing to Paris, where it remains. The idea of variety in costume began among the patricians in Gaul; yellow hair and veils, the stole, and the corset, or *strophium*, were worn; also, the first sewn (as opposed to draped) linen leggings from which stockings were derived. In costume, as in most things, the dark ages were far behind Roman culture and had not yet reached medieval grandeur.

Friday, March 16, 1945

Voice class.

Then an acting class in which Mr. Ben-Ari gave us several exercises for centering attention, but mostly he talked about various directors' methods, especially Vakhtangov's. Vakhtangov was a pupil of Stanislavsky who later broke with the Stanislavsky method and wanted to do away with naturalism to create a theatre of "fantastic realism." He believed that the theatre must adapt itself to the actor's imagination, which is much closer to Piscator's theory than to Stanislavsky's. Fantastic realism requires more depth on the actor's part, just as Piscator's methods, if they were genuinely carried out, would require of the actor inspiration as well as imagination. Therefore, Mr. Ben-Ari concluded, Stanislavsky is a good basis for any method of acting. We then did some exercises that we invented for each other.

An acting class with Miss Wyler. We began work on Thornton Wilder's *The Happy Journey from Trenton to Camden*, setting the action and fixing it. She showed us how to mark our scripts, indicating our cues as well as our lines, diagramming all our moves and actions.

Mr. Gassner gave a lecture on Shakespeare, speaking of "the ordinary guy" in his work, not the wit. Shakespeare invented no plots, nor did he originate a style – only in his depth of characterization was he an innovator.

Sunday, March 17, 1945

Twelfth Night to illustrate the March of Drama Shakespeare lecture. Double casting gave us a chance to compare interpretations. At the matinee, I appreciated Priscilla Draghi's Viola because her performance approached my own interpretation, whereas Grace Huffman's Viola was thoughtful, more adult and less impulsive. Eugene Van Grona as the Duke was really superb. Charles Coleman, a lovable Sir Toby Belch. Elaine Stritch was a perfect fool (that is, she acted the perfect fool perfectly) and her singing was enchanting. Jimmy Walsh played a proud, puffed up Malvolio, whereas Eugene had played him with a pathos that verged on making him too attractive.

Of greatest interest are the setting and the style of the production. Julian Beck, who saw the matinee with me, saw Helen Hayes' *Twelfth Night* on Broadway several years ago, and said that only this March of Drama production reveals Shakespeare's real humor. Leo Kerz's designs were the most original part of the production. Instead of weighing down the light spirit of the play with drapes and flats, he placed a screen stage center and hung fishing nets above it. Slides were projected on the screen – not to show the place, but the essence of each scene.

Many of the comic effects, such as Malvolio's imprisonment, were achieved by playing behind the screen in silhouette.

Monday, March 19, 1945

Dancing with Madame Piscator. Though I am improving at the *barre* work, the steps are often too difficult for me to follow.

A make-up class, in which my attempt at late middle-aged make-up yet again proved a failure. I looked somewhat less dissipated than last week, but in place of dissipation, I looked dirty. I worked on that until my skin hurt.

Current Plays was a discussion of current flops, and one forthcoming one. Roselyn Weiss, who is a recent graduate, spoke to the class of her experiences playing the title role in *Sweet Genevieve*, which had a short run on Broadway. I wish I had such an opportunity.

In directing class, we went on with Alexander Dean's book: elaborate manipulations of people, continually demonstrating emphasis and focus.

Mr. Piscator has so much to teach, so much knowledge to feed us, that it seems pitiful that we must spend our classes on Mr. Dean's technical manipulations.

Tuesday, March 20, 1945

Directors' Council, with the usual scoldings and assignments of jobs for Lope de Vega's *Sheepwell*. In this class, and later in Theatre Research, Mr. Piscator read us a letter from a soldier, a former student at The Dramatic Workshop, Gilbert Seymour. He wrote from the battlefield of the vastness of things, of the limited and warped perspective people have who have not seen the world's greatness and been part of the world's fight. "How far the world's fight is from me! I am glad when the radio says that the news is good and that now victory is nearer. I say hurrah but I am not filled with the emotional impact of great things. I am ashamed to admit it, but it is too far away." Seymour, too, had not understood the meaning of Epic Theatre, but on the battlefield he felt that the world and the vast problems that compose it are the vital spur for the theatre. He writes that if he cannot return to a theatre where these ideals have meaning, a theatre of purpose, then he would as soon choose some other field where he might play some part in the development of his time. "Thus," says Piscator, from my point of view misguidedly, "war teaches nobility."

We started a discussion on *Twelfth Night* but comparisons (which Piscator hates) crept in. In the library, Nisha Rosenberg and I read a scene between Manuela and Frau Birnberg from *Mädchen in Uniform*. The quality of great drama is lacking here – perhaps I miss the poetry and the grandeur of the classics with which we are so busy right now.

In stage design class, Mr. Kerz looked over our assignments. The long hours I had spent were not completely wasted. He said the others who had tried it were wrong and I was right. He said so and handed the drawing back. He showed us how it should have been done, and then taught us how to make a floor plan and an elevation drawing.

Wednesday, March 21, 1945

Voice, with the ruination of many lovely poems.

Dance with Madame Piscator. I'm surprised that my improvement has no effect on my posture or my movements outside of class. Perhaps I am expecting results too soon, but I should at least feel some ease of movement. Perhaps I am too tired to give my body a chance at grace, and now I will be working even harder on *The Sheepwell*. I read for several parts, without success. I'm afraid that it was Miss Montemuro who was responsible for my not being cast.

An acting class with Miss Wyler. First we did our *Happy Journey*. This time I got a chance to play Arthur, the 10-year-old boy, and at last was fully absorbed in the part. Steffi played the mother and Miss Wyler noted that I made good contact with her. My only problem was with Alice, the Cat, for I teased her like a little girl rather than like a little boy.

We then did a scene about a telephone call. One person asks another for use of their telephone, which is refused. We varied the characters and the plots. The final variation was a dramatic scene for Steffi and me. My friend asks to use my phone, which I must refuse because my father is inside the house, drunk, and I cannot let her in. She tells me of the call's urgency and I am so moved that I confess the reason I cannot let her in. I overdramatized the scene because of my habitual reticence at improvisation. Using Pancho as a model, I visualized that drunken poet as a father, loved as one would love such a father, and ashamed as a child would be of such a father.

I felt the love and shame with too much intensity. I have only to look over my frightening semi-sane diary of last year to realize that. This teaches me that whereas certain gestures and reactions are exaggerated or at least enlarged on the stage, there are also those that must be made smaller, condensed and refined. Yet I also made it too poetic, too beautiful again. I promised myself that for my next reading, I would choose something completely unpoetic to prove that I could do it. In playing tragedy, my difficulty lies in trying to make even real tragedy beautiful, and I have aimed too much at beautifying real life.

In Styles Through the Ages, we covered the Flemish masters of the 17th century – Brueghel, Rubens and Van Dyck – comparing them with their contemporaries Rembrandt and Velázquez. Brueghel had a tendency to moralize in *The Parable of the Blind Leading the Blind* and even in *The*

Harvesters. We compared his detailed, big *Slaughter of the Innocents* with Rubens' paintings of the same subject. Brueghel's was bright and living and intense, whereas Rubens', with its curves and heavy baroque lines, had no emotional effect.

A comparison of Brueghel's *Christ Driving the Money Changers out of the Temple* with El Greco's had the same results. Brueghel does not show two opposing forces but a group of earthy, ugly, prosaic people opposing the spiritual and holy. *His Christ Bearing the Cross* is a panorama, a festival, with many people and many details not connected with the small figure of Christ: a depiction of the indifference of the people to the great event. As for Rubens, his voluptuous, obscene women do not raise my estimation of him. Van Dyck, on the other hand, is I think an amazing artist. His drawing of the heads of three Negroes combines superb technique with a modern quality.

Voice class. I couldn't keep myself from doing some other work in class, since I consider it a chore to sit through a voice class, so Miss Montemuro justifiably asked me to leave. I would gladly not come to any further classes, but . . .

In History and Sociology of the Theatre, we discussed the psychology of the actor. We used the whole class time to define psychological types into which we could group actors. We discussed the introvert and extrovert types, concluding that almost all actors are extroverts for obvious reasons, though Dr. Zucker said the complete extrovert was as rare as he would be unpleasant. Sidney Schwartz said that he was a complete extrovert, but Dr. Zucker assured him this was not so. We classified four types and gave examples of each: the choleric, i.e., the irate, quick-tempered, aggressive type like La Guardia and Toscanini; the phlegmatic, i.e. the unemotional, like Joe Louis; the sanguine, i.e., the quick-witted like Roosevelt and Wilkie; the melancholic, as the name implies, like the late Nijinsky. The actor may be any one of these types, but must understand them all.

A class in costume design for which Mr. Kerz had assigned homework. I worked for several hours in the library of the Metropolitan Museum of Art doing research on togas, and finally found one that I succeeded in turning into an afternoon dress, but Mr. Kerz thought it old-fashioned.

We then discussed medieval dress. This was the first period in which dresses followed the line of the figure. The Oriental influence and Oriental materials such as heavy brocades were perfectly in harmony with the heavy

Gothic architecture. Tunics, double sleeves, jackets of fur, made the clothing expensive and voluptuous, and so hard to make that styles changed slowly.

Friday, March 23, 1945

Voice class, worse than yesterday. We did as exercise, among other things, a fragment of a lovely little poem by Edna St. Vincent Millay, "like lead into the dust . . ." Miss Montemuro made such an abomination of it that I could not possibly read along with it, and I left the class again. If this keeps up!

Mr. Ben-Ari's class consisted of each of us inventing an improvisation which he then assigned to someone else to carry out. I had chosen an improvisation of a girl in a room waking up to find the house on fire, which Arla Gild did spectacularly. It was an effective exercise and a challenge to our imaginations. Mr. Ben-Ari then did a prison scene with Eleanor and Arthur.

Before my next acting class with Margrit Wyler, I wrote the song for *The Sheepwell*'s wedding scene. It begins:

> In knighthood's most valiant tradition,
> He came to woo the maid.
> In maiden's most charming position,
> She blushed and was afraid.

My attempt at "additional dialogue" for Lope de Vega.

In acting class, we did some readings, most of which were undeveloped, with the exception of Charlie Coleman's nose speech from *Cyrano de Bergerac*, and Eleanor's misinterpreted but lovely reading of Julie at Lilliom's death. I had hoped to do a scene from *Having a Wonderful Time*, just to prove that I could be unpoetic and completely naturalistic, but Eugene Van Grona sat in on the class and I was glad that I was not given a chance to read, as his presence made me too self-conscious.

In The March of Drama, I saw the most evocative performance I have seen in school. Mr. Gassner spoke about the late Elizabethans and Marlowe, underscoring their earthiness and their rebelliousness. He read us some heretical, anti-church writings attributed to Marlowe, which made why he was under arrest for heresy at the time of his death fully under-standable. We then saw a version of Marlowe's *Dr. Faustus*, excellently abridged by David Weiss. But the performance of Charles Zimmerman as Faustus was the most moving performance I have ever seen anywhere. Mephisto was played by Barbara Sisson, who played a devil for whom one had compassion. The conventional masculine devil is, after all, not the only choice and Barbara was very convincing, especially in her "unhappy spirit who fell with Lucifer and are forever damned with Lucifer" speech, where the pathos of wickedness struck with full force. The angels were respectively too good and too evil, as they should be. Garence Garie played Molière's Angelique as the good angel, while Estelle played a very modern evil one in a red evening gown. The Seven Furies brought to mind a slightly ridiculous night club revue. But Charles Zimmerman was incredible in his emotional definition of the role. The final speech of Faustus burned like a pyre, it is beyond description, I can-not possibly tell how moved I was. The lines followed each other in pangs. The passing of time was as painful as Faustus' soul being torn from him in that last, unbearable, unforgettable cry of "Mephistopheles!" It was as inspirational a moment as the theatre can hold. I could not want more.

Saturday, March 24, 1945

Working on the sets for *The Sheepwell*, I learned for the first time what a set consists of. We hammered and sawed and I became acquainted with that ingenious invention, the jigsaw. I worked on this all morning until a colleague broke the device. We worked with a student who is majoring in set design and has quite a bit of experience. She had been at the Goodman Memorial Theatre School and described it as a very well-equipped school with all the facilities, but no idealism and, therefore, completely static. The progressive spirit of The New School and its idealistic, young approach to theatre lured her here. How gratifying it is to build sets, to hammer and nail when you feel this forward movement.

After a morning's work, I went to see the rehearsal and Margrit Wyler asked me if I wanted to be in the crowd scenes, and of course, I was delighted. I wrote another song, unfortunately not good, and got right on stage. I do not object to playing in mob scenes – *au contraire*, I remember

Piscator repeating the old saying, "There are no small parts, there are only small actors."

Sunday, March 25, 1945

Sheepwell rehearsal. My role is that of a peasant girl, which at least allows me some characterization. I have a playmate, Pedrito, and so I have built quite a character around the young Manuela Malina (my own invention). Piscator saw the rehearsal and after making many corrections, spoke to us about the play, its meaning, its importance. He said that Lope de Vega's *Sheepwell* was not the story of an individual, but the story of a people. The town of Fuente Ovejuna was a drama of the people. The Russians called this play "the first proletarian drama." Piscator staged the scenes in which the mob "took part with such care and intelligence as to make them meaningful to us, so that we became not walk-ons, but historical fact."

Monday, March 26, 1945

A dance class with Madame. I find the class work easier, but I had expected that a certain amount of improvement in my movements outside class would be noticeable. Perhaps I ask too much, too soon.

In make-up, I have finally arrived at a decent middle-aged woman. I have lost the "fallen" look and emerge at a stage where I can hope to grow old gracefully.

In Current Plays, we discussed production costs and, taking *Twelfth Night* as an example, figured out expenses, and assuming that the sets cost no money, except for the designer's work, we arrived at the fantastic sum of $30,000 at the minimum. And is there such a question as: "What is wrong with the theatre?"

We rehearsed *Sheepwell* at a studio on Sixth Avenue and Eighth Street, blocking out the rest of the scenes and having a very jovial time about it. I left rehearsals so as not to miss directing class, but when I arrived, Mr. Piscator was not there and Chouteau worked on a scene from the Dean book with several sub-plots in it – a prize fighter pictured in several moods, the victors and the crowd, the vanquished and the energetic autograph seeker.

After the class, I spoke with Eugene Van Grona as we walked up to 62nd Street together. *En route*, he described to me his attack on a part. Coming to the school as a dancer, he knew nothing about acting and could not speak properly. He worked and worked for a year to reach this point. Never considered for a romantic role (though he is physically perfect for them, but has been typecast in roles as men with putty noses), he studied Duke Orsino, but when *Twelfth Night* was done again, he was assigned his customary Malvolio. But asked to be heard also as the Duke, and given the chance he was prepared for every line and gesture and knew the role, not only outwardly but inwardly. His performance of the romantic Orsino certainly won *my* heart.

Tuesday, March 27, 1945

In Directors' Council, we attempted to assign further crew staffs and, as usual, came to no conclusion, especially as Mr. Piscator was not there. Our Theatre Research class, likewise, missed his presence. The discussion of *Dr. Faustus* lacked his impetus. Charlie Zimmerman shocked everyone with the announcement, "The first thing I did was not to read the play." He went on in this caustic vein, attributing the acting to a momentary inspiration. Mr. Piscator will fume at this, but then again, he has not seen the performance. If Charlie left it to inspiration, then inspiration certainly was punctual and obliging.

After the class, we rehearsed *Sheepwell* until it was time for stage design class. Being determined to prove to Leo Kerz that my work is serious and that I do study to the best of my ability, I worked long over my assignment until I brought to class such a finished piece of work that even he had to take note of it. He said he "appreciated the work you put into it, but that (of course) it was not right." It actually was, but not to his specifications. I realized my mistake, though admittedly, it was a hard class, dealing with differences between drawing elevations and an interior decorator's design.

Wednesday, March 28, 1945

I did not attend voice class and rehearsal interfered with my dance class, so that I am not attending very many classes, as *Sheepwell* has precedence. In acting class I just had time to read and left for the Seder . . .

Instead of *Having a Wonderful Time*, I did a scene from Irwin Shaw's *The Gentle Hope*. Miss Wyler was very satisfied. I managed to keep it down to earth and was able to believe it completely. If I could reach that point of saturation in the role in everything I do, I will have accomplished my aim. Another encouraging incident occurred during this reading. I started to laugh at one point, but the immediacy of my immersion in the role and situation managed to overcome it. Miss Wyler said that complete focus can help in that direction.

Thursday, March 29 and Friday, March 30, 1945

Absent for Passover.

Saturday, March 31, 1945

Rehearsal with Mr. Piscator. I shall try after this week to take at least some notes during Mr. Piscator's rehearsals. He gives so much and I forget, alas.

Sunday, April 1, 1945

Rehearsal. I have a line all my own, or rather, a word. When my little boy playmate is tortured, I must scream, "Pedrito!" I am really most happy about it, for it gives me so much more to build on. I really feel part of this play. Rehearsals are, of course, engrossing and in my way I can do so much to wield, mold, create out of nothing. It is so invigorating to act without a role, for here the role is within me as I stand on the stage, even without speaking. I understand now why there are no small roles.

Monday, April 2, 1945

No one was there when I came in early to work on the set. So Miss Wyler let Steffi and me sit in with the acting class. Joan, a Canadian girl with a very clear voice, did Portia's mercy speech without real belief or interpretation. She then improvised the scene with Hal Tulchin, who surprised me with his ease in improvisation. Jo Deodato read from Odet's *Waiting for Lefty*. I feel I could do better than they, for although the readings were intelligent, they lacked the feeling for truth.

Rehearsal now takes the place of most of my other classes, and I was busy shouting for the *Commendador* and screaming at the torture scene until my directing class in the evening. This was one of the best classes I ever had. We reached the chapter on picturization in the Dean book and Mr. Piscator made it a significant class. We defined picturization and then did some exercises. One of the students in the directing class and I enacted several scenes of relationships; I was scolded as a daughter, then as a wife.

Other groups worked out various scenes until we came to the "farewell." Here, Mr. Piscator spoke at length about the variations of farewells. In his humorous, casual tone, he said "Bye, I'm going to the drugstore," and then answered himself, "Goodbye." He went on like this with a description of goodbyes for an hour's walk, an overnight trip, a week in Washington, a boat to Europe, until he said, "Now we come to the final big farewell, the funeral. So," he said, "we have goodbyes from the drugstore to the funeral, but some actors play the drugstore like the funeral and the funeral like the drugstore." An actor does not find this in the text and this is where picturization comes in. The whole story of a final parting can be shown in the lines of the actor's body, in a handshake. Now Mr. Piscator approached me and leaned toward my seat, straining his arm forward almost painfully with the most direct gaze, with which he seemed to take in every atom of my face and more. I gave him my hand and the whole class felt the finality and harsh sadness of it. It was one of those rare occasions when an artist conquers you completely and makes reality of the situation. It was, for me, a momentous thing.

We then worked on Dean's farewell scenes. First, of a boy going to school or the drugstore while I, his mother, mix a cake batter. Hal played the son nonchalantly. The son going to war presented more of a problem. Eugene Van Grona played it with us, Hal and Eugene shaking hands while I cry on one of their shoulders. The question arose – on whose? We tried both ways and finally realized that our failure lay in having forgotten to determine which one was playing the son. I became very confused (Gene wore a soft, deep cologne), and I hardly knew how to go on. Mr. Piscator tried it with us and showed us how it should be done.

We then did two scenes from *Twelfth Night*, one with Eugene as Malvolio and one as the Duke. Malvolio's scene was the delivery of the ring. I hope someday to be able to play the role of Viola. As the Duke, Gene was splendid, except that Mr. Piscator criticized his seated position as "unroyal" and pointed out the quality of grandeur that can be achieved by a more stately posture, and remarked, "It's interesting that he's a dancer." Last week, Gene told me that when he first started acting, he was so "movement conscious" that he had to work hard at forgetting movement. I might remember this in learning to speak less poetically. Priscilla Draghi played the bedroom scene with him and was very charming, though Mr. Piscator wanted her to show more love toward him when he did not notice it. Such as when taking off his boots, "Approach it as 'his foot'." I am so sure I could do that role. As Gene said, "I shall study it in advance," and try for it next year. That gives me a whole year.

Tuesday, April 3, 1945

In Theatre Research, Mr. Piscator spent the two hours talking about his "political theatre." It was one of the most inspiring lectures. I tried to write down the essence of what Mr. Piscator said:

> Art in itself seems a beautiful accomplishment of life, even when it does not criticize life. We begin with the question of how art should be used, and from this follows the question, "How should life be used?" Can we make progress in life or only in certain scientific discoveries? Is man little or is he big? For what purpose has he created something greater than himself, for some X, for some God? We die children of 70 years. We conquer nothing. Art is conquered out of the universe, out of that in man which is greater than himself. Art goes beyond the walls, where even our brains cannot go. Genius – is it a sickness, a deformation of the individual? Genius and insanity are balanced on a knife blade.
>
> Lenin called the idea of God into question. We have turned back to what we see. We know that other things exist, but what we see is organizable: society, justice, an end to wars. Shall we reach, as men, what we have thought as men since the beginning, since Plato and Christ? But the doubters say, "Who gives me the next piece of butter?" The victors are the powerful who make wars, and the others are "the masses." Thus both art for art's sake and art with an aim start from

the question, "Can we progress or shall we be driven by unknown forces, by Christ's fantastic teachings, by God, by that revolutionary book, the Bible? There is betrayal everywhere, from the drugstore to The New School: the Pope in the fantastic Vatican wears good clothes. Christ is a bestseller who asks for eternal peace. We kill 1000 with one shot.

The realists say at least we are on the right side. One knew about Iowa, but not Iwo Jima. Four thousand men died and now we know about Iwo Jima. This is progress. The crosses in Strasbourg are progress. 13 million died in the last war, perhaps 30 million in this one! Progress? Behind all this, the XYZ power, God. The *Venus de Milo*, and *Parsifal*, below us in the dirt, unlooked at. Such progress! The realists hold that art is above life. Let the people come out of their darkness to see beauty and art in theatres and museums. Then let them return to their dirt. The dirt is unchangeable. Thus speak the realists.

But there are those who say we need not separate art and life. Life in itself is art. Let us build life in an artful way till we need no art. Art may be seen as an excuse for our imperfections. The human spirit can build, at its highest points, manifestations of the spirit – cathedrals, the Acropolis. We cannot build the pillars of the Acropolis today. Although the Bank of Athens is built to the same measurements as the Acropolis, the spirit is lacking, the harmony of spirit and technique. We made of art a special thing, as we did of religion. Religion became an institution and the spirit flew out. The spirit flew out when we divided art and society.

Can we build society like an eight-cylinder car, by understanding its elements? Can we do this without considering spiritual form, which governs human happiness? Spiritual meaning, growth and intelligence. We need art to complete the incompleteness of life. But first, we need society and security in society. We perfect the world through the nation and through the self, and we must take a step toward this in our theatre. Political theatre is art theatre.

There are those who say that theatre is not art because it is a pro-grammatic form. In music and painting, you can be abstract or sheerly beautiful. But the theatre is thoughtful, every word opens a world of thought with an analysis of thought. The art theatre was always bound to thinking, and always seeking for truth. Thus the art theatre was always a political theatre. The theatre turns, even unconsciously, to politics. Recently in Russia, the Communists started to use theatre consciously again, to show two sides, good and bad, presenting problems and suggesting solutions. To avoid the negative is not to build the positive. How do we build the positive? After the disastrous war from 1914 to 1918, the struggle for clarity began and our political theatre began. Reinhardt continued the beautiful theatre, but we returned to the theatre to fight.

Theatre, too, is like an opium for the people, musicals, even the classics, like the church which kept the real religion hidden in ceremony. The church, the inn and the theatre are three vital buildings in any city. We must make art that is conscious. Clarify, like Lear in the storm, his revolutionary cries unheeded.

Only once in Brussels, a revolution started in a theatre. When *La Muette de Portici* was given at the Theatre de la Monnaie, and the audience stormed out of the theatre and started the revolution that liberated Belgium from the Dutch.

But today, not only the high admission prices, but also the absence of spirit prevents us from realizing a people's theatre. The money, the ideology and the spirit are in the hands of another class, and in the midst of this stupidity, we have war. Art, conscious art, political art needs the necessity and the desire for change. One side here fights for social change, the other does not need it.

Art is not made consciously to point out the moral necessity of what an artwork must be. In this way, the propaganda picture emotionally kills the intellect. To understand, we must remain objective. If we are drawn in, we no longer think. The war movies merely upset us with how many dead people lie all around, and still the hero gets the girl. The real causes of war must be made clear to move an audience to action.

Romain Rolland said, "Action springs from the spectacle of action." The political theatre exists to take the theatre out of political *argument* and into political *action*. But we do not arise, we do not move. All the action of the world is in this room. We must face up to this fact. Then art conquers art, for our art is in our life and is no longer an outside thing. Then we can conquer by wisdom and bring art back to beauty.

This is the point: Political theatre is for me the only art theatre. There are some who would demean the art theatre. Why build a love story and then construct a social implication around it? No, we must build a case, clarify it, build around it.

Epic Theatre has no enclosure, it is complete. The word "politics" comes from the Greek "polis," meaning "the whole city," all the surroundings. Every event has a relation to the case. It means more than one plot. I used all I had. I said that the actor must demonstrate, use film, design, use the audience to describe the impact of the story. Emotion by thought, as in *Nathan the Wise*. We have not reached the beginning of that theatre. 1890: The Volksbühne, *The Weavers*. 1890: naturalism, Zola, Antoine. In Russia: Tolstoy, teaching through his plays, *The Fruits of the Enlightenment*, Schiller.

In the French Revolution, the theatre failed its mission. These are the ancestors of our political theatre. We should study the theatre in two ways – technically, and to give content to it. Study in our age and time should lead us to the problem of content so that these problems might lead us to greatness. He who wants nothing is nothing. We are as great as our cause. Art grows only under the sun of idealism. The ancient Greeks called it "the perfection." If you are not married to your art, your art is dead. Stay with art like a priest.

What must we do to deserve such a teacher?

Wednesday, April 4 and Thursday, April 5, 1945

Absent two days for Passover and to digest that lecture.

Friday, April 6, 1945

Our first full dress rehearsal of *The Sheepwell*. My absence has not been too much of a problem, for it seems (one fears to say it, according to the old actors' superstition) to be going well. Mr. Piscator is, of course, not satisfied, but considers it adequate. This run-through lasted from ten in the morning until the March of Drama lecture at eight. It seems like an endless play. Not Gassner, but Paolo Milano spoke of the Spanish theatre. Most of his speech was given over to the life of Lope de Vega. This man, perhaps a genius, was not only a prolific writer but a prolific liver, lover and father. His plays number circa 2800 and his *amours* are scarcely dwarfed by such a number. Yet he became a priest and died, as Dr. Milano puts it, "in the arms of the Holy Roman Catholic Church." I could not stay till the end of the lecture, as I had to return to rehearsal, which lasted until three in the morning. My voice is ruined with screaming "*Fuente Ovejuna*" and the tiredness of hard work.

But Mr. Piscator, like the miracle of energy that he is, still directed with a vigor that none of his 20-year-old students could equal.

Saturday, April 7, 1945

Before the performance, a rehearsal in dress but not make-up. The play is still loose and needs more work, but this is not possible. When we were photographed, I felt very professional for some foolish reason. Only a half hour between rehearsal and performance call. Mother called for me and I ate, very excitedly, some macaroni at the Waldorf Cafeteria, with my costume under my coat and strange white cotton stockings and *hurachas*. Then, to the theatre, where we are told our make-up is too light. We all set about mixing Max Factor 8 and 7, and I found a ruddy, very dark tone, almost too Spanish. Vicki Paul, the lead, was not half so nervous as I, while Harriet Charney, the second lead, was sick, as was half the cast. After the play started, with the audience not too responsive, I awaited the crowd scenes as though they were my solos. Finally, the welcoming scene at the entrance. I was so excited that the shouting came easily, but the letdown came when I had to remain quiet as the action proceeded. This was the only point during which my bogey-man, the nervous laugh, tried to intrude – but I drowned him immediately. All went well in the wedding scene and I successfully delivered my single line, "Pedrito!" in the torture scene. To my future success I say, "Katherine Cornell, I started as an off-stage groan."

Sunday, April 8, 1945

Run-through and performance. Until tonight I wasn't aware that the second night is always the worst performance because of the so-called letdown. This performance seemed to me to be a 100 percent better, and

98

the difference lay mainly with the audience. Last night the audience found the play inappropriately amusing and laughed, even during such tragic scenes as the rape and death of Jacinta, and at the torture scenes. But tonight, the audience liked the play and even hissed Harold Dyrenforth on his curtain call, in real blood-and-thunder melodramatic style.

It brought to mind the U.S.O. in Hempstead and Carl and Don Del Rio, whom the soldiers hissed when we meagerly attempted to present *He Ain't Done Right by Nell*. If I directed that same play now, applying the knowledge that I have gained in this short time, how much more unified, comical and professional it would appear. How much better my approach will be in two years. *Sheepwell* was an invaluable experience and I am sorry it is over. For me, the letdown comes now. And the sore throat, for in my enthusiasm for the *Commendador* and for my role, forgetting Miss Montemuro's warnings, I screamed myself hoarse and can hardly speak.

Dance class. Terms like *rond de jambe*, *attitude* and *plié* become part of my vocabulary. But the correct execution is not yet achieved. If I had even a short class daily it would be helpful or if I could practice at home, but time presses terribly and the summer comes.

Make-up brought about a general strike. Most of my classmates complained that they had hurt their skins with the *Sheepwell* make-up and did not wish to irritate them further. Of course, this is a rather feeble alibi for laziness, since our fondest ambition is to do one or two shows a day. Esther made up Helen Braille, from early middle age to old age. I am tired of middle-aged make-up, for once achieved, it is always within my grasp.

Current Plays shows Mr. Ince in the role in which my first impression had visualized him. He is producing *Margret* and discusses his problems of casting and financing with us. This simple two-set, ten-character play will cost a minimum of $50,000 to produce. The other side of the man-you-want-an-appointment-with became humanized, as do his problems in casting. He lamented the difficulty of being gentle with the hundreds of actors that want a reading. Still, Mr. Ince says he wants a "new" actress for Penelope in order to give a young actress a chance. But theatre as a business still brings a bad taste to my mouth, left there by Genius Inc. and the St. James Hotel, where I hung out for years of making the rounds, surrounded by an odor vaguely like bad and watered gin.

From the prosaic to the divine, we come to directing class, where we worked on problems of background action. Eugene Van Grona staged a scene. Taking his idea from *Waterloo Bridge*, he made his main action a prostitute and a prospective client. Gene cast me as the girl and Louis Guss as the man, and we had a lot of fun doing it. Another scene was set in a department store. I played a salesgirl and Esther Nighbert played a shoplifter who stole a pin from my jewelry counter. She was gently but firmly arrested by Eugene. Six people then mutually suspected each other of a theft, very successfully. We played a scene from *Twelfth Night*, the comedy scene with the three comedians behind the screen and Malvolio finding the letter. Eugene, who is working to change his Malvolio for future productions, found the scene very difficult, and Piscator found many faults in his performance.

Tuesday, April 10, 1945

Directors' Council. At last I have a job! I am assistant director for the reading of Euripides' *Electra*, but as it is Miss Montemuro whom I assist, I can only hope that I will have no difficulty. It is good to have the opportunity, and I will try to make the most of it, though *Electra* is rather a hard thing for a beginner.

In Theatre Research class, we discussed *The Sheepwell* with the actors commenting on their roles. Vicki Paul, as Laurencia, said that what she needed was an extra 20 pounds. I know what that means. Mr. Piscator added that of course, she was absolutely a city type, though she played the rural girl as well as she could. Although he does not believe in type-casting, he realizes that the slim, chic Vicki is not destined to play peasant women. Bob Carricart, speaking of his part, said that he knew that all the world loves a lover and was confident that the audience did likewise, and relying on this, he relaxed and played the lover. To which Piscator added, "Yes, even when you were tortured you smiled very carefully to show your nice teeth." Mengo, played by Louis Guss, was the only really perfect piece of casting, and it certainly was a fine portrayal. Louis was able to justify all his actions.

The guest actors then commented on their roles. Dennis MacDonald met a particularly daunting challenge which he overcame masterfully. Having worked with Dennis before on a play called *Comic Supplement, or, My Mother-in-Law*, which I performed for soldiers as part of the war-effort under the sponsorship of the American Woman's Service Organization (and which was rather unsuccessful), I admired his capacity

100

for characterization. In *The Sheepwell*, he played two roles incorporated into one, and also played the judge. The two incorporated roles were conflicting characters, and the fact that Dennis could assimilate them at all was an achievement in itself. His diligence and thoughtfulness are admirable.

Two years ago Dennis had just come to New York from Iowa and all of us who worked with him saw every chance for his success. Now for two years he has done very little work on Broadway and still has not reached a point of steady employment even though, because of the war, there is a male shortage on Broadway. What peril, then, do I face, much less able to play a stock role, nor as versatile nor as physically attractive and, worst of all, a girl?

Ray Hinkley, another guest actor, was saluted for being wounded in action, having sustained a broken wrist when he was "slaughtered" by the ladies of the cast. He is a war veteran playing his first role. He put too much into it, playing almost too intensely. Harold Dyrenforth, who was not present, was criticized by Piscator for playing "too much the Nazi officer." Mr. Piscator thought of the role "more in Charles Laughton's vein." The criticism that I agreed with entirely, was that Harold had played the part too attractively, making the *Commendador* so charming that the women's disdain seemed almost a lack of taste. We will continue criticisms next week.

March of Drama and a discussion of the Commedia dell'Arte program. We discussed the possibilities of demonstrating the Commedia style with a series of satirical sketches on former productions. We started off well with a hilarious *War and Peace* narration by Esther Nighbert. With our many improvising comedians, I think that the program should be quite successful.

In Stage Design, Mr. Kerz showed us some of the highly inventive designs he has made for ballets and plays. For the Joos Ballet, he made a thrilling newspaper setting for a theatre in Johannesburg. His haunting *Winterset* showed more than mere skill but rather an imaginative genius. His use of color and his perception of stage space struck me particularly. Like his taste in the theatre, his designs have about them something broadly open to new conceptions, a freedom and an outgoingness.

In the evening, Adolph took me to see the Margaret Webster production of *The Tempest*, which was brilliant in many ways, but which merits criticism as well as praise. The set was a unit on a turntable, which never explored its own possibilities. Arnold Moss was quietly powerful, more so than I imagined in reading *The Tempest*. His strength was more completely mental than my imagined Prospero's. As for the part nearest my heart, I thought Zorina looked lovely as Ariel but lacked the poetry. Her delivery was clear and intelligent but it always remained the delivery of lines. Though my classroom recitation of her lines sounded more sincere, I was not as technically certain of myself. The one line, "My liberty!" she spoke perfectly, whereas I had understood what I wanted to convey but could not do it.

Canada Lee as Caliban pounced and grunted and was dressed in some sort of spangled finery which I did not understand at all. His performance did not live up to his Bigger Thomas in *Native Son*. Miranda and Ferdinand were sweet in roles that allow so little. The "bad men" merged so that they were just a group lacking definition and characterization. The magical spirit of the play did not come through. I feared that it was my critical attitude that prevented me from entering into the spirit of the play. Miss Webster put Prospero's speech, "We are such stuff as dreams are made of," at the close of the play. I felt the magic then for the first and only time. Effects alone cannot convey magic. It takes good acting.

Wednesday, April 11, 1945

A voice class which I attended for two reasons, though I have missed most classes until now. First, I must do *Electra* with Miss Montemuro, and secondly, the fact that my vocal cords are completely ruined by such a simple job as hailing the *Commendador* for two evenings. On this basis, seven shows a week with a three act part would finish my voice in one week. Much as I disapprove of her methods, I must learn the voice control that Miss Montemuro can teach me. We discussed *Electra* and possibilities of casting. The fact that I have not read the play made things difficult, but I shall read it tonight.

A dance class with my usual problems in trying to follow steps. Madame Piscator then discussed the idea of a dance movement program with me, thinking that I might be able to write the narration against which the movement was to be played. I would love to do it, but haven't been able to find a theme and hope that Madame Piscator will give me a basis to work from.

Acting class with Margrit Wyler. Eleanor Epstein did Curley's wife's speech from *Of Mice and Men*, which I had worked on for the Experimental Showcase. For some reason, she was as unconvincing in the role as I had been. Some improvisations with Arthur Greene making a farce of any given situation, which his talent for caricature justifies. Evelyn Bigge played a simple scene which achieved a certain naturalness and an inherent, frank charm, though her deeper talent does not yet come through. Arla again proved herself towering over the rest with her facile ease in acting, seeming almost too true. For next week, we are each to prepare a scene and I will dare to essay Viola, though with tremendous misgivings. I am terribly anxious to make a good impression in it, anticipating next year's production of *Twelfth Night*. My chances of playing the role are slight, but studying it can do no harm.

Styles Through the Ages presented France in the 18th century and achieved the seemingly impossible when Dr. Zucker showed us how to differentiate between the styles of the several Louises – the baffling differences between Louis XIV, Louis XV, Louis XVI and Napoleon's neoclassicism. Louis XIV's period is dominated by pale cream and pale rose and gold, with the rectangle the predominant form. All the decorative overflow is gathered somehow into the rectangle. Louis XV diffused the rectangle, lost the styles completely in curves and pastel, and silver or gold dominated. This style is the same as rococo. When Louis XVI's reaction to all this confusion set in, the rectangle returned, and colors became grey and pale and simpler. In Napoleon's time, the Louis XIV designs started to repeat themselves, but with the addition of some Egyptian motifs and pineapple designs and the use of black and deeper shades. These periods were illustrated with slides of rooms from the Palace of Versailles that made the subject very clear. The pictures of the garden and layout of the house and plazas and the fountains and stairs were so lovely, that I long to see the original place. Perhaps if they are not too ruined by the war, I shall have my wish.

In contrast to the architecture and decoration, the paintings were weak and dull. Perhaps I shall someday learn to appreciate them, but today Watteau, Lancret, Chardin and Boucher seem like so much whipped cream. Fragonard particularly is fluffy and completely insignificant. Chardin's drawings are perhaps the only real art by any of these men. The sculpture of the period, with its modest neo-Greek goddesses, is even more tasteless. I fear to judge too harshly that which is recognized art, lest I someday realize suddenly the beauty in that for which I felt only disdain (how many times has this very thing happened in Dr. Zucker's course?). I feel the pangs of penance already.

Thursday, April 12, 1945

It is difficult to describe a day like today, starting with the early classes on what was then a rather ordinary school day, but which now seems tinged with foreboding. It all started simply with a voice class, after which Miss Montemuro discussed the Greek play with me. A change from *Electra* to *Medea* has altered our plans. I felt badly about this, as last night's reading of *Electra* left a deep impression with its passion and unashamed tragedy, usually so masked in modern acting. But *Medea* will be played by Margrit Wyler and this is sure to be a wonderful experience. We cut the three-hour *Medea* to what it's hoped will be less than an hour or 45 minutes, a painful task. Every bit of poetry seems to cry for inclusion, each seeming the loveliest line in the play.

In my History and Sociology class, we spoke of the theatre as the stage vs. the drama, the question being whether the main effect of the performance was a sensual or intellectual one. The class seemed to sway towards the sensual, while only four of us (myself included) preferred the intellectual side. Choosing between a good play with a message or a sheerly beautiful poetic fantasy, all but three students (myself included) chose the sensual play. The rest of my memory of this class is completely blotted out by what followed.

Lola Ross and I went out for coffee and had to hurry back, as I had an early stage design class with Mr. Kerz. We got into the elevator and I felt relief to see that Mr. Kerz was just on his way to class though it was late. Hal Tulchin was in the elevator and as Lola got out, Hal said to her, "Have you heard the news?" but she was gone before he finished. He turned to me then and said, "President Roosevelt is dead." Shock! And then a protest reaction that I'm being fooled. I believed him, of course, but so wanted him to be jesting that I insisted he was not being truthful. His face told me that I was being unjust. Mr. Kerz, as we left the elevator, looked at me and said, "Yes."

I walked to the classroom and sat next to Hal. Mr. Kerz asked for a cigarette and then said, "Most of the teachers have postponed their classes this evening because of the death of President Roosevelt." He was interrupted by the caught breath of the class and one voice that said, "No!" What I felt at that moment and for the rest of the evening I cannot describe. I won't say shocked or stunned or use such words. The terrible impulse to laugh, the laughter that is my sublimated way of crying, struck me terribly. Mr. Kerz said something further about class and we left with disbelief and sorrow. I went to find Lola and as we met in the hall we both laughed, a harsh, almost hysterical laugh, and still I cannot say what I felt. It was sadness, shaded with fear.

Friday, April 13, 1945

A voice class with a somewhat slow tempo, but people are far less affected by Roosevelt's death than I am, though I try to cover it.

An acting class with Mr. Ben-Ari. We start to speak of *Sheepwell*, but we all felt that we wanted to "do something." Mr. Ben-Ari gave us an exercise about the theatre. Arla was to come for her "big chance," an audition with Mr. Big, but because she was late, loses her opportunity. I was to be a preceding applicant. Charles played Mr. Bigshot. Again, I encountered the problem of letting what I know in real life interfere with my acting. Coming in to introduce myself, I knew beforehand that I would not be accepted, and my imagination would not run counter to this Broadway instinct. And try as I might I could not be eager. Arla, on the other hand (who has never been auditioned by Bettina Cerf and The Theatre Guild), approached him with utter hope and belief and, on being told she was too late, pleaded so magnificently that he seemed a beast to reject her. And when he did, Arla sat down on the stage and cried, but really cried to the point where she could not stop when she left the stage.

Arla is, of course, a terrific actress. I could not cry real tears on the stage, nor would I want to, but to be able to master the technique is admirable. She claims to have done it because she felt it, though I am inclined to think (I am not sure) that feeling it so completely is not a good thing. We then did some improvisations on *The Sheepwell*, creating a well in the center of the stage, and did some actions in connection with the well. Steffi pulled up water, Charles tried to whistle a song, and drank some water to whet his whistle. Ethel washed her face, I remained my little Manuela of the *Sheepwell*, age 10, and played with a cat, finally walking the cat on the edge of the well, and shrieking with horror when the cat fell into the well. Mr. Ben-Ari's only criticism was that a reaction does not come as quickly as mine did, since it takes a moment to realize something before we react to it. I felt freer in this than in any other improvisation, probably because I had a few minutes to plan my actions and did not have to grope for words.

Between classes, Miss Montemuro cut the script of *Medea* into about a tenth of its length, or so it seemed. To omit verses again seemed cruel, but it means that we can present the full story instead of an excerpt.

In Miss Wyler's Acting class, we went on with our *Joan of Arc* speeches, which we are supposed to know from memory. Steffi did hers first, with Ethel Sheppard as the Inquisitor. Steffi did an excellent, though unpolished job. She played it well emotionally, but not technically. Margrit Wyler criticized her particularly for not knowing what to do with her body. Well do I know the feeling! Steffi, being tall and quite big, feels clumsy, while I feel so slight, so scrawny, that I am tempted to draw myself together to seem more massive, lest my extended limbs make me feel like a line-drawing figure in a diagram.

Ethel was told to work on an annoying mannerism, that of moving her head up and down as she speaks, a trait carried over to the stage from her daily life. Eleanor was the Inquisitor when I played Joan. Worried about time, I gave it much less than my best, though I am surprised at the new ease in reading and of flow of speech that memorization brings. Where I knew the words, I had the power to move in any direction that I pleased, which gave me a feeling of security I never felt before. Miss Wyler said that my understanding of the lines was complete, but my tendency was to scream intensity instead of projecting it. This tendency to shout also seems to express anger where none is intended. I feel that my errors were mostly due to lack of planning in tempo and volume, which I believe is better off "fixed" than left to chance.

In the evening, Mr. Milano spoke on the Commedia dell'Arte. A theatre of improvisation with only a vague scenario to guide the players. I recall how well I improvised as a little girl in the Broadway Central Hotel with Rachel Falk from around the corner. Settling a plot in advance, we played for hours, days, sometimes even for weeks, on the same plot and characters with an infinite variety of situations, characterizations and dramatic effects. I wonder now at how an instinctive ability can be lost through learning and sophistication. Our naïve belief in the story and our deadly seriousness were amazing. Avis Jean Weiser occasionally played these stories with me and, last of all, Marguerite Ditchik, but already with a more inhibited sense and with much less variety than with Rachel. And now I cannot improvise. For me, improvisation, like the Commedia dell'Arte itself, is a dead form, forced back to life sometimes but never fresh again.

After the performance of *Sheepwell*, The New School closed, and Workshop classes were canceled for two days until Monday because of Roosevelt's death.

Monday, April 16, 1945

The most wonderful dance class I ever had. Lanie Van Grona, Gene's wife, taught. She possesses not only Madame Piscator and Eugene's dancing knowledge and ability, but also a masterly clarity of explanation. She did an amazing group of exercises which she referred to as the Swedish method. I have never felt such a looseness, freeness and power in dancing as I did then. A deep understanding, too, of the origins of movement. The realization of which part of the body leads in certain movements was both enlightening and overwhelming. I did well, too, until we came to fixed steps. Again I could not follow. But the vigor and energy and splendor of her dancing captivated me. She is very like Eugene, she could almost be his sister, although she seems the stronger of the two. I can easily visualize them dancing together. Oh, if I could dance! I would work so hard. The most living expression is movement. Speech is an artificial invention, it is small and precious when compared to the true and godly expression of movement. What sacrilege against the theatre does this passion lead me to express? I will think of this again in a more objective humor. Till then, I will revel fully in my infatuation.

Being in too large a mood for the make-up class, I found painting minute crow's feet with carefully placed highlights utterly unbearable, and having done it once, could not possibly do it again. I finally found a way out by painting my face red, with very black eyes and lips. I know that such stunts are all wrong and are a psychological regression to something that I swore off long before coming to school here.

In Current Plays, Mr. Ince continued his discussion of the forthcoming production of *Margaret*, after which we started to cast *Medea*, including the chorus and the men.

Directing class focused on "area," this time on its importance in mood values. Dean's book assigns a particular atmosphere to certain stage areas. These are purely technical rules, and not without exceptions. Perhaps they are more or less superfluous. The imaginative director would hardly, while working on a production, plan areas for mood value, nor would he be insensitive enough to bring a ghost on downstage right. We demonstrated by playing an identical action in different mood areas. Harriet Charney and I first played an argument about directors, then changed it to a more violent action, where Harriet and I had a genuine "female fight." I cannot say that I did not enjoy it. A more virile fight between Jimmy Walsh and Bob Carricart developed into a scene involving two soldiers, a Nazi and a *saboteur*. Though an interesting improvisation, it didn't prove anything as far as the mood values of areas are concerned. We discussed the scene placements in *Sheepwell* and then did some of the scenes from *Fuente Ovejuna*. After the actual performance, to see a piece of it out of context with all its imperfections is a disappointment.

Tuesday, April 17, 1945

Directors' Council. Harriet Charney finds *Medea* interesting and will probably share the assistant directing job with me, or so blows the wind.

Theatre Research. Mr. Piscator spoke to us of Roosevelt and his significance to us as artists. The notes I took of Mr. Piscator's talk are worth noting here. Being direct quotations and mostly out of context, the grammar and meaning is sometimes obscure but, in general, Mr. Piscator said:

> We should consider the life of a great statesman as proceeding from the same historic necessity as the work of an artist. Man is the continuity of a tremendous mass of people. Like leaves on a tree, they come and they go. But what they build is greater than any one man. Roosevelt's greatness was the touching vision of an artistic soul. His speeches held the trembling touch of something underneath his words, an idealistic vision of humanity's future. His face like an actor's but dominated by a thoughtfulness that could be read in his expression. His heritage for you should be to see such a man from your standpoint, as a comrade, as a real friend, as an example. We are not

singular. As Roosevelt built for 12 years a thinking world, so you must build a constructive world with art. My energy is to give to you what I learned 20 years earlier. To make you 20 years richer. You live little lives where you must live great lives. The theatre is in actuality the construction of life, and this is a great, tremendous thing, Roosevelt was an artist as well as a politician. He is buried in you now.

When Mr. Piscator says these things, I feel as if I am capable of so much. That's why, when I would so much like to listen, I take notes instead, for then I can have them always, almost to hear him again.

We went on with criticisms of individual performances in *Sheepwell* and came to Jimmy Walsh, whose ability as an actor far exceeds the performance he gave. When Laurencia had been raped and returned, accusing her father of not protecting her nor attempting to defend her, Jimmy failed to express the emotions that a father in this position must feel.

Mr. Piscator asked, "Have you a daughter?" Jimmy laughed and said he did not, but he had a dog. Mr. Piscator answered that even this might help him to understand the situation. Mr. Piscator told of a dog he once had, a lovely little Dachshund named Trilby. He had to throw stones at the dogs who constantly circled the house, looking for Trilby, especially one enterprising "dirty little mongrel with two black eyes." One morning, though, he awoke to find, as he put it, the most horrible sight he could imagine, "This filthy old dirty Mephisto and my Trilby. So I kicked the Mephisto out, but the damage was done. Little Trilby had puppies and she died. This mating was just not meant." Though Mr. Piscator embellished this story with all the humor and charm at his command, his point was that we learn to act from all things, and our love towards an animal can be parallel to that for a human being. Then he told us of a Doberman that he had, a dog he loved dearly, that was killed by a car. Mr. Piscator said that at the death of the dog, he felt as deeply as though it had been a human being. If he had to act his feelings at the time, he could not do it, so full was the emotion he felt. Jimmy realized that he never really felt or portrayed his role in *Sheepwell*.

The March of Drama class time was used to cast *Medea*. Margrit Wyler, our Medea. Miss Montemuro and I listened to tryouts and cast Harriet as the leader of the chorus, Marian Cohen as the nurse and Louis Guss as the king, Creon. As for Jason, we have certainly no actor among the students who can stand up to Margrit Wyler, and so we will use an outside actor.

In Stage Design, Mr. Kerz showed us, as examples to discuss, some *Theatre Arts* design prints ranging from the modern Japanese theatre to Meyerhold's biomechanical constructions. None of them were realistic and none of them struck me as particularly beautiful. Meyerhold, whose theories impressed me so, seems in this instance to go to an extreme in ugliness. The set looked like a *ballet mécanique* with a large cast completely unindividualized, unemphasized, but rather portraying a complex sort of arrangement less aesthetic than a blueprint. But I should not judge a man's staging abilities by two pictures of a single play. Should Piscator be judged for *The Sheepwell*?

In the evening, Lola, Sidney and I went to the ballet, and managed to sneak in at the intermission to see the last three numbers of an all-Tudor program. The first was a splendid new ballet (its second performance) with a psychological basis, called *Undertow*. Though the characters were given mythological names from obscure legends, the story of the psychological development of a boy was amazing, even if sometimes the narrative remained ambiguous. The opening birth scene was a masterpiece and the choreography was consummate. It was quite modern in the Tudor style, though the backdrop was medieval, complete with towers and bats. Kriza did some stupendous dancing, but I must see *Undertow* several times to appreciate it fully – to understand enough to realize how much I do not understand.

During the intermission, I saw my ballet teacher of two lessons but many happy times, Madame Beatrice Stavrova. She was the Russian ballerina who first taught me the basic principles of ballet. I am hopeful of meeting her again, and perhaps taking some lessons. She invited me to her box, but then I could not find her again. *The Judgment of Paris* was a little light breathing space before the exotic and exquisite *Pillar of Fire*. *Pillar of Fire* was breathtaking, with Nora Kaye dancing Hagar and Janet Reed as the little sister. Nora Kaye is the only ballerina that has ever impressed me as strong and real and human. The whole ballet was lifelike and true, although expressed within the aesthetic form of ballet.

Wednesday, April 18, 1945

Voice class is more successful now that I am working with Miss Montemuro and, incredibly, it is very helpful. Actually, I have been working on my voice ever since the laryngitis of *Sheepwell*. I do not carry it over to daily speech, though, and neglect is worsening my speech.

In Dance class, I worked harder than hard after making the directing book for *Medea*. The ballet still inspires with that strange inspiration that makes everyone who sees the ballet wish to be a dancer. Lola was even more enthusiastic than I. I feel perfectly happy doing *barre* work, but fixed steps are impossible. At any rate, I used up all my energy and a day loomed ahead.

An Acting class and *St. Joan*. Cherie Ross did St. Joan to Hal's Inquisitor and did not find the strain, the importance of the scene. Lola tried it and, though experiencing the feeling deeply, was technically unable to portray it, though it seemed to well up in her. Arla Gild gave it a big emotional try and certainly did it well. She is a completely successful emotional actress. Her realism is surprisingly convincing, but the more I learn of acting, the more I temper my feelings with the intellect. I am eager to think, and the more I think, the better my work, although Piscator claims that intellectual acting is not the best. But he admits that there are actors who have created great parts completely intellectually. In Arla's expressiveness, as wonderful as it is, I doubt if a consistent 200 performances would not almost break her, provided she could evoke the emotion as strongly each time (and I believe she can). I read the Inquisitor and Miss Wyler liked it very much, best of any she had heard, but said "Here your stylization comes in well." My "stylization," which I am trying to overcome, is my "style" and no doubt is a protest against this infernal naturalism, though not intentionally so. In working on *St. Joan* at home, I have been as realistic as possible without being too unrestrained, while with my Viola, I have yet to find a character. I am not very far along with Viola but once I have shaken off the remembered intonations of Priscilla's and Grace's performances, I will find my own way.

In Styles Through the Ages, Dr. Zucker discussed 18th century England. Being tired and seeing nothing interesting in 18th century English painting, I did not gain much from the lecture. The paintings all seemed the ancestors of the bad picture postcard and greeting card picture, with the outstanding exception of Hogarth, whose satiric painting bordering on caricature and his copper engravings were really captivating, despite the moralizing implicit in the care and observation that they showed.

Thursday, April 19, 1945

Voice class, with the last of the phonetic alphabet, which I had the advantage of knowing all along. Perhaps now we can do phonetic reading which I like, though I tend to speak it somewhat pedantically. In my free time, I worked on *Medea*. Margrit Wyler, even in these early stages of reading, creates a wonderful character with her beautiful voice.

In History and Sociology, we discussed dramaturgy, or the play as opposed to the theatre. There are two schools of thought about plays. The first states that drama is a form of literature and that a play is to be read; in other words, that drama is for the library. This theory was, in fact, supported by such men as Aristotle, Lessing and Voltaire. But most contemporaries agree with the second: that the theatre and not the bookshelf is the ultimate goal of the play.

Dr. Zucker then spoke about the elements of drama: exposition; the older form of introduction by secondary figures, such as the conversation of servants, or the more modern explanations by the characters themselves; characterization and the importance of the plot; these were some of the topics covered. As an example of an almost perfectly constructed play and perfect drama, we are going to study Eugene O'Neill's *The Great God Brown*, which Dr. Zucker considers one of the finest modern dramas.

In Costume Design, we tried to make up for lost time by diagrammatically drawing the main trend in costumes from 1600 to 1890. The changes seem to take place so fast, Elizabethan dress changes quickly to the French pre-revolutionary elaboration, then suddenly, revolution, the Empire, the bustle, and the gay 90's. We drew these on the blackboard in turn, and my old love of picture-making (I won't say drawing) came suddenly to me and made me fill my notebook with Mephistophelean faces instead of the costumes of 1690–1725.

Friday, April 20, 1945

Voice class.

Acting class with Mr. Ben-Ari. We reviewed the discussions of the beginning of the semester to discover what progress we have made with our individual problems. I claimed that, although I had improved so much in acting, I was still frightened at the idea of improvising. Thereupon, I was given an improvisation to do, and it did prove very difficult.

I was to have received a letter from my husband and learn that he is in a German prison camp. I go into church, light a candle and pray. Foolishly, I tried to be Arla instead of myself, but more than all this was the long inbred refusal of my hands to cross myself, and of my knees to kneel before the crucifix which my imagination saw. I tried several times to do these things but my hands trembled and my knees buckled instead of kneeling.

I have no sense memory for such an action, always a taboo, and one of those things that sets us apart from our Christian friends – what can I remember? I remember my high school friend, Mariya Lubliner, who, in a panic about not getting into heaven, converted to Catholicism in the church on 96th Street and Amsterdam Avenue.

I went to the church with her once and watched her kneel and cross herself. I tried to base my acting on what I had observed, but the fact is that I had observed too critically, and was too put off by my observations to enter into her belief.

After much effort, I finally succeeded in carrying out the various rituals and kneeling to pray, though I thought more about my inability to evoke tears than the actual prayer, which I finally succeeded in thinking silently. The class immediately noticed that I was more interested in the church ceremonies than in my husband.

In Miss Wyler's Acting class, Charles Coleman and Joel Rene both read "If music be the food of love," but achieved merely intelligent readings. Neither approached Gene's grasp of the spirit. Steffi read Eliza Doolittle from *Pygmalion* and Miss Wyler says the fault lies in her heavy movements, but I think she cannot give her the brusque delicacy, the rosy-eyed dirt of Eliza. We then did an improvisation in a restaurant, in which I was asked to be the waitress, and Miss Wyler said that I showed excellent observation in the way that I handled my invisible props and in my attitude towards customers and the hostess. Miss Wyler was not aware of two years of such work in which I developed these skills until they were completely automatic. Here I was able to "believe" or "live" my part. For as soon as I looked upon the students as customers, they became just that and I treated them accordingly. (How many of them have I served at Valeska Gert's Beggar Bar?) This ended a short class, shortened by a *Medea* rehearsal.

In the evening, *The Second Shepherd's Play*, a medieval drama, was done for March of Drama. Dr. Tannenbaum, an authority on Shakespeare and on pre-Shakespearean drama, gave a lecture that consisted of an outline of the drama up to the middle ages. *The Second Shepherd's Play* is really a charming comedy. The earliest English farce, it bears all the signs of slapstick and has a touchingly naïve plot. The characters, though, are masterpieces, every one. Laura Curly gave a free, uninhibited performance as the lusty, ugly, full-bodied Jill, the unpleasant, nagging wife. The three shepherds were played by Charles Coleman who, as usual, gave an extraordinary performance with his natural good humor. Joel Rene did well in his first role, though he still lacks that either-you-have-it-or-you-don't quality that makes an actor and is beyond words. Arthur Green, on the other hand, is improving tremendously and if his temperament develops along with his histrionics, he may succeed. Buddy Stratton played opposite Laura as Mac the Sheepstealer and fulfilled the role with a great deal of humor. The casting created a comic effect, for Laura is five foot one, while Buddy is about six foot two, and the difference was exploited fully.

The staging and direction show that Esther has the capacity for great things. Besides her natural talent, she almost is unique in taking from Mr. Piscator all that he has to give, and in really working in school, not trying to do as little as possible. I feel that she is the only one who approaches my love for Mr. Piscator and the School.

Saturday, April 22 and Sunday, April 23, 1945

Medea rehearsals.

Monday, April 23, 1945

Dance class. Madame Piscator terrifies me at times with my own incapacities. My *barre* work is improving rapidly, whereas my steps are still unbelievably clumsy. As much as I loved my early school, Hunter Model, I did resist drilling the steps they taught us in gym class (so the knowledge of my right side and my left side would become instinctive despite myself, because it would help me so much in my life). Now in my eighteenth year, I find myself in the awkward position of again not being able to tell left from right without hesitation, and consequently not capable of mastering elementary steps. I remember how I used to fake the little tap dancing steps we had to do in gym class at Hunter. But once I had to learn a "break," it was the only step I ever knew. I can still do it. It is still the only step I know. My love for dancing and my really sincere efforts make my failure all the more disheartening. So disheartened was I, in fact, that I stayed away from my make-up class – as well as avoiding *Medea* rehearsals.

In Current Plays, we discussed "failures." The class had seen enough of them to be an authority on the subject. Most of them were such pitiful little attempts at theatre that we wondered how a playwright and a producer and a director could all be so mistaken, when every theatre-goer could see how bad the play was in the first act. We spoke of believing in, or "being inside" a play, i.e., not following critically but partaking in the action. Virginia Baker and I both admitted that we followed plays from the outside, though we tend to believe in the movies. I think this is a matter of non-resistance. I do not wish to judge the movie because I don't consider it worthwhile. I am unfamiliar with the techniques and accept almost anything they offer for what it is, since it is lifeless and "canned" anyway. Therefore, since it is intellectually uninteresting, my emotions can freely range the story without critical interference.

In directing class, we continued with the technical side of staging, which according to Dean, is the most uninteresting. But Mr. Piscator prefaced the lesson with a brilliant speech about stages and space. He said: "The stage in itself has no architectural space, it is a dreamlike, empty room and our force must build the space."

Then he described some of his productions and some of Meyerhold's from the point of view of the stage space. In a production of *The Lower Depths*, he used an enormous flight of stairs, a device derived from his teacher, Leopold Jessner. In the darkness actors sat on the stairs and with small electric lamps lit their faces as they spoke, till the day came and people went to work up the steps, moving through streets and houses. Those on the lower steps went to their labors slowly; and more slowly, down lower still, those who did the lowest kind of work. Then, forever in the darkness, were those who had no work: the last, lowest steps, the "lower depths." In the revolt scene, the actors came running down the steps toward the audience until guns had to be aimed from the orchestra pit to protect the audience from the massed fury.

These "Jessner steps" were also employed in *Oedipus the King*, where the hero as king stood on the top step and with each fall from honor or position went down one step till he stood, blind, at the bottom. This is an almost primitive but direct use of the value of levels. We demonstrated level values in a much smaller way from the Dean book.

Tuesday, April 24, 1945

Directors' Council. In Theatre Research, we concluded the discussion of the never-dying *Sheepwell* and went over the performance of *The Second Shepherd's Play*. Mr. Piscator was quite satisfied with all the actors. Arthur Green's performance was compared to his work on *Sheepwell*, in which he presented a deeper characterization by placing a comic character in a tragic situation. Arthur's comedy skills made him try to turn his comic student into a tragic figure. Today, he told Mr. Piscator that it was impossible to mix comedy and tragedy. Mr. Piscator smilingly refuted this very authoritatively spoken statement and told us some of his experiences with audience reaction.

In the tense situation, there comes a sudden relaxation – laughter. From this relief, the emotions are almost immediately tensed again. Having relaxed, the audience can return to the deeper situation with a fresh view, and is more aware of the depth of tragedy by the humorous contrast. Mr. Piscator then began to talk very mysteriously about our "guest actor." As we had no guest actor in the production, it took us quite a time to realize that he was speaking of Charles Coleman, whose make-up had been so clever that during the performance Mr. Piscator had asked Chouteau, "Who is this?", and in her mischievous humor she replied that it was a guest actor, and he took her at her word. The fact that Charles can so conceal his real self, which Mr. Piscator knows well, is a good sign from the acting viewpoint.

In March of Drama, we were assigned duties for *The Circle of Chalk*. My lot falls to costumes. The costumes are to be hand-made for this performance, with the aid of a hired seamstress. Though I am promised I will only have to paint on the costumes, I fear I shall be asked to sew. Oh, dread and bane! Perhaps I shall have the opportunity to change to props, which is fascinating in its go-get-it-or-make-it spirit.

In stage design, we worked on the problems of a simple setting. We were given a unit set consisting of three arches to construct five scenes in various parts of a castle, using only plain drapes or cutouts or a cyclorama. The simplest effects are the most successful, but the tendency to clutter is absolutely painful. A harbor, a vault, a terrace and two interiors remain: a home assignment.

Wednesday, April 25, 1945

Voice.

Then a Dance class and due to the lack of a teacher, Alice Blue took over. Alice has had quite a bit of success as a dancer, her movements are sweet and delicate: surely not the result of her early training with Fokine, but probably of her own adorable nature. We tried doing some coordination exercises and some of her routines, but these consisted of fixed steps which were too much for me.

Acting class was done together with the "B" acting group, in order to save Margrit's energy for *Medea* rehearsals. I was glad that I was not asked to do Viola, being still somewhat wary of the opinions of these older students. Not that I fear judgment; *au contraire*, the judgment of Margrit Wyler or Erwin Piscator is precious. But the rashness of a young person who is not, but believes himself to be your superior, is definitely to be avoided. Many students did readings, alternating between the newer and the older groups, and the difference was not too great.

Mimi Rosenberg did the Martha role from Irwin Shaw's *Bury the Dead*. Mimi reached deep enough to get at the emotion involved and to a certain extent convinced me of the lower class woman she was trying to portray. Mimi's acting consists more of heart than of theatre.

Cherie then tried a scene from *The Man Who Came to Dinner*, playing the role of the actress – but approached sophistication from a naïve point of view. Margrit explained that seemingly false sophistication is, though not real to the sophisticate, at least a real pose, and must be played with as much sincerity in the posing as any action that the character requires.

Myrna Seld did the telephone conversation of the same character. Being naturally more sophisticated than Cherie, she succeeded in bringing the illusion to life, for though she would vehemently deny it, her voice often carried some of the "*But really!*" in it. The exuberance required for the scene was also well done. I wonder, though, whether Myrna could do something deeper, for she is one of our logical, modern, Huxleyan minds, and I cannot visualize her in a rending passion or with any real emotion besides anger.

Gerance Garie then read Olwin's description of Martin's death from that fabulous jigsaw puzzle *Dangerous Corner*. The character, of course, is a cool one, but Gerance played her as an unemotional one. I felt that she was repeating a story she heard and not telling of an incident of which she was part.

Anna Curtis Chandler, "the storyteller," has still left her imprint in my mind as far as her art goes. I still have a tendency to read like her. A few weeks ago, I read a poem of Ezra Pound's to some people. After my reading, one of them said, "Doesn't she remind you of the woman that used to tell stories in the library some years ago?" I asked if she meant Anna Curtis Chandler and of course I was right. Miss Chandler was my teacher five years ago and my reading remains under her influence. How amazing is the importance of the teacher!

In Styles Through the Ages, Dr. Zucker showed us the negligible, uninteresting art of America in the 18th century, the most exciting example of which is Mr. Stuart's Washington, that has become so well-known as to be painfully stereotyped. The others were so unimaginative that I cannot even recall one of them, nor did I take notes.

Thursday, April 26, 1945

Voice.

In History and Sociology, we continued our conversation on the ingredients of drama by reading O'Neill's *The Great God Brown*, a drama whose greatness amazes me afresh at each reading. Virginia read Dion in her stirring voice. Arla read the other woman and Louis Guss and Charles Coleman read the men's roles. We found it an almost perfect example of a play. The first scene already showed how Eugene O'Neill used every line with fullest forethought: in the whole scene there is not one line that does not either establish a character, or further the understanding of the audience as regards plot and environment, and in foreshadowing the outcome of the play. It is a simple scene in which no action takes place. Two families, two businessmen ambitious for their sons' careers, two rather sentimental mothers and an ordinary young girl loved by both boys. We have the sensitive, the beautiful, the untouchable in one camp, and in the other the prosaic, the philistine. We meet the young Brown, nice, simple, and the young Dion, spiritual, poetic, doomed to misfortune by a fragile soul. All this is brought out in a simple scene with tremendous impact.

In Costume Design, we made diagrams of men's costumes from 1450 through to the 1900's and found them as various as their female counterparts. In 1450, men looked very much like British sailors, the tight trousers and fitted top and V-neckline bringing to mind today's limey. In 1500, a robe was added. In 1625, the doublet and hose started to tend toward "the Puritan costume," which remained the style in England, while the French began to beribbon themselves with the Restoration bows which, modified, became what we know best as "the early Colonial costume." From there, it was only a step of modification (elimination of the ruffles, narrowing of the jacket, and the addition of trousers) to modern dress, not to forget the 1900's, with their tasteless patterns and straight cut. During the class, while drawings were being prepared on the blackboard, Mr. Kerz compared the European pre-war theatre with American theatre. Arbitrarily, I took the side of the European theatre, though he countered every point I made with three better ones. His knowledge of theatre and modern plays is enough to make me feel humble on a subject that I thought I was quite an authority on. The studying I have yet to do overwhelms me.

Friday, April 27, 1945

Voice class.

Acting class. Lola and I did an improvisation which I felt was a great improvement on any of my previous improvisations. We were to plan it ourselves and our basic theme was this: I come to tell a man's wife that I love her husband. I enter the woman's apartment and introduce myself. I come in nervously, but I am fully prepared for a scene, and for asserting my love, and my right to love, no matter how she counters my remarks. I ask for the man and then, on being told he is not home, I sit and prepare to let go my speech when Lola named a girl whom I (in my character) knew and suggested I go there, as he often spends his evenings with her, or perhaps with another young lady, "He does run around so." Thus, the clever bitch completely stumped me and forced me to retreat in a huff, and then, to add insult to injury, the moment I am gone she called the husband from the next room. Though she ruined my dramatic scene, I must admit she did show quick thinking.

I underestimated the dramatic quality of the scene. Afterwards, when Lola and I sat down to discuss it, Lola told me about an exact parallel from her life, that was both true and personal. The story is exactly the same, except that Lola spoke not as the wife, but the other woman. My reaction was so completely different that I realized I had not allowed myself to think on stage. Here is the thought process that I could have gone through: the wife is a predetermined obstacle. The girl knows he is a married man, her victory is in winning him from the wife. But another woman is a new factor. Here, jealousy and anger would come in. For the other girl is in the same position as she is and, therefore, a rival. To be one of many would be heartbreaking for the girl, a completely new reaction. She might even have cried, or become hysterical.

Steffi and Charles Coleman also did a very fine original improvisation. Charles played a drunken husband and Steffi, the wife. Charles did a wonderful drunk scene and Steffi, as usual, reacted perfectly. Their playing together was interesting to me, for Charles acts as I do, mentally, while Steffi puts herself into her role completely. Perhaps I shall do this when my technique is far enough developed that I can act naturally without thought, though Charles acts with pure technique, and does so successfully.

The afternoon was spent preparing for *Medea*. Involving light rehearsals, some simple sets and much excitement. Mr. Piscator came to rehearsal and under his searching sensitivity even the perfect performance of Margrit benefited from his criticism. We had thought it perfect, but in this perfection, Mr. Piscator found room for improvement. His grasp of Medea's character is uncanny. I would have thought that no man could understand a so thoroughly feminine passion.

March of Drama and the *Medea*. Margrit's performance was absolutely stunning. Not only her acting and voice, but she actually looked like a savage, gorgeous queen. Never has anyone been so striking. Jason almost reached her pitch. David Lewis played him with a quiet tension. Charles Coleman read a dignified Creon, but Medea could not be overshadowed. Throughout, it was Medea's presence that was felt. Through her, the others, the men, lived. Margrit Wyler gave impetus to the whole cast.

THE REPERTORY
OF THE
DRAMATIC WORKSHOP
1940—1952

PREMIERE PERFORMANCES IN NEW YORK

Borchert, OUTSIDE THE DOOR
Bruckner, CHAFF
Bruckner, THE CRIMINALS
Frisch, HOUSE IN BERLIN
Gabrielson, DAYS OF OUR YOUTH
Herczeg-Herald, THE BURNING BUSH
James, WINTER SOLDIERS
Kaestner, EMIL AND THE DETECTIVES
Klabund, CIRCLE OF CHALK

Matthews, THE SCAPEGOAT
Neuman-Piscator, Tolstoy's WAR AND PEACE
Pagodin, THE ARISTOCRATS
Palma, THERE IS NO END
Penn Warren, ALL THE KING'S MEN
Salacrou, NIGHTS OF WRATH
Sartre, THE FLIES
Shaw, VILLAGE WOOING
Yordan, ANY DAY NOW

EXPERIMENTAL PLAYS
(Authors are Members of the Playwriting Classes)

Abel, HANDS AGAINST ONE
Arluck, WOLF ARE YOU READY?
Bennett, NO HIDNG PLACE
Bradford, CHAMELEON
Cunningham, MARIE'S NEW DRESS
Druck, CRISIS AT QUIET REST
Druck, HALF A LOAF
Ehrlich, KING OF THE HILL
Gillivan, ALONG THE WAY

Gregory, THE LAST ENEMY
Irving, JOHNNY CASEY
Mark, WHEN YOU HEAR THE SIGNAL
Orlovitz, CASE OF THE NEGLECTED
   CALLING CARD
Peterman, MOMENT OF DECISION
Pitcher, SNAKE, SNAKE
Pitcher, THE CHIMES
Pollock, WEDDING IN JAPAN

Shore, WHO ARE THE WEAVERS?

CLASSICAL AND MODERN PLAYS

Anderson, Stallings, WHAT PRICE GLORY?
Aristophanes, LYSISTRATA
Benet, THE DEVIL AND DANIEL WEBSTER
Calderon, THE GREAT WORLD THEATRE
Chekhov, A MARRIAGE PROPOSAL
Carroll, ALICE IN WONDERLAND
Conkle, PROLOGUE TO GLORY
Coward, PRIVATE LIVES
Galsworthy, ESCAPE
Gogol, THE INSPECTOR GENERAL
Gozzi, TURANDOT
Hauptmann, HANNELE'S WAY TO HEAVEN
Heiyermans, THE GOOD HOPE
Hellman, THE LITTLE FOXES
Hoffman, THE SEA SERPENT
Kesselring, ARSENIC AND OLD LACE
Ibsen, GHOSTS
Kingsley, THE WORLD WE MAKE
Laurents, HOME OF THE BRAVE
Lessing, NATHAN THE WISE
Lope de Vega, THE SHEEPWELL
Millay, ARIA DA COPA
Maltz, PRIVATE HICKS
Miller, ALL MY SONS

Moliere, THE IMAGINARY INVALID
O'Casey, JUNO AND THE PAYCOCK
O'Casey, SHADOW OF A GUNMAN
Odets, WAITING FOR LEFTY
O'Neill, MOURNING BECOMES ELECTRA
Patrick, THE HASTY HEART
Pirandello, TONIGHT WE IMPROVISE
Saroyan, TIME OF YOUR LIFE
Saroyan, HELLO OUT THERE
Segall, HEAVEN CAN WAIT
Shakespeare, MACBETH
Shakespeare, MIDSUMMER NIGHTS DREAM
Shakespeare, ROMEO AND JULIET
Shakespeare, TAMING OF THE SHREW
Shakespeare, TWELFTH NIGHT
Shaw, ANDROCLES AND THE LION
Shaw, THE DEVIL'S DISCIPLE
Shaw, MAN OF DESTINY
Shaw, THE MILLIONAIRESS
Sherwood, THE PETRIFIED FOREST
Steinbeck, OF MICE AND MEN
Treadwell, MACHINAL
Tolstoi, THE CAUSE OF IT ALL
Thurber-Nugent, THE MALE ANIMAL

Wilder, OUR TOWN

MUSICAL PLAYS

Arden-Harburg-Herzig-Saidy, BLOOMER
   GIRL
Hoyt-Carter-Selden, TEXAS STEER
Myer-Eliscu-Gorney, MEET THE PEOPLE

(Original Revue), MIDDLE MAN,
   WHAT NOW?
Kaufman-Ryskind-Gershwin, OF THEE I SING
Hart-Rodgers, CONNECTICUT YANKEE

SUMMER THEATRE PRODUCTIONS

Barry, PHILADELPHIA STORY
Booth-Luce, THE WOMEN
Coward, BLITHE SPIRIT
Denham, LADIES IN RETIREMENT
Franken, CLAUDIA

Holm-Abbott, THREE MEN ON A HORSE
Miramova-Leontovich, DARK EYES
Williams, THE CORN IS GREEN
Sternheim, MASK OF VIRTUE

24

Plate 16 Full repertory of plays produced at the Dramatic workshop, 1940–1952.

Plate 17 Architect Joseph Urban's theater at The New School.

Plate 18 McGrew mural in the Joseph Urban theatre.

Plate 19
Piscator
with
Simone de
Beauvoir
and Saul
Colin.

Plate 20
Piscator
with
student.

Plate 23 *Frankenstein*, The Living Theatre, 1967.

Plate 24 *The Money Tower*, The Living Theatre, 1975.

Plate 25 Piscator in jail, 1930.

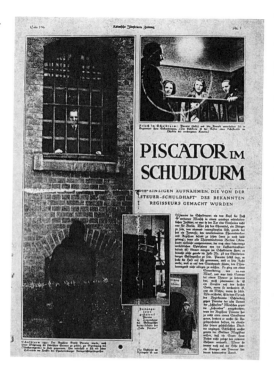

Plate 26 Judith Malina and Julian Beck in jail, 1971.

Plate 27 Judith Malina and Maria Ley-Piscator teaching at The Dramatic Workshop II in 1990.

Plate 28 *Eureka!*, The Living Theatre, 2008.

Plate 29 Judith Malina, Brad Burgess and Tom Walker rehearsing *History of the World*, 2011.

Plate 30 Judith Malina and Brad Burgess performing *Occupy Your World*, an expression of support for the Occupy movement, 2011.

part 3

The Ongoing Epic

We were a generation of young actors, actresses, stage designers, musicians, and Judith and Julian made a place for us. Even though so much of what we did in the early 60's has become common in theatres everywhere, The Living Theatre is still experimenting – with social political themes, with improvisation, with audience involvement, with high poetic theatre.

Robert De Niro

The work that Piscator initiated is continuing its transformation. The years of his return to Germany proved yet another painful journey – though through his perseverance, they ended in success.

When he lamented his failure in his diary on the plane back to Germany, he did not realize that his life's work still lay before him. The 11 years that he spent despairingly as a freelance director spread the message of his work to many cities, and influenced a whole generation of actors. The three great productions that he directed when he was finally given the West Berlin Volksbühne resulted in a reinvigoration of political theatre, and the reawakening of street and site-specific Total Theatre techniques; what Brecht called "his great scenic innovations."

I conclude this work by boldly listing the plays of The Living Theatre over a period of 65 years, pointing out the scenic and theatrical devices that have their origins in Piscator's experiments. There are many theatres that have drawn on Piscator's creations, but here I write of the theatre that I know best.

In 1990, at The New School, I taught a class together with the aging Maria Ley-Piscator on Piscator's work. Madame Piscator called the class The Dramatic Workshop II, for she never gave up the idea of reviving the school . . . In that class we taught the ongoing resonance of Piscator's work, analyzing and rediscovering the ideas of such a progressive theatre.

End of the Notebook and First Workshop Plays

On April 27, 1945, in the midst of our work on *Medea*, I stopped keeping these notes because I became too deeply involved in the production activities to afford the luxury of the perpetuation of the moment that the diary form represents. I wanted to give all my energies to the work at hand.

I have had many regrets at the abrupt ending of these notes. But when I entered into the tremendous here-and-now of play production, I had no desire to write, only to be part of the action.

When I stopped keeping the notebook on April 27, I was already working on props for Klabund's *Circle of Chalk*, and then in May, I was given the role of The Spartan Woman in Maria Piscator's metallic-plastic and cellophane production of Aristophanes' *Lysistrata*. Then in June, I played one of the students in *The Corn Is Green*, singing "All Through the Night" with the direction of Chouteau Dyer's Miss Moffat.

Those were the plays in which I participated in the first months of my studies at the Workshop, but by no means all the plays that I saw there. For Piscator's didactic theory held that it was necessary to be trained in all the classical, academic and traditional theatrical forms in order to bring forth the new. That season at the Workshop I saw Molière's *The Imaginary Invalid*, O'Neill's *Mourning Becomes Electra*, Shaw's *Androcles and the Lion* and Ibsen's *Peer Gynt*.

My first performance in a Dramatic Workshop event was as a member of the chorus in the March of Drama reading of Racine's *Esther*. We had only a few rehearsals; I record two in my notebook. I soon encountered my breaking-up problem, and tried to understand it and to overcome it, though that was not completely accomplished until years later. Fortunately I was one of a chorus, and able to let other voices take over and hide my shame. No one seemed to notice it and, if they did, they said nothing. Throughout my time at the Workshop, I managed to keep Piscator unaware of this flaw in my acting. He had little patience with such things, expecting the same stern discipline from his actors that he always demonstrated himself.

My next theatrical assignment was work on the costume crew for *The Imaginary Invalid*, with a rather elaborate period wardrobe. We did what was termed "a tour," to a public school in Brooklyn. It was my first, though not my last, for later I spent much of my life on tour, dealing with such practical limitations as inadequate dressing-room space, or functioning with a large cast and only one mirror and no water. It was good training, though I complained of it at the time in my notebook, because it caused me to miss my classes. It was hard for us to understand, at first, why Piscator always put production work ahead of class work.

This performance was also the first audience-involvement event in which I participated. The fact that it was a performance for children, albeit of an adult play, allowed for a looseness of form, and though Molière's lines were not always accurately spoken, the actors encountered the children in the aisles, leaping from stage to house, enacting the relationships of the conflicting characters with amazing gusto, creating a bedlam that delighted the children.

In 1968, when bedlam in the theatre delighted The Living Theatre's audiences in *Paradise Now*, when all the rules were broken, everything seemed possible. Piscator never saw this production, nor do I think he would have recognized how many premises of his philosophy it hinted at fulfilling, but for me *The Imaginary Invalid* was a tremendous lesson in the possibilities of what can happen when actors feel free and uninhibited on the stage.

These productions were created around a heavy schedule of classwork, so designed that the productions were integrally part of the instruction.

Julian Beck

I attended these performances, which were part of the Workshop's core program called The March of Drama, with Julian Beck, an abstract expressionist painter and my soulmate from the moment we met in 1943 until his death in 1985. He was to spend many hours at the Workshop, seeing all the productions, sitting in with me in many classes, sometimes assisting with production work, and though he never enrolled in any courses, he garnered more from Piscator's teaching than many of the latter's students. And through the testimony of Beck's later work as a director, producer, and stage designer he could be said to be one of Piscator's most faithful disciples.

Julian was especially impressed by Piscator's single-minded political commitment, which was always in the foreground of his theatrical aesthetic. Just before I entered the Workshop, I attended Peggy Guggenheim's Autumn Salon at the Art of this Century Gallery, where Julian's painting was exhibited alongside the works of Motherwell, Baziotes, Rothko, Jackson Pollock and de Kooning. And from there a relationship developed between

The Living Theatre and the New York School of Abstract Expressionism that has often sustained The Living Theatre, in the way that Piscator's work was enriched by his interactions with George Grosz, John Heartfield and the Dadaists.

By Any Other Name and Maurice Schwartz's Yiddish Art Theatre

When the summer break came, The Dramatic Workshop closed, or rather moved to a playhouse in Sayville, Long Island, where Piscator ran a summer theatre in which I could not afford to participate. So I spent part of the summer in a comedy, *By Any Other Name*, at the Cherry Lane Theatre, where The Living Theatre was to play its opening season some six years later. Then I spent the rest of the summer playing one of the angels in Maurice Schwartz's *Three Gift*s (*Dray Matones*) at the Yiddish Art Theatre on Second Avenue.

Maurice Schwartz was a legendary figure in the Yiddish theatre of New York, rivaled only by members of the Adler family. In what was later to become Loew's Second Avenue movie house, Schwartz produced the Yiddish Art Theatre for 30 years, playing Yiddish works as well as Shakespeare, Ibsen and Wilde in the Yiddish language. From Maurice Schwartz I learned a different discipline. It derived from the Yiddish Theatre of Vilna, and is the style they created for their famous production of *The Dybbuk*. It is an endless struggle between outcry and restraint. The Jewish outcry overcoming the restraint of oppression.

In October the school reopened, and I began to understand how the productions of The March of Drama expressed Piscator's vision, like the stages of a vast initiation from Aeschylus to O'Neill. That month I worked backstage on Molière's *Imaginary Invalid*, and the next two months I played a small part in Pirandello's *Tonight We Improvise*, a play that The Living Theatre was to produce twice, in 1955 and 1960.

Piscator's Basic Question: The Role of the Audience

In "The Theatre of the Future," published in *Tomorrow Magazine* in February 1942, Piscator wrote:

The aim of drama is to involve the audience in the action, and the history of theatre is simply the history of greater or lesser triumph in . . . audience participation.

In that same essay Walter Gropius, the architect who designed Piscator's never-built Total Theatre, wrote:

We intend, by these technical means (projections, scaffolds, movable structures, etc.) to force the audience into close contact with the scenic action, to make them participate in the playing, and not to allow them to hide behind curtains.

The use of the word "force" is significant.

Because when it came to "participation in the playing," Piscator felt the need for control, to protect the rehearsed work, rather than dealing with the chaos of the spectator's improvisation.

Piscator understood both the social necessity of escaping from the elitist architecture of the traditional theatre, and the revolutionary imperative of participation. He struggled all his life to find means, dramaturgical or technical, to fulfill this imperative, and invented the most extraordinary devices to bring it about. Only one thing – the most evident and available step – he did not and he could not take. It remained for his students, for his artistic progeny to bridge the gap between the audience and the performer.

Becoming a Director: A Confession

I had enrolled in the Workshop as an acting student, since I had been brought up to be an actress. But after only a few days at the Workshop, and a few days of watching Piscator at work, I was certain that I needed to work in a broader field, with the wider scope of the director who absorbs the whole play, and can transmit its meanings to the actors and the audience. And who can, when necessary, reinterpret the playwright's meanings, search out the historical truth, and in the use of setting, lights and sound, relate the play's expression to the time and the environment in which it is performed. I wanted to be a director.

As briefly documented in my Notebook, with great trepidation I went to Piscator's office. Imperious, seated in front of his map of wartime Europe, he heard my request with cold regard. "Women," he explained, with a certain impatience, "lack staying power in the theatre. They tend to get married and give up the work. So it is better you stick to acting." I was stricken. What could I say when my mother's example seemed to prove his contention, and how could I convince this misogynist of the sincerity of my intentions, and of the endurance of my dedication to the theatre?

Shamefacedly I admit now that I used an old tactic that women often stoop to, in order to gain consideration from the men who feel that they do not belong in certain exacting professions, which they believe to be exclusively man's domain. I cried. And I got permission to take Piscator's directing course.

The Inspiration of Joseph Urban's Architecture

The New School for Social Research was designed by Joseph Urban in 1930, and is a thrilling example of the great vision of modern architecture during its pioneer stage. It was the first such facility developed exclusively for adult education, and is hailed as an outstanding example of the "International Style" of 20th century architecture. Its dramatic spaces are in themselves an inspiration to students, including its sunburst auditorium, where we performed our plays, its moving social murals by Orozco, and the splendid Benton Room with Thomas Hart Benton's marvelous panorama of American humanity. In later years, the Workshop was located in The President Theatre, a small midtown enclave of serious work in the midst of Broadway, and then in The Rooftop Theatre on the Lower East Side in an old Minsky vaudeville house, where Piscator thought to assemble again his long-hoped-for "proletarian audience."

When I attended my first classes in the Urban building, I found it a miraculous place, in which every space, and every wall was created to convey an aesthetic that was basic to the education we were receiving. A fit place to house Piscator's teaching.

Eleanor Fitzgerald

Eleanor Fitzgerald, always called Fitzi, was one of the remarkable theatrical figures of the time. She'd had a long career at the Provincetown Playhouse when Eugene O'Neill and Edna St. Vincent Millay were carrying the banner of art theatre during a dry time, and later wrote a book about the Playhouse. She was also the longtime lover of the anarchist Alexander Berkman.

She was one of those energies that attaches itself to certain men of genius, who she can then encourage and assist. According to Maria Piscator, e.e. cummings said of Fitzi that "She was the incarnation of the mystery of individuality, of a nightly sorrowing and rejoicing, a prodigious, generous, fearlessly unique and passionate human being." Piscator sometimes made fun of her going out "for a liquid sandwich," but he valued her highly. I used to sit on a little shelf in the back of the box office and listen to her stories of life and love, and theatre.

For Piscator, she ran the box office and the subscriptions, organizing the audiences for the plays. She did this work because she adored Piscator, and it fulfilled her need to be near a man of greatness.

When Piscator and Albert Johnson agreed to create a theatre school, it was Fitzi who said, "We must make a school that is a theatre, because Piscator must have a theatre to work in!" It was her insistence that finally established The Studio Theatre at the Workshop. After the fiscal failure of The Studio Theatre – and Piscator's work was constantly crushed by theatre economics – a more modest plan developed: The March of Drama.

The Classes

The March of Drama

Our classes began at ten in the morning, and the Workshop day ended at eleven in the evening, or after the performance on Fridays (see Figure 4 opposite).

It was The March of Drama that proved to be the seed of "the school that was a theatre." A linear and pedagogical idea, The March of Drama presented a panorama of the history of the theatre from Aeschylus to the present. Piscator's school could not present this as a history course without relating it specifically to modern times, through the eyes of Marx and Toynbee, through the lessons of fascism and socialism, through two world wars, and our hopes for the future. Recreated on pp. 130–31 are two pages of the school catalogue, showing the scope of this vast pageant.

	MONDAY	TUESDAY	WEDNESDAY	THURSDAY	FRIDAY
10–11		Directors' Council B.R.	Voice C D.S.		Voice C D.S.
11–12		Theatre Research B.R.			Acting D
12–1		Theatre Research B.R.		Voice C D.S.	Acting D
1–2	DANCE		Dance	March of Drama	
2–3	Dance B D.S.	March of Drama D.S.	Dance B D.S.	March of Drama	Acting D
3–4	Make-up B	March of Drama D.S.		March of Drama	Acting D
4–5	Make-up B	March of Drama D.S.	Acting D	Hist & Sociology of the Theatre	
5–6	Current Plays		Acting D		
6–7		Stage Design		Costume design	
7–8		Stage Design		Costume design	
8.30–9	Direction D.S.	Styles thru Ages A			March of Drama
9–10.30	Direction D.S.	Styles thru Ages B			March of Drama

Figure 4 Judith's weekly schedule.

On Friday evenings, either John Gassner or Paolo Milano discussed a period, and outlined the historical perspectives. They analyzed the specific work to be shown as an example of the style and the politics of the time. Gassner and Milano, two of the day's leading figures in theatrical history and criticism, presented each period within its economic and cultural context. They showed us the Epic quality that positions drama in the changing stream of history, and how it deepens our understanding of the fabric of the time. After Milano or Gassner gave their talk, one of the directing students presented a reading of the designated play, performed by Workshop students.

THE MARCH OF THE DRAMA

A. GENERAL SURVEY. 2 hours.   John Gassner, Paolo Milano

Required for all students enrolled in one or more courses in the Dramatic Workshop who have not completed their first year. The fee to them is nominal.

Members of this class are considered not as students but as audience and participants in play readings and discussion of dramatic works of art which constitute a kind of living history of the theatre, stressing characteristic expression and style in the various stages of its development. The course may be thought of as the nerve center that unites all the separate branches of dramatic study in the drama itself.

Masters of the Drama by John Gassner is used as preparation and background for understanding the cultural and social forces to which the theatre has responded in various epochs. The course is supplemented by Dr. Zucker's course in styles through the masterpieces of the arts, and by the course in dance styles of Maria Ley and Vincenzo Celli.

FALL TERM

Lectures	Readings
I Primitive rites and passion plays: functions of drama	
II Aeschylus and the beginning of tragedy: the dramatist as thinker; drama and Epic Theatre	Agamemnon
III Sophocles and the development of dramatic technique	Antigone
IV Euripides and modern drama: the problem drama; the psychological drama	Trojan Women
V Aristophanes and Roman comedy: the functions of comedy	Lysistrata
VI Oriental drama, sensuousness, ethics and mysticism in the theatre	Shakuntala
VII The Medieval drama: communal theatre	Everyman and the Second Shepherd's Play
VIII Commedia dell'Arte and the Renaissance	
IX Lope de Vega and Calderon: the golden age of Spanish theatre	The Sheep-Well
X Marlowe and the rise of Elizabethan drama: the theatre of will and self-assertion	Dr. Faustus
XI Shakespeare: the drama of individualism; the art of characterization	Richard II
XII Shakespeare and the modern world. Ben Jonson and the last of the Elizabethans	King Lear
XIII The classical French drama – Racine, Corneille, individualism and order	Phaedra

XIV	Molière and the comedy of society	Misanthrope
XV	Congreve and Restoration comedy, Lessing and the Enlightenment; rationalism and the drama	The Way of the World, Nathan the Wise
XVI	Goethe and romanticism: the drama of aspiration	Faust
XVII	Victor Hugo and the decline of romanticism: Scribe and the rise of the "well-made" play	Hernani

SPRING TERM

I	Ibsen: the rise of realism in modern society	Peer Gynt
II	Ibsen: the development of realism, character and society in the realistic theatre	Hedda Gabler
III	Strindberg and the naturalistic theatre – Zola, Antoine, etc. The rise of naturalism	The Father
IV	Hauptmann: the meaning and modification of naturalism	The Weavers
V	Neo-romanticism: Maeterlinck and Rostand	
VI	Pirandello and Benavente: cerebral drama	Six Characters in Search of an Author
VII	Russian realism from Gogol to Tolstoy	The Inspector-General
VIII	Anton Chekhov: the drama of attrition	The Cherry Orchard
IX	Maxim Gorky and the Soviet drama: new aspects of realism and communal theatre	The Lower Depths
X	Expressionism: Wedekind, Kaiser, Toller, Capek, etc. The interior drama; dramatic distortion and emphasis	From Morn to Midnight
XI	The rise of Epic Theatre: Brecht and Piscator; epic concepts of the drama	An American Tragedy
XII	Giraudoux, Bourdet, etc.: French drama in the twentieth century, drama and entertainment	Amphitryon 38
XIII	The awakening of the English theatre: Shaw and his precursors	Pygmalion
XIV	Bernard Shaw and the comedy of social criticism	Saint Joan
XV	Twentieth century English theatre: Galsworthy, Barker, Barrie, Masefield, etc.	Strife
XVI	Eugene O'Neill and the awakening of the American theatre	Desire Under the Elms
XVII	American drama since 1918: Anderson, Howard, Rice, Paul Green, Behrman, Kaufman, Barry, etc.	Winterset
XVIII	New forces in American drama: the social drama, the living newspapers, and Epic Theatre	Awake and Sing

Figure 5 Lecture Programme for The March of Drama, Fall term and Spring term, taught by John Gassner and Paolo Milano.

Each student director tried to use his or her hour on the stage to get beyond the semi-circle of chairs and the actors reading, script in hand. There was no budget for these March of Drama readings, but the director could add a shawl, a crown or a special chair brought from home, or add a bit of music on a flute or a record. And the director could cast students who agreed to learn the lines and get off book, and then what was to stop them from moving around? And soon, adding a few lights, the readings illustrating the March of Drama lectures became full weekly productions.

The trend was unstoppable. The best of these productions became The March of Drama Repertory, and there it was – the school that was a theatre.

Theatre Research

The Theatre Research class was Piscator's seminar. It was the platform from which Piscator communicated his ideas to us, and taught us to clarify and express our own ideas. "The purpose of Theatre Research is to establish a philosophy of the theatre," he said.

I quote from the school brochure: "Theatre Research: Mr. Piscator's lecture and discussion period serves continuously to coordinate all the studies and activities of The Dramatic Workshop and to relate them to a coherent philosophy of the theatre. Based on criticism of the production program, it investigates and interprets every aspect of the theatre as a classic heritage, a contemporary art and a social and moral institution." It was the one class that the whole school was expected to attend.

On the day after Franklin Roosevelt's death, Piscator used the Theatre Research class to speak to us of the life of the deceased president to attune us to the historical dimension; that is, to a sense of being inside the historical process. We all live in history, but we can do so fully aware of the process of which we are a part, or we can live the unconsidered life, and feel neither our participation, nor our responsibility.

Theatre Research Critique

The Theatre Research assignments were very specific: we had to present a written critique of The March of Drama performance of the preceding Friday evening. Piscator said:

Criticism is not the ignoble thing we read today in the newspaper, it is a noble mission to the theatre. There have been great critics like Aristotle and Lessing. Without Lessing there could not have been Goethe or Schiller. We criticize with prejudice – taste is prejudice. But we must think dialectically (Hegelian) – that is, we must think from more than one point of view.

If we found these ideas difficult, and we did, we were given the following outline to apply to our critique of the plays:

I. The Play's Necessity

  A. The playwright's original purpose
  B. The play's message in terms of today

II. The Playwright – his world, his point of view

III. The Play

  A. Plot: story of the play in one paragraph, stating situation, conflict and outcome
  B. Action: how the plot is developed, detailed description of the story
  C. Style: several characteristics, specific exceptions

IV. The Performance

  A. Direction

      a. Dramaturgy – adaptation, cutting
      b. Style – does performance achieve the prescribed mood and message?
      c. Of actors, casting, coaching
      d. Staging – total concept

  B. Acting – describe one actor in detail, all in general
  C. Design – of setting, costumes, props
  D. Lighting
  E. Sound and Music
  F. Technical execution

V. The critic's personal opinion

  A. Objective: does the play achieve its necessity?
  B. Subjective: how would you have done it?

Figure 6 Piscator's suggested outline for Theatre Research Critique assignments.

I took this outline quite literally and it was a heavy task to cover all the points every week, along with our classwork and our rehearsals for the next March of Drama play. I did try to do all the research: the world and points of view of all the authors, from Sophocles to Goethe, from Marlowe to O'Casey – and tried with the help of Gassner and Milano to analyze each work. Piscator liked my essays and asked me each week to read them aloud to the class. But later on, for the very reason that I followed his outline so closely, he complained that I was "a typewriter director."

Years later I learned that those youthful essays were placed in the Piscator archives at the Akademie der Künste in Berlin, where they are open to scholars and researchers. And some 60 years later I find that I still have in my possession eight of these Theatre Research papers: *Nathan the Wise*, *Faust*, Piscator's film, *The Revolt of the Fishermen*, *Mourning Becomes Electra*, *Claudia*, *Gaol Gate*, *Private Lives*, and *The Cause of It All*.

Several of my classmates presented excellent critiques, though they tended not to use the outline so methodically, and paid more heed to the performances. I tended to emphasize the literary, historical and dramaturgical material.

Following the readings of one or two papers came Piscator's discourse on the play in the light of history. With history as the background, the Epic play is a kind of panoramic tapestry against which the ideas in the foreground are enacted by performers who are aware of their context, and guided by the director who has made coherent the three elements of the Piscatorean performance:

1. The epic background
2. The immediacy of the performance
3. The usefulness of the performance to the spectator

Piscator's categories: The Past = History interpreted by:

1. the playwright
2. the director and set designer
3. the performers
4. the spectator-participant

The Present = The play in the theatre:

1. Total Theatre
2. Participation of the spectator
3. Political/Social interpretation

The Future = The political results of Total Theatre

The Plays

The Sheepwell (Fuente Ovejuna)

Fuente Ovejuna, The Sheepwell, by Lope de Vega, was the first full production in which I performed at The Dramatic Workshop in April, 1945. The play, which Lope de Vega drew from the history of Andalusia in the 15th century, is a romance about a tyrannical overlord, and the resistance that a town called *The Sheepwell* puts up when a young couple defy the overlord's seigneurial right to spend the wedding night with the bride. The tyrant is killed and the townspeople are tortured to reveal the name of the killer. They answer with one voice: *"Fuente Ovejuna."*

In "The Proletarian Theatre: Its Fundamental Principle and Its Tasks," published in 1920, Piscator wrote:

> It will be possible to make every play into an instrument to strengthen the concept of mass struggle, to deepen revolutionary insight into historical necessities . . . In this way a large portion of world literature can be made to serve the cause of the revolutionary proletariat, just as the whole of world literature can be used for the political purpose of propagating the concept of class struggle.

In *The Sheepwell* the class struggle and the solidarity of resistance are basic to the plot, though as always Piscator made changes in the script.

I was given the role of a child, one of the people of the village of Fuente Ovejuna. In his first talk to us Piscator pointed out that "the people are the true protagonists," and that we who play the masses are playing the leading role. In my youthful exuberance I thereupon worked on my ensemble role as a full characterization, creating a name and a history for my character, and felt rewarded when I was given a single word to cry out, a line all my own, calling out my playmate's name, "Pedrito!" when it was his turn to be tortured.

Piscator staged the crowd scenes himself, with particular attention to the social implications of every move, making sure that we were cognisant of the political significance of each move.

Piscator staged the tortures in shadow-play behind a white screen. When one by one the villagers are asked, "Who killed the Commendador?" we answered, in chorus: "Fuente Ovejuna!" That is, all of us in the village, together, were responsible for the act of rebellion against the oppressor. All the actors leaned in, watching the victim. The torturers began with de Vega's dialogue, but as each victim approached, freezing in various positions of torture, and uttering a scream, the tempo increased, until at last the question, "Who killed the Commendador?" and the choral shout that answered it became quite frenzied.

Piscator opened *The Sheepwell* on April 7th in The New School's Urban auditorium. We performed it again on the 8th, and it was scheduled for the 13th and 14th. But the 12th was the day of Franklin Roosevelt's death, and classes were canceled and the school and the theatre were closed, while the city and the world went through its state of shock.

Franklin Roosevelt's Death

On the 17th, classes resumed, though we did not re-open *The Sheepwell* until a year later. In his Theatre Research class Piscator gave one of his most memorable discourses on "the life of a great man," urging us to be inspired by him to "lead great lives."

I did not share Piscator's unqualified admiration for FDR. My father had been dedicated to the lifting of the immigration quotas, which would have saved countless lives. But petitions and protests and appeals were to no avail. Roosevelt defended the legal limitations that prevented masses of Jews from escaping from their Nazi persecutors.

For Piscator, however, Roosevelt represented the great wartime leader, the Agamemnon of our age, and Piscator's sense of history moved me to tears.

We performed *The Sheepwell* again a year later, on the 6th, 7th, 13th and 14th of April, in The President Theatre. Then again a year later, in 1947, from March 26th to 30th at The Rooftop Theatre. I had the good fortune to perform my small role in all of these and to hear my song, "In knighthood's most valiant tradition," which Piscator had asked me to write to describe the courtship of the young lovers, sung by the talented Elaine Stritch. I thought it unfortunate that Piscator valued me more as a writer than as an actress.

136

THE PISCATOR NOTEBOOK

The Living Theatre's *Seven Meditations on Political Sado-Masochism* had its earliest roots in this play. Julian Beck, who saw several performances of Piscator's *Sheepwell*, felt that its charge of social responsibility left a lasting impression, and for me the echoes of Piscator's *Fuente Ovejuna* are audible in all The Living Theatre's plays.

Lysistrata

Lysistrata was a production directed by Maria Ley-Piscator, and it was all glittering decor. It was given only one performance, in the dance studio on May 25, 1945. Arla Gild played a tough Lysistrata. I was given the role of the Spartan Woman, which I suppose was a joke, since I was very small and frail, and the stereotype of the Spartan Woman is tall, strong, and ruthless. The staging was full of fuss and fancy; silver paper and strips of confetti entangled us – like the sexual desire we were suppressing in order to stop the war.

Many years later, in the days of the Vietnam anti-war movement, when I participated in The Women's Strike for Peace, there were frequent discussions of the possibility of a sex strike, as in the plot of the classical *Lysistrata* story. But at the Women's Strike Center on Eighth Street in Greenwich Village, the women of the peace movement felt it was inappropriate for them, because their partners were all also anti-war activists.

Yet in 2003, when the Iraq war was in full murderous swing, there were hundreds of productions of *Lysistrata* done worldwide in one month, in a protest called "The *Lysistrata* Project."

In the 1945 Piscator production, in spite of the fluff and glitter, the anti-war theme hardly needed emphasis. Although Piscator, in his supervisory position, came and talked to us about what a bold, pioneering play it was, that could speak of a peace action 2000 years ago, not like Antigone's individual rebellion, but rather a women's resistance strategy that was organized into a mass movement.

The Spook Sonata

At the end of the year I was given my first directing assignment, Strindberg's *The Spook Sonata*. At the first rehearsal Piscator came to talk to us about his performance as Arkenholtz at his theatre, The Tribunal in Königsberg, in January of 1920, when he was 26 years old.

By telling us that he himself had played the hero, Arkenholtz, at the very beginning of his career, he meant to make it clear that a high standard would be demanded. He explained the significance of this mysterious play in the context of Königsberg in 1920: a play about the guilts and crimes of the past poisonous society, and how the still-untainted youth must struggle not to be caught up in the shame of history. The First World War was behind them, but close enough to cast its polluting shadow on the young people. The idealistic vision of a new philosophy saves the young hero from the spooks of the past.

He described the opening scene: how the young Arkenholtz has just become a hero by rescuing a child from a fire, and then leaving the scene before he could be thanked or honored. Having established himself as a heroic youth, he must confront the worst aspects of the old rotten society, and the sins of the fathers envelop him. The decadent society, full of secret guilts and murders, tries to seduce him. A beautiful young lady intrigues him – but he recognizes her defect, his purity transcending all the evils around him. He is the wood of the ark which will bring the survivors to a new world. He represents what the progressive artists and thinkers of that time called "The New Objectivity."

Piscator had joined the Communist party two years before he played in *The Spook Sonata*. He never spoke of that affiliation in those pre-McCarthy days in America, when Brecht and Eisler would soon be called to appear before The House Un-American Activities Committee. Yet he was able to convey to us the profound social implications of this story of love and decadence, as was surely the playwright's intention.

I was not yet really ready to direct this masterpiece, but a strong cast sustained me. Eugene Van Grona, the accomplished dancer who had decided in mid-life to become an actor, played the old man Hummel, though I thought he should have been Arkenholtz since I was so taken with his heroic style after seeing him dance "Rhapsody in Blue" as a solo on the vast stage of Radio City Music Hall. Anna Berger, who has remained my lifelong friend, played the Cook, to whom she lent that fantastic dynamic between character and persona on which she later built a brilliant career in the theatre and in Hollywood. I was just beginning to learn the role of the director in relation to the actor.

I staged it with ladders, atop which the ghosts sat, perched above everyone, yet present for everyone. Piscator loved my ladders. They were a poor-theatre equivalent of the Jessner steps.

Because it was a March of Drama reading it was performed only once, on the 14th of December, in 1945. But it was produced again at the Workshop in 1948, after I had graduated. Howard Friedman directed it and asked me to play both The Young Lady and The Mummy. His Arkenholtz was Louis Criss and his Hummel was Alexis Solomis.

The Spook Sonata was a seminal play for The Living Theatre. We produced it at The Loft Studio in 1954. Julian Beck's dark set, which I described in my diary as "a black cavern, deep, dense, charred . . . stained with luminous points of violet, orange, green and gold," was a reflection of the scenery Piscator described to us almost ten years earlier, in which "the chairs were like spiders, infesting the old house as manifestations of the decadent society."

Alan Hovhaness wrote a profoundly appropriate score for The Living Theatre's production, and Richard Edelman played an Arkenholtz of a stature that could surely have stood up to Piscator's, though our aesthetic was not knowledgeably that of The New Objectivity at that time.

Piscator showed us how Strindberg's tortured world, as well that of the classics, or of the modern playwrights, were all available to an Epic interpretation. When Piscator performed the role of Arkenholtz, he was between the Dada events that he organized with Georg Grosz in Berlin in 1919, and the Dada events in the Burchard Art Gallery that he directed in June of 1920. The theatre of Strindberg, mixing the Romantic and the Freudian/psychological, is far from the outrageous experiments of the Dadaists, and yet during this time Piscator also directed Wedekind, Kaiser, Gorky and Upton Sinclair! In The March of Drama and in his Theatre Research class, Piscator taught that all plays can be developed from a political point of view, because every drama contains the conflict that demonstrates the economic and hierarchical relations and struggles common to all humanity.

Hannele's Way to Heaven

On the first three days of February, 1946, I played Flossie in Gerhard Hauptmann's *Hannele's Way to Heaven*.

It was at one of the rehearsals for *Hannele* that the full meaning of the theatrical commitment was borne in upon me. At the end of the rehearsal,

Piscator announced that our next rehearsals would take place on Friday evening and Saturday morning. I had often worked on the *shabbos*, excusing each incident as a special case, an exception.

Perhaps it was the spirit of this deeply religious play, though, about a young soul striving towards purity, that roused the thought that I had tried to put aside – that the choice was between the theatre and the *shabbos*.

But since I had already made my decision for the theatre, the best I could do was light the *shabbos* lights in the dressing room, or in a hotel room, which I have managed to do all my life. I made a cartoon image of a young woman, with a picket sign in front of a synagogue, horrifying the pious men with her slogan: "When my work is prayer and praise I will labor seven days."

Hannele's Way to Heaven was first produced at the Workshop in January, 1944, where in the dual role of the Schoolteacher who saves Hannele, and the Christ figure who protects her from her abusive father, Marlon Brando's talent burst upon the world. A famous agent, Maynard Morris, came to see him at the urging of Stella Adler, and found him breathtaking. It was done again at the Sayville Summer Theatre, and was already a part of the Brando myth when we played it in February, 1946, just after Marlon had entered the world of Broadway and Hollywood.

Hauptmann's great masterpiece, *The Weavers*, a compassionate dramatization of the Silesian weavers' revolt of 1844, was staged by Piscator in Berlin in 1927. Hauptmann was a profound social thinker, as well as a dramatist capable of exquisite spiritual writing.

The Aristocrats

The Aristocrats by Nicolai Pogodin is a gigantic play about the building of the White Sea Canal, using prison labor. A Soviet document of the "Five Year Plan" and its labor expediency, it dramatizes the struggle of the Soviet Union to fulfill a technologically difficult project by sheer will, guts, and the abusive use of forced labor.

I played an underage prisoner and had some delightful comedy scenes with Anna Berger, who played a more experienced prisoner trying to break me in. Sixty years later, we still enjoy re-enacting the scene in which she teaches me how to spit and how to knife a man. Piscator didn't want the play to be realistically coarse, and I wondered at his hesitation in showing the crude desperation of the prisoners' lives. Chouteau Dyer, who was responsible for much of the direction of *The Aristocrats*, composed a little ditty for us female prisoners to sing as we marched to work with our shovels:

> See the bitches who dig ditches
> In the grass,
> We are stuck in muddy water
> To our . . . knees!

But Piscator thought it too offensive, and much to our regret insisted on cutting it.

And once again, alas, Piscator showed greater interest in my writing than in my performance. He asked me to write a cantata for the chorus, that would set the play in its Epic context. I wrote an oratorial cantata beginning:

> There was a merchant named Bakin,
> And he lived in 1789,
> And the merchant Bakin
> Went to the Tsar and said:
> "There is gold and copper and oil
> Deep in Karelia,
> Bring it to The White Sea,
> For the good of Russia,
> And for my trade . . ."

And it went on to trace the history of the White Sea Canal, which was of course not built under the Tsar, but by the Soviet Union. The play takes no notice of the oppression of the prisoners, nor did Piscator emphasize it, nor did my cantata acknowledge it. Rather, the production showed the triumph of the communist work ethic, and recalcitrant prisoners were shown to be uncooperative louts, who were soon won over to a better attitude.

The set was an exemplary Epic construction. It was played on a wooden turntable, built over the stage of The President Theater. The turntable was not mechanized, but was pulled by hand, by the actors, heaving together on two ropes attached to pulleys. We used to complain that it was harder than building the White Sea Canal.

In Maria Piscator's *The Piscator Experiment* she writes of the *Aristocrats* set:

The stage was open and bare. Atop the turntable were four screens attached to steel pipes and mounted on dollies, guided by four actors into various positions and formations. Changing images were projected onto these screens, as yet another form of narration. The turntable allowed the stage and the screens to move independently. They formed walled rooms or rows of trees. While one screen showed a slide of the prison barracks, another showed a map of the territory; a third projected statistics relative to the progress of the canal, and the fourth a picture of the workers and their slogans.

Piscator's "Technique as an artistic necessity" did not always require huge budgets. In the final scene of triumph, when the canal was finished, the actors marched forward, the screens became great banners leading them, and they sang the final verse of my cantata, in the Soviet heroic style:

This is a play about people,
People who worked,
People who prepared for a victory,
People who prepared for peace
– after war –
People united.
It is a story dedicated
To the unity of people,
And the unity
Of all people!

The Aristocrats was first produced on April 10th and 26th, 1946, at The President Theatre. It was reviewed in the *New Yorker Staats-Zeitung* by Julius Bab on May 2nd, memorable to me because it was the first mention of my name in a newspaper review. It was performed again on the 5th of May, and on the 19th and 20th of December. Then in January 1947, when I had officially graduated from the Workshop, and when Julian Beck and I had already begun to make plans for The Living Theatre, it was re-opened at The Rooftop Theatre, requiring several rehearsals to adapt it to the much larger space. We performed it again from January 15th to the 19th, and from the 22nd to the 27th, and in February on the 1st, 2nd, 8th and 9th, as well as the 15th and the 16th, which is the last date I recorded for this long-running play.

Agamemnon

Howard Friedman, philosopher, and my special friend among the students, directed The March of Drama's *Agamemnon*. He cast the powerful black actor Marcus St. John as The King, and I played Cassandra, in a costume that my mother pieced together from some old curtain material. In keeping with Friedman's scholarly approach, Cassandra spoke her first lines in Greek:

> Apollo, Apollo my guide,
> Where hast thou led me,
> And to what house?

As was his custom, Piscator came to speak to the cast about the play, so that our motivation should be clear to us. He said:

> The kings are related to the gods, and cannot be gainsaid. If we defy one god, we can only do so with the help of another god – for the Greek gods were engaged in a rivalry more severe and unyielding than any mortal strife. And we can side with one against the other and gain valuable alliances. The Trojan War is a story of such alliances. These strategies and stratagems continue today without the sanction of gods or demons, the terrestrial rich and powerful taking the place of the heavenly forces, still ruling us and our passions without surcease.

Friedman, a true visionary, was convinced that only Brancusi's *Bird in Space*, that magnificent work of pure form suggesting motion even in its stillness (which redeems the concept of minimalism from much of the foolishness committed in its name) could convey Piscator's analyses of Aeschylus' masterpiece. He commissioned a sculptor to make a wooden life-size copy and painted it gold . . . It stood downstage center, dominating the stage as an image of divine and mortal strife. In the vertical image of flight and the poetical image of the bird, it implied the transcendence of that strife.

Agamemnon was performed only once, for The March of Drama on May 31, 1946.

The Circle of Chalk

Klabund's version of the Chinese classic *The Circle of Chalk* was first directed by Max Reinhardt, with Elizabeth Bergner as Hi Tang, at the Deutsches Theater, in Berlin in September, 1925.

In 1931 a "counter-play" to Klabund's, called *Tai Yang Awakens*, by Frederich Wolf, was directed by Piscator at the Wallner Theater in Berlin. Wolf countered with a story about Chinese labor conditions in which the heroine organizes a strike among the workers in a spinning mill. Wolf was a lifelong friend and colleague of Piscator, and a leading protagonist in the long struggle to bring Piscator back to post-war Germany, against resistances from both Piscator and the orthodox German communists.

Tai Yang was designed by Piscator's collaborator, John Heartfield, who filled the stage with banners emblazoned with political and statistical inscriptions which also served as screens for projections, a Piscatorean technique foreshadowing the set for *The Aristocrats* at The Dramatic Workshop.

In London, *The Circle of Chalk*, with Anna May Wong in the lead, was produced at the New Theater, with Laurence Olivier as Prince Pao, directed by Basil Dean.

On March 24, 1941, Piscator opened Klabund's *Circle of Chalk* at The Studio Theatre, directed by James Light, with Dolly Haas in the leading role, and it was thereafter kept in the repertory of The Dramatic Workshop. It was the second production at The Studio Theatre, following *King Lear*.

By the time I entered the play James Light was not present. Chouteau Dyer did the stagings, and Piscator oversaw everything. Priscilla Draghi played Hi Tang.

The play tells a story of murder, and of the parentage of an infant, resolved as in the Solomon story. It is about a brave individual who searches for life solutions in a world wracked by economic injustice and inequities.

At first I was put in charge of the prop table, full of fans and lanterns and all manner of *chinoiserie*. That was in May 1945, and I was still new at the school, and thrilled to be backstage.

Later, in December 1946, I played one of three Teahouse Girls. In this production, the commentary on the class structure was vivid. We sang together in light Asiatic tones:

> To the men Tong's courtyard thronging
> I'm a toy that can be bought,

To their lust, and to their longing,
Yielding all except my thought.

It's interesting how we tend to remember the songs, long after the story has faded.

Klabund was the pseudonym of Alfred Henschke, a college classmate and, like Frederick Wolf, a close personal friend of Piscator. Klabund was a poet and a pacifist, married to the famous actress Carola Neher.

In 1944 Brecht wrote *The Caucasian Chalk Circle*; an adaptation of the Klabund play. Written while Brecht was living in America, he intended it for Broadway, but could find no producer there. It was first produced at Carleton College in Northfield, Minnesota in 1948, in Eric Bentley's translation. Bentley directed it for the Hedgerow Theatre in Philadelphia, after which it became for a time Brecht's most popular play in the USA.

The Flies by Jean-Paul-Sartre

Piscator's production of *The Flies* is an extraordinary example of the taking of a classical myth, and shaping it to shed light on contemporary politics and philosophy.

There's a popular saying, "We never tire of the *Oresteia*." Which is to say that the ancient plays still yield endless interpretations, profound and frivolous, progressive and reactionary, political and philosophical. Sartre used the figure of Orestes, and the Furies that pursued him, to show us the existential possibility of our liberating ourselves from the burdens of our guilts and our past crimes. In freeing himself from his Furies, Orestes frees his people from tyranny.

I played the Chorus Leader (Korephon) of *The Flies* (I like to boast that I played the title role).

We wore black bodysuits and our faces were masked with black netting. We buzzed and danced about the sleeping Orestes and Electra, chanting, "We shall settle on your rotten hearts! Like flies on butter . . ." When Orestes rejects us in the end, we leaped across the orchestra pit into the house and vanished up the aisles.

Every few performances one of us didn't quite make the leap, and landed in the pit with an injured ankle. Consequently, the number of Furies kept diminishing. Orestes' triumph over his guilt was a risky business for us.

Piscator asked me to write a cantata relating the classical story to the circumstances of occupied France, where the author had been a prisoner-of-war, before he escaped and joined the resistance movement. He intended the play to reflect that experience. I wrote the cantata but in the end, Piscator had a better idea. As a prologue, he projected documentary footage of the Nazis marching down the Champs Élysées and under the Arc de Triomphe.

The Flies was first produced by Charles Dullin in 1943, in the Théâtre de la Cité, in occupied Paris. Maria Piscator believed that it was only because of the Germans' desire to assert their cultural superiority that they did not stop it. She writes in *The Piscator Experiment*: "*The Flies* was more than an existential credo, it was a pledge to the resistance."

However, the use of the film in Piscator's production caused controversy. During the dress rehearsal, several people, John Gassner among them, objected that the prologue's impact weakened the classical structure. News of the controversy reached Sartre and he sent Simone de Beauvoir as his emissary to New York.

Piscator suggested that they present two versions at the previews, with and without the film. It was evident that the audience was more enthusiastic when the play was preceded by the film.

And Simone de Beauvoir, too, approved it, calling the production "one of the few theatrical experiences that lift the theatre beyond its self-satisfied mindlessness, and gives the audience an active role again." De Beauvoir came backstage to praise our work, and then posed with us for photos under the *papier-mâché* statue of Zeus, with Piscator and Maria Ley, and with Maia Abiliea, Dan Matthews, who played Orestes, Carol Gustafson as Electra, Jack Burkhardt as Zeus, Walter Matthau as a humble soldier and Frances Adler, of the famous theatrical family, as Clytemnestra.

Waiting for the camera, I heard de Beauvoir say to Piscator, "This play does not take place in the past, but in our future – it is the moral crisis of our future . . ." And Piscator politely contradicted her, "No, it is the moral crisis of the present that we are playing here."

In the program it reads, "Directed by Paul Ransom under the supervision of Erwin Piscator." I quote Maria Piscator's *The Piscator Experiment*: "Supervision was Piscator's way of saying, 'We work collectively, as a group, together, as a unit and as one person. Theatre is a collective – the most challenging, and also the most ambivalent, since in the final analysis, one will has to prevail.'" As I recall the rehearsals, Piscator was a mighty supervisor. Paul Ransom conducted the daily rehearsals, but Piscator's will prevailed.

The Flies opened on April 17, 1947. It played its last performance on December 21. It was my last play at the Workshop with the exception of one performance of *The Spook Sonata*, directed by Howard Friedman for The March of Drama.

During this period, Piscator was deciding whether to return to Germany. And in Germany decisions were being made about inviting him to the various theatres where he might take over the directorship, as part of the rehabilitation of German culture. The comrades who were reconstructing the theatre life of the Russian Sector, which was later to become East Germany, were not favorably inclined toward Sartre and existentialism. Existentialism, like surrealism, focused on the individual rather than the collective. They were even critical of Wilder's *Our Town*, because the dead speak at the end and this violated their sense of realism. Brecht's *Antigone* came under fire for exalting the choice of a single person. And Sartre's Orestes makes his existential choice a personal choice, betraying a dangerous individualism, even though it liberates the people.

The criticisms of Piscator's production of *The Flies* made it difficult for him when he returned to Germany. Many did not trust his political position, just as they didn't in the United States. In America he was distrusted as a potential communist, in Germany there were suspicions that he was not communist enough.

This was the reason that, after Piscator returned to Germany in 1951, he had to work in provincial theatres, waiting 11 years before being given his own theatre in Berlin.

Tonight We Improvise – Pirandello: Breaking into the Audience

It was Luigi Pirandello who was able to bring the basic theatrical questions into the theatre without thereby losing the poetry. And it was in Piscator's production of *Tonight We Improvise* that Julian Beck and I first confronted the question of who the actor is in relation to the spectator.

Tonight We Improvise was Piscator's great Pirandellian production in which he could experiment with the major theatrical concepts that concerned him, and that later became central also to the work of The Living Theatre.

In *Tonight We Improvise*, the fiction and the reality of the theatre collide with the reality of the actors' and the spectators' here-and-now. Often we don't know which reality to believe in, or rather, we don't know how to reconcile the duality of the actor's real presence with the fictional personage.

At the Workshop I played the role of an absinthe-drunken customer in the cabaret where the protagonist Samponetta encounters his soulful Chanteuse. The Chanteuse was played by our classmate Elaine Stritch, the niece of the cardinal, who was later to gain fame on the Broadway stage. In *Tonight We Improvise* she sang a song that Piscator asked me to write for the occasion:

> I sold my soul for love and now I've lost it,
> I burned my only bridge before I crossed it,
> I had a soul and down to hell I tossed it,
> Now there's no world to win anymore,
> But I don't want to sin anymore.

Tonight We Improvise is, as its title suggests, a play about the theatre. The actors play out a family drama, but they always remain actors, and the director maneuvers them, even though the director is also played by an actor. In the end the realities fuse, and the leading actress, abused and dying, delivers Pirandello's great monologue on what the theatre really is. The role was written for Pirandello's beloved Marta Abba, a formidable actress who allowed no other actress to play the role in her lifetime, even after she was much too old to play it. Since she lived to be 88, she thereby relegated the play to the libraries, or to such school performances as the Workshop's.

At the end of the second act the family attends the theatre. It is part of their mother's scandalous Neapolitan behavior, regarded as improper by the Sicilians. The mother, her daughters and their boyfriends, Italian air force men, enter the back of the actual house and cause a disturbance. It is one of the mixed realities so important to Piscator, and one of the reasons why The Living Theatre later chose to produce this play twice in its history.

The Living Theatre's *Tonight We Improvise* changed the Director's name from Pirandello's Hinkfuss to Beckfuss, not only to include the directorial concepts of Julian Beck's theatre, but also to maintain the Germanic roots which Pirandello must have intended by giving him such a name. Most critics suggest it is a reference to Reinhardt.

The Living Theatre's first production of *Tonight We Improvise* was at The Loft Theatre on Broadway and 100th Street, in 1955. There I played

Mommina, the role that Marta Abba coveted and that was played by Priscilla Draghi at the Workshop. In our first *Improvise* production the performance that the family went to see consisted of a film which Julian made with an 8mm camera, including some animations of abstract drawings and some images of the Madonna. He called it "Sicily, Land of Passion." In 1960, at The Living Theatre's 14th Street home, the family visited the opera instead, with Jerry Raphael, as Pagliacci, lip-synching to a scratchy record.

In 1955, The Living Theatre was already searching for a more profound role for the spectators than either Piscator or Pirandello had allowed them. When we entered the theatre from the back of the house, Mommina, the most flirtatious of the sisters, sat on a spectator's lap. Her jealous boyfriend demanded that she get up, but she asked for the spectator's protection. The spectator then had to make a choice of what kind of a scene to play, and decide how afraid he was that he might really be menaced.

Faced with the spectator's response, neither Pirandello nor Piscator was willing to confront the challenge of the audience's improvisation and potential irresponsibility. To deal with this required the whole ensemble to be committed to the experiment, and greater confidence in the audience than Piscator could muster. The Living Theatre, on the other hand, was committed to just that experiment.

Kandinsky's Great Insight

In 1888, at the first Impressionist exhibition in Moscow, when Kandinsky stood in front of Monet's painting of a haystack, he had one of the great realizations – perhaps the seminal revelation of modern art.

Kandinsky saw that the paint was more pertinent to the art than the subject matter. And art was never the same again.

In the same way, Piscator, when he formulated the principles that he called Objective Acting, realized that the presence of the audience is more pertinent to the actor than the fiction of the drama.

The paint Kandinsky saw was real; the haystack was a construct of the mind, conveyed to the observer by Monet through the medium of the real paint.

The presence of the audience is real; the dramatic fiction is a construct conveyed to the spectator by the author, the actors and the director.

In *Actors on Acting*, Piscator says of the Objective Actor, "He acts with the knowledge that life is more important than the play, but that at the same time, it is understood that at that particular moment, there is no more dignified example of life than this particular play. It is the finiteness of the theatre versus the infiniteness of life."

Piscator and the Audience

Piscator did not teach a particular acting technique. It was important to him that the teachers in his school introduced us to many different disciplines. Piscator taught a young actor to be aware of, and attentive to, the audience. He asked the actor to place the center of his attention not on the center of the stage, but in the center of the spectators. He urged the actor to look the audience straight in the eye, and not to let his eye "glide over the heads of the audience as if they weren't there at all."

Piscator wrote:

> I am a little ashamed of such behavior because it seems humiliating for the actor. He loses contact with the audience and places himself in a false and unfair position. See how the situation changes when his eye meets the audience. The whole stage seems to come alive. Through the directness of that glance a truth establishes itself between the actor and the audience and brings back a vital contact, and a greater reality to the action.

Objective Acting is not performance technique, it's an aesthetic political position.

Among the acting teachers in The Dramatic Workshop were leading proponents of the work of Stanislavsky, Meyerhold, Vakhtangov and the *Commedia*. These included Stella Adler, who taught there before my time, Herbert Berghof, who remained as a guest actor after he founded his own studio, and Lee Strasberg, with whom I took two classes before I decided that his Method wasn't my way – in spite of the formidable contribution he later made with The Actor's Studio.

What mattered to Piscator was intensity without emotion in the communication. If this was authentic, it would induce the actor to find the means to make the communication complete. But Piscator stopped at the glance, at the contact of the eyes. Why? Can't the actor speak directly to the spectator? And above all, why can't the spectator talk back, express herself, argue, shout . . . perform?

Because Piscator, whose whole epicenter was the audience, also feared the audience. As he wrote in *Actors on Acting*:

> If we want an intelligent audience, for whom the theatre is more than entertainment, we must tear down the fourth wall from the stage.
>
> (Cole and Chinnoy 1949)

In 1929 he had already written:

> The lifting of every barrier between stage and spectator, the drawing-in of every single spectator into the action, forges the public into a whole mass, for whom collectivity does not remain a learned concept, but an experience of theatre.

The stage was a closed space. We actors were locked into the safety of the innocuousness of its proscenium, its curtains, its enclosing lights and outer darkness, as part of that imprisonment which kept us safe but distant from the pangs and perils of life.

Piscator's theatre forced open the door of that space, and in that breach, which cost us our secure tradition, was a liberation that changed theatre forever. The actor can no longer pretend to be someone else; her presence is non-fictional because we stand in the light of reality. Now acting can no longer be pretending. Though we can show the spectator the character of Hedda Gabler or Julius Caesar, we can do so only in the sense of a Piscatorean narrator who confronts one reality with another, and shows us how and why it is the same and how it is different.

That is, I am not Antigone, but I give you my understanding of what Antigone felt, of what Antigone knew, of how Antigone moved, and finally, of what she did when she defied authority.

In 1927, Piscator said, "The masses have recognized the importance of our theatre. They know it is part of the battlefield where the battle of their fate is being fought."

There were two periods of great disappointment regarding the audience in Piscator's career. The first, which he described in 1929, was his disappointment that the proletariat, the working-class audience, did not come to his Berlin theatre, even though be offered seats at low prices. He lamented:

Unfortunately, the workers themselves withdrew their support, and in spite of intensive promotion in all the unions and workers' organizations, the theatre remained empty. As far as it is in my power, the theatre will again become an instrument of struggle. But my will alone is not enough in the long run. The workers must finally recognize that the Piscator stage is something for which they must fight. The more seats in the theatre that are occupied by workers, the better the Piscator stage can express its struggle. A revolutionary theatre without a revolutionary public is nonsense. It's up to you whether the curtain must fall in the bitter acknowledgment that though the time is ripe for revolutionary theatre, the proletariat is not.

What a tragic passage!

The second and even more tragic disappointment was his realization that the German people were willing to allow Hitler and Nazism to come to power.

He considered these two failures the justification for his conviction that a narrator is necessary in the theatre because the audience needs an "explainer." He felt that the audience could not be trusted to "make their own decisions" on the basis of the information presented.

This loss of trust in the audience, which Piscator would have been the first to acknowledge, is tantamount to a loss of trust in the people, and was costly for Piscator's faith in his own work. Thus the fascist period was historically a failure for everyone.

And yet if we are discouraged, it is a victory for fascism, and ultimately we will not let that happen. Piscator did not entirely despair of the spectators, though he felt he must give them more guidance.

Objective Acting

Epic Theatre, in Piscator's view, requires "a new actor." Neither the declamatory style of the classical actor, nor what Piscator called "the Chekhovian actor hypnotizing himself behind the fourth wall" could serve the purpose of Epic political art.

Brecht's contention that the way out of the cul-de-sac of Stanislavsky's system was alienation, seemed to Piscator a romantic concept, which he believed "was formulated on the basis of oriental classical theatre" – though he agreed with Brecht that "the action should be set before us, rather than involving us by means of empathy."

Piscator said:

> I want to get hold of the complete human being. I will only separate
> intelligence and emotion in order to unite them again on a higher level.
> To do this the modern actor needs superior control, so that he will not
> be overcome by his emotions. He needs what I have called "The New
> Objectivity."

"The New Objectivity" was a phrase that inspired artists at the time of the
Bavarian Soviet Republic, proclaimed in Munich in April 1919, when the political freedom of an experiment in anarchistic social organization coincided
with the work of the artists in search of new forms.

At that time, the artists actually took over the government, meaning to
use the experimental boldness of artistic creativity in the political arena. But
the effort ended in a bloody massacre, and among its visionary leaders, the
poet Erich Mühsam and the playwright Ernst Toller were arrested, while
the philosopher Gustav Landauer was stomped to death by right-wing storm
troopers called the *Freikorps*. During his imprisonment, Toller wrote the
political drama *The Transformation*, which was performed in Piscator's theatre, Die Tribune, in September 1919. The concept of "The New Objectivity"
lay dormant for several decades.

I never heard the phrase "Objective Acting" at the Workshop. I heard it
later from Maria Ley, and read Piscator's description of it in his article in
Actors on Acting.

Too much mystery has been made of Piscator's theory of Objective
Acting. Objective Acting means performance which does not ignore the audience behind a fourth wall, but takes its presence as a primary motivation.

Objective Acting means theatre inspired by the spectator, transformed
by the spectator, and responsible to the spectator. In this it differs from
Stanislavsky's concept, in which the actor relates first to the fictional character and to her personal engagement with the fiction.

In Thea Kirfel-Lenk's valuable study *Erwin Piscator im Exil in den USA*,
she discusses Piscator's essay on Objective Acting, saying:

> Piscator made it emphatically clear that one of the two polarities in
> the theatre is the spectator, who has the same stake in the matter
> that's being dealt with on the stage as the performers. For the per-
> former the center of his attention must lie in the spectator's space
> (*Zuschauerraum*) and not, as Stanislavsky taught, on the stage.

He must draw the spectator into the process of the action (*Spielprozess*); he must enable him practically to look over the shoulder of the actor, activating all his senses, in order to participate together with the actor in the unfolding of the life process.

Naturally, the prerequisite for this is to get rid of the "as-if" stance that is rooted in naturalism and is still at home on the American stage, where it forces dissembling, because it denies the presence of the spectators.

Piscator saw the performer, above all, as the trainer of the spectator, teaching him to be an intelligent partner, from whom he wants to learn something about the "wonders of the world."

This contact effects the capacity for recognition and decision-making in the spectator as well as the performer. They must be partners, the one is incapable of objectivity without the other; only together can they create a verisimilitudinous picture of reality.

(Kirfel-Lenk 1984)

Mel Gordon, in his course at New York University on "The History of Performance," told his students that Objective Acting is a myth, and that he would reward with an "A" any student who could find a satisfactory definition of it. One of his students, my daughter Isha Manna Beck, interviewed Maria Piscator on the subject. She reported: "There is in Madame Piscator's archive a metal cabinet containing several hundred file cards (Madame Piscator says there are 300) on which are typed acting exercises which she says she is willing to open to research. How many of these exercises were actually created by Erwin Piscator, or whether some or all of them were derived from his theories after his lifetime, or after his departure for Europe, when Madame organized The Piscator Institute, is not yet known."

Maria Piscator died in 1999, at the age of 101, and her extensive archives have since been deposited in various institutions. In her later years she was much concerned with Piscator's papers. Most of them were already placed, in her lifetime, at the Akademie der Künste in Berlin, and at the Morris Library at the Southern Illinois University at Carbondale, but for years her dining table was covered with photographs and manuscripts which she and her assistants and interns were endlessly putting into order. I remember well the filing cabinet containing the 300 cards of which she spoke to Isha Manna, though she never spoke to me of its contents, knowing that I would have immediately asked to see them. This was at the time that I was teaching a course on Piscator together with her at The New School.

My sense is that Maria Ley-Piscator was deliberately obfuscating the content of Piscator's theory of Objective Acting, perhaps because she herself did not grasp its intentions, or perhaps because she did understand the political significance of Objective Theatre and, as always, meant to protect Piscator from a dangerous expression of his political ideals.

Theatre, like poetry, exists primarily as a form of communication. Thousands of people experience pure poetry, walking in the woods while chanting great lyrics, madrigals and epics, but if it is not communicated it bears fruit only for the poet.

But the artist, having put her soul into words, commits these words to paper, or speaks or sings them into some listener's ear, and moves not only herself but another . . . It is this other who is the object of Objective Acting.

The "other" of Objective Acting becomes the center of the actor's attention, and thereby creates a social, that is, a political field. Objective Acting is political theatre. The political significance of Objective Acting lies in the roles that the participants take in the social structure of the theatre. The Objective Actor is no longer merely the paid employee of the audience, but a partner in an exploration in which both of them are taking part. The interactive audience member is no longer a passive observer of the action, but a driving force that guides the direction of the drama and energizes the actors. In this way, the play becomes an example for our lives, reaching toward that utopia in which the old structures of domination and submission – as we live them in the midst of the class struggle – are replaced by a new, more fruitful relationship that unifies the persons present.

Objective Acting is not a technique. It is not a way of teaching and not a method. It is the recognition on the part of the actor of all the people present, and an obligation to express to them her personally held belief, her own truth. When this level of recognition is matched by the other actors, as well as the director and everybody else involved in the production, then Epic Theatre becomes possible.

Between Two Worlds

One afternoon, a few days after the end of the war in Europe, Piscator called five of us into his office; some of us were his favorite students, and some were German-speakers. I don't remember everyone who was there, but I do remember Gene Van Grona, and Chouteau Dyer. Piscator began with a discourse about the end of the war, explaining that he wanted us to feel our responsibility to being present at this moment of history, at the beginning of a new chapter in the story of the world.

Now that the war was over, he told us, he would soon be invited to return to Berlin to take up his post at the Freie Volksbühne, and he was asking the five of us to accompany him as his staff! We were awe-struck at the thought of working with Piscator in the newly liberated city; of transforming the capital of Nazism into our brave, new world.

There were, he said, still many questions to be resolved. I believed he was speaking of returning to the Eastern sector, to which he had the strongest ties. The dividing wall would not be built for more than a decade, and he awaited a call from somewhere in Berlin (East? West?) but it never came.

We prepared ourselves for a great adventure. We waited. Weeks passed. Piscator's face grew sadder. He never spoke to us about it. Or at least, not to me. As months passed, his expression changed from one of hope to one of despair. Years passed, and still the invitation did not come. Meanwhile, I graduated from the Workshop in January 1947, and began creating The Living Theatre with Julian Beck, leaving all thoughts of going to Germany with Piscator behind me.

What I did not realize was that Piscator was following the news with a growing inner conflict, that he was living between two worlds; the fleshpots of New York and the smoldering ruins of Berlin.

He had, in fact, been invited to Berlin, but not on the terms that he sought. On June 4, 1946, the playwright Friederich Wolf wrote to Piscator, offering him a chance to direct a film in Berlin: "We are starting our own Defa-Film Company. Wouldn't you enjoy seeing your old desolated, but nonetheless vital and indestructible Berlin once again? I have written a treatment for a film which deals with the last days of Hitler-Berlin and the first days of our new Berlin, that is, May 1st to July 1945. All we need is a director. Piscator?"

Piscator hesitated to respond to this offer for many reasons, one of them being that he was unlikely to get a re-entry visa if he left the United States, and another, his uncertainty about the political situation in post-war Germany.

Hermann Haarmann, in *Erwin Piscator und die Schicksale der Berliner Dramaturgie* (Haarmann 1991), gives us Günther Weisenborn's description of the new beginnings of theatre in Berlin in 1945. In the ruins of the Eden Hotel, where the dust and smoke of the last days of Nazism were still lingering, and where the window glass was replaced by cardboard, they served a kind of cocktail that was called the Hotdrink, made of warm water and some chemicals. Here, amid the ruins, the director Karl-Heinz Martin called together such anti-fascist theatre people as survived in Berlin, and they appointed themselves "The Board of Theatre Workers" and began the reorganization of the German theatre, and German culture.

They included Boleslav Barlog, who became the director of the Schlosstheater; Fred Winsten, who became the director of the Theater am Schiffsbauerdamm, staged Sartre's *Flies* there in 1949, and then became the director of the East Berlin Volksbühne in 1950; Wolfgang Langhoff, who took over the Deutsches Theater; and Ernst Legal, who succeeded Jessner as director of the Staatstheater.

They discussed the reconstruction very practically, sitting there with their Hotdrink. A few actors still owned bicycles (a precious commodity) and they rode through the ruins of the city, reporting on all the theatre sites:

"Roof still sound . . . stage floor only partly destroyed . . ."
"Curtains gone . . . seats missing . . . house still usable . . ."

Piscator was not there. He was in New York, squabbling with Brecht over the staging of *The Private Life of the Master Race*, even though the Berliners were counting on him. He had in fact been preparing to return to Germany for a long, long time. In "Theatre for a Post-War Europe," he wrote, "On January 12, 1943, Albert Basserman wrote in my guest book, after we had been discussing this same subject all evening, 'Today we have founded the first Post-War Theatre.' To which Kaiser added, 'Count me in!' and Elsa Basserman, 'Me, too!'"

But when the foundations were laid, Piscator was not there, and years of correspondence ensued in which Piscator hesitated, while Brecht and Wolf and many of his friends urged him to come. Wolf wrote to him:

Could we fish you out of your two theatres and bring you to a ruined Berlin where you would find many things lacking, but at the same time an infinite number of new and genuine tasks? Could you abandon the security of your position over there in favor of our somewhat loose situation here?

On August 14, 1945, the Hegel Theatre in Berlin opened *The Threepenny Opera* under Karl-Heinz Martin's direction, without Brecht's presence. It was bitterly denounced by the comrades, who felt that "*Erst kommt das Fressen, dann kommt die Moral*" ("First comes food, and after that morality") was a sentiment unworthy of the new Germany, and "*Verfolgt dem Unrecht nicht zu sehr*" ("Don't persecute injustice too severely") was "an insult to every anti-fascist and resistance fighter."

On June 4, 1946, Friederich Wolf wrote to Piscator that his play *Professor Mamloch*, the story of the moral struggle of a Jewish professor who opposes armed resistance to National Socialism in the 1930's, had opened in Karl-Heinz Martin's Hegel Theatre, in January 1946, and ran for 50 performances to sold-out houses. It was a play that Piscator had directed in Zurich in 1934.

On April 17, 1947, Piscator opened Sartre's *Flies* at The Dramatic Workshop in New York, which, like Brecht's *Antigone*, was criticized by the German comrades as furthering the "cult of personality," and as constituting a "call to individualism." Actually, Piscator's interest lay in the examination of existentialism and its liberation from guilt, a view that did not find favor with the tendencies of the time.

On October 31, 1947, Brecht, after testifying before The House Un-American Activities Committee, abruptly left the USA for Switzerland, where he created his *Antigone*, which opened on February 15, 1948, in Chur. Not until October 1948 did Brecht return to Berlin, where he opened *Mother Courage* on January 11, 1949. On February 9, 1949, Brecht wrote to Piscator:

> Now I'm three months in Berlin. I've staged Courage, and the results of my observations are as follows: It's very necessary and altogether possible to bring the theatre here back into the swing of things. The public, that is, the public of the working people, is very good. There aren't many actors and almost no directors . . .

Haarmann, quoting this letter, asks, "With such an encouraging invitation, how could he hesitate?"

During the years between the war's end in 1945, and Piscator's return to Germany in 1951, the artistic and fiscal fate of The Dramatic Workshop was continually threatened. Since 1944, when the Workshop was threatened by the unions, and Piscator asked The New School for $20,000, and was refused, the Board had been contemplating closing the Workshop. Finally, the fire-regulations (always the last resort) made a theatre in The

New School impossible, leaving moot the question of "student decorum," and the accusation (or observation) that the Workshop held too many "egocentric anti-social individuals." I take it that this included myself and my friends, who were already beginning to yearn for the more liberated lifestyle and artstyle that the 1960's were to bring us.

Working at The President Theatre and The Rooftop Theatre, the Workshop could not maintain a presence in two theatres after its final separation from The New School. Caught between these troubles and the growing menace of the Congressional witch hunt, Piscator left New York, leaving The Dramatic Workshop in the hands of Maria Piscator.

Piscator's final Dramatic Workshop production in America was *Macbeth*, on February 28, 1951, at The President Theatre. Soon both The President and The Rooftop Theatre had to be given up, and Maria Piscator moved the Workshop to small quarters on two floors of the Capitol Theatre Building, where it survived a few seasons. Julian Beck and I staged Capek's *R.U.R.* there, in difficult circumstances, and in the end we helped Maria Piscator carry out costumes and props when she was finally forced out. "How Piscator would laugh, if he could see us now," she said with a tragic laugh, her arms piled high with satins and tinsel crowns. But we all knew he would not have laughed, because it was the end of The Dramatic Workshop. Throughout the rest of her very long life, Maria Piscator spoke of creating Dramatic Workshop II, and schemed to involve all her friends and former students in this. But sadly, without Piscator's charisma and theatrical genius, it could not be.

Piscator: Success and Failure

Was Piscator's failure really his success? His 12 years in America were a Calvary of struggle and persistence, but also an unacknowledged influence on the entire course of modern theatre.

Piscator succeeded in opening the fourth wall, in legitimizing political content in the theatre, in using all the technological means available to make the stage a dynamic organism and not "a picture." Through the goals of Objective Acting, which makes the audience its object, he opened the door to audience activity that went beyond the traditional limitations of the divided house.

Our theatre is a house divided.
There are two distinct groups present:
Those on the stage and those in the house,
Those who are being paid to be here and those who have paid to be
here,
Those who have prepared, and those who have come to be surprised
by the action.
Those who speak, and those who are expected to remain silent,
Those who are in the light, and those who are in the dark.

This is of course a microcosm of the class system, and of our whole social structure. The class system that we want to do away with.

Piscator's Return to Germany – and to Berlin

Piscator never relinquished his hope that his theatre could enact the visionary ideals with which he set out in the 1920's. Seeing recent theatrical history as a matter of continuity, he wrote to Wolf, "We must begin again where we were forced to leave off, and we must be glad if we can begin there and don't have to go still further backwards . . . We know that we must be more careful and more realistic than we were in the twenties . . ."

In May 1947, César Klein, who had designed Piscator's *Michael Hundertpfund* back in 1926, wrote to him, saying, "The Germany you left has died." Included with the letter was a list of the eight theatres that were operating in Berlin, and then the list of the artistic directors of each of them. By 1947, all these positions were filled. Piscator never got an invitation to run any of them. He had the impression that he had been "purposely overlooked."

Piscator waited too long. He did not seize the opportunity of participating in the reorganization of the Berlin Theatre. Brecht wrote to Berthold Viertel: "By the time Piscator left New York, it was too late for him to be installed as director of one of the theatres. In 1949 there was still flux, but already too much is fixed. Production possibilities have become positions, jobs . . ." Many opportunities were offered to him, but none with the kind of financial security that he demanded, nor in the position that he believed he deserved.

On October 6, 1951, Piscator flew to West Germany. He was 58 years old and had been gone for 20 years. On the plane he made notes describing his despair:

. . . against this flight, this direction, this goal . . . What goal? What shall I do there? Stranger than strange seems this land towards which this plane takes me. My calling? But no one has called me, neither in the East nor in the West.

Yet the archives of the Akademie der Künste in Berlin, and the Morris Library in Carbondale, are full of invitations to direct films and plays, even an offer from Brecht to direct a play at the Berliner Ensemble – but none to take over the Freie Volksbühne.

Willett cites the list Piscator made on the plane, recounting the insecurity of his civic status:

1. Germany: deprived of citizenship
2. France: identity card
3. America: denied citizenship
4. A German once more
5. Israel: no answer
6. Likewise from the East: no answer
7. They recommend: Chile or . . .

Haarmann writes:

> Piscator was in no way greeted with open arms. The political climate, and the growing tension between East and West, was not fertile ground for an artist who, through all the experiences of his exile, remained an advocate of political theatre.

He settled in Dillenberg in his old family home, near his birthplace, and 60 days later, at the Hamburg Schauspielhaus, he opened a play called *Virginia* which was "a resounding failure and became a great liability."

After that failure, he found himself working as a freelance director, dependent on lesser provincial theatres. It was a fate he had always dreaded. For 11 years he directed plays in Marburg, Giessen, Oldenburg, Mannheim, Tübingen . . . And though he wrote to his wife Maria in New York with bitter complaints about this itinerant work, one cannot help but think that Piscator's vivid presence must have diffused a good deal of Epic energy into the provinces.

He appealed to the Berlin Senate's Director of Public Education, writing, "I am forced to do work that contradicts my tradition and my work-methods;

traveling from city to city can never produce an artistically integrated concept, and therefore cannot serve German theatre culture as it could . . . I would think that Berlin could find room . . ." and so on.

Not until 1956 could Piscator even put on a play in Berlin. On May 4th he finally did *War and Peace* at the Schiller Theater, where it was fiercely attacked. Leading critic Friederich Luft said Piscator's effort to put Tolstoy's masterpiece on the stage "was like trying to empty the sea with a small pail."

Despairing, Piscator wrote in his diary in June 1956: "In Russia I received the death-blow; in France – in spite of my name – two years for nothing; in America I couldn't even land. The conditions were impossible, and my personal inability to adapt, 14 years of battle to the death, and Germany, after 1951 – dead. My death will be Danton's death."

But finally, after years of despair, he was given what he needed. Perhaps it was because the socialist Willy Brandt had been elected Mayor of Berlin. Brandt wrote to Piscator on the latter's 70th birthday:

> Be sure that we are all happy to have you back in Berlin, not only because your name represents a piece of the continuity of our liberty-loving Berlin tradition, but because we believe that we here in Berlin have a series of tasks before us, among which is the formulation of an aesthetic for the 20th century. For the time is past that art could be deemed as disinterested amusement. And that these times are over, my dear Erwin Piscator, is decisively your doing.

Perhaps it was through the continuing efforts of Brecht and Wolf and other friends, or perhaps it really was the eventual recognition of Piscator's enormous talent, or possibly it was the fact that the Freie Volksbühne had got through three unsuccessful directors in the preceding four years. But in the spring of 1962, it was announced that Piscator would take over the Freie Volksbühne.

Now everything was new and everything was possible. Willett says, "For the first time in his life he was able to stage plays that met his requirements . . ."

He worked in these optimal conditions for four years, until his death in 1966. He created six plays there, of which three have had a major impact on theatrical history: *The Deputy*, *In the Matter of J. Robert Oppenheimer* and *The Investigation*.

All three of these plays are valuable documents of modern history. They allowed Piscator to use the full scope of his techniques in a big theatre, with excellent actors and enough of a budget to fulfill his vision. They are all plays about persecution. *The Deputy* deals with the Catholic Church's and the Pope's refusal to intervene during the persecution of the Jews in the 1940's. When Rolf Hochhuth brought the script to him, Piscator said, "It is a play like this that makes it worthwhile to work in the theatre." It raised a storm, and has been called "the most controversial play of our time."

In the Matter of J. Robert Oppenheimer by Heinar Kipphardt tells the story of the persecution of a scientist who, while trying to resolve the moral problems of scientific discovery, becomes the victim of a witch-hunt.

The Investigation dramatizes the Auschwitz Tribunals of 1963 to 1965, in Frankfurt. It was Piscator's last success, a vast courtroom drama uncovering the crimes of the concentration camps, with a text that playwright Peter Weiss drew from the records of the war crimes trials of former SS members. Written in the form of an oratorio, or a "scenic cantata," its terrible facts and the gruesome self-justifications of the Nazis were interspersed with intense musical sections by the great Italian composer, Luigi Nono. It was music of an emotional quality that contradicted Piscator's theories of objectivity, as if the enormity of the subject did not allow us the privilege of remaining "cool" while considering the inhuman heat of the death-camps' ovens.

The Living Theatre was on tour with *The Mysteries*, *The Maids*, *The Brig* and *Frankenstein*, at the Akademie der Künste in Berlin, when Piscator's *Investigation* opened. If he did not come to see our plays, he had the excuse that he was working on a major production, but the fact that he *never* came to see a Living Theatre play is a great sorrow to me. Our *Frankenstein* ended its run at the Akademie der Künste on the 17th of October, 1965, and *The Investigation* opened at the Freie Volksbühne on the 19th.

When I attended the play, I never imagined, of course, that it was the last time I was to see Piscator. He greeted me before the play with the same gruff scolding that was his customary way of speaking to students, even those whom he liked. It is a distressing German habit that displays intimacy with a rude kind of gruffness. He scolded me for not mentioning my beginnings at his school in my interviews with the press during our tour. I think I did speak of Piscator because I always speak proudly of Piscator, but couldn't help what the press chose to print. But it's sad for me that even during our last encounter, I was never really able to express the extent of my esteem.

The set for *The Investigation* was a huge courtroom that seemed to enclose the audience. It was wonderful to see Piscator working in a space that could encompass his epic, panoramic vision after years in the limited New School auditorium, and the small President Theatre and the decrepit Rooftop. Here was space. And behind the semi-circle of the interrogated, Piscator's stage designer Hans-Ulrich Schmückle had suspended huge screens, on which the faces of the accused were televised, so that even as they spoke we could examine their expressions in a manner beyond what the theatre usually allows. By using the technique of the cinematic close-up, Piscator permitted the audience to share in the investigation.

Nono's sounds were overwhelming, electronic noises that contained all the cries, screams, groans and shrieks of human suffering. The Living Theatre had worked with Luigi Nono on a piece called *Escalation*, based on a descriptive text by Herman Kahn, in which the acting ensemble, without any musical accompaniment, created, under Nono's conducting hand, a sound piece that escalates from limited aggressive warfare to the last gasps of total nuclear destruction. Nono was a dedicated political artist, a Communist, who unlike Piscator never hid or obscured his commitment or his affiliations. The Living Theatre was also preparing a major dramatic work together with Nono and the writer and former partisan leader Giovanni Pirelli, which never came to be because The Living Theatre's pacifism was at risk of being compromised, not by the principles, but by the tactics of Pirelli's armed liberation fighters.

In *The Investigation*, Piscator, collaborating (as he had always hoped to) with the best progressive artists of his time, succeeded once again in showing history, dressed in the garments of art, as the powerful force of enlightenment.

It is significant that three of the outstanding political dramas of our time, plays that are now produced in many languages on stages all over the world, and are taught in colleges as the best examples of the validity of contemporary political theatre, were brought to the stage by Piscator: *The Deputy*, *In the Matter of J. Robert Oppenheimer* and *The Investigation*.

Eric Bentley

Eric Bentley's *The Playwright as Thinker*, published in 1946, was perhaps the single most influential book in rallying the American theatre towards political commitment and historical responsibility. At The Dramatic Workshop, its publication was considered a major event, and its texts discussed as fundamental theories.

In 2005, when I talked to Eric Bentley about Piscator, he laughed mischievously: "He challenged me to a duel!" Bentley's mischievousness is legendary. At 94, he is spritely and seems almost untouched by the usual debilities of age. Cheerfully, but with the bitter kind of humor that derives from the cynicism of the 40's and 50's, he recounted the story of his first communication with Piscator.

In his book, Bentley had referred to Piscator as a communist, and Piscator had panicked at the threat of being exposed and losing his precarious foothold in the United States. It was through Saul Colin that Bentley received the challenge, and he answered simply, "Swords or pistols?" "Words!" came the answer from Piscator, through Saul Colin, inviting him not to a duel but to a debate.

Saul Colin was one of the many assistants that Piscator attracted. Colin was a man with a history. In his administrative position at the school, he never made much of an impression on me, even though I had heard that he had been Pirandello's secretary. Bentley, always the historian, reminded me that in that capacity he had supported fascism and denounced such leftist playwrights as Odets.

Colin, said Bentley, had aspired to become Einstein's secretary, because he wanted to attach himself to the most historically significant person he could find. He pestered Einstein so annoyingly for the job that, according to Bentley, Einstein lost patience and shouted, "Saul, if you don't shut up, I'll kill you!" So Colin settled for working for Piscator.

I asked Eric to tell me about the debate, and what he believed Piscator's work meant at that time. He said the debate was to take place on the stage of The Rooftop Theatre, on the set where we were performing *The Sheepwell*. Eric remembers seeing our performance of the Lope de Vega play, but sadly, I did not attend the debate. Perhaps I had a rehearsal that night; or perhaps we students were not invited. Again, I asked Bentley what was said, and why Piscator, who admired him, wanted to challenge him. But instead he told me of the antics of Saul Colin at the meeting of these two mischief-makers.

Bentley said, "I agree to the debate, but only on the condition that you get me tickets to Gielgud's *The Importance of Being Earnest*." It was the most popular play of the season, and was entirely sold out. Julian and I had ordered tickets far in advance, and saw it at a matinee on April 24, 1946. (I played a performance of *The Flies* that night.) Colin thereupon called the theatre box office and said he was Mr. Gielgud's secretary, and needed two tickets for Eric Bentley. The ruse worked and Bentley accepted the debate.

Once again, I urged him to speak of Piscator's work and influence. "Piscator," he explained, "lost out to history. Today, Meyerhold and Stanislavsky are more effective, because Russia got there first. It was in Russia that revolutionary theatre started. But of course, they killed Meyerhold, whereas Piscator got away and lived to fight another day. It was because of Germany that Piscator lost the middle part of his creative life." I suppose he was referring to the part of his life that he spent at The Dramatic Workshop.

Bentley continued: "I was surprised at his commitment to Soviet Communism, but he never got beyond the 1930's in his political thinking. In some ways Piscator wanted to be more Stalinist than Stalin. He felt that he was a communist before Stalin was born. Though of course he had no ties to any communist group in the United States."

This was certainly not the Piscator we knew at The Dramatic Workshop. I remember seeing a play of Eugenio Barba's at The Odin Theatre in Holstebro, at the end of which the whole social structure collapsed, and the set and the props all lay in a heap center stage. An actor who played the Writer, who spent most of the play sitting at a typewriter, rose and, observing the debris, noticed a small pamphlet. It seemed to be *The Communist Manifesto*. He looked to the right and to the left, and when he was sure that he was unobserved, quickly hid the little pamphlet under his shirt, and walked away from the destroyed world with the *Manifesto* hidden close to his heart. When I saw the play in Denmark, I thought of Piscator, and how he was in New York, with a hidden agenda under his always well-laundered white shirt.

But Bentley had a different perspective on a time and a territory that he has studied closely. Bentley's wife was the daughter of Hallie Flanagan, whose book *Arena* not only chronicled the courageous work of The Federal Theatre, of which Flanagan was the founder and director, but stands as a milestone in our understanding of the theatre yet to come. Bentley, among his dozen books on political theatre, is also the curator of *Thirty Years of Treason*, a magisterially comprehensive volume of excerpts from the hearings that took place before the House Committee on Un-American Activities. Bentley believed that:

because Piscator could not go beyond the politics of the 1930's, a fellow-traveler was the same for him as a communist, and there are profound moral questions which he did not approach. For instance, the Marxists simply never understood anti-semitism. Even Brecht's play on Hitler makes him out a fool, whereas it was Hitler that pushed Krupp around.

When I first met Piscator he offered me a small job, at $50 a lecture, which I refused. Many years later, it was I who brought Piscator the text of *All the King's Men.*

But Piscator was always forthright; Brecht was not forthright. Brecht promised the Soviets that be would never criticize Stalin, in return for an exit visa to the United States . . . But you see, that was because Brecht felt that he was able to handle the vagaries of the Soviet system – but Piscator, oh, Piscator wanted to be a statue of Schiller.

Piscator's Influence

The difficulty of discussing Piscator's influence on modern theatre is that it is so diffused, so universal, that the dramaturgical theories and dramatic forms are hard to isolate. It could be said that modern political theatre was invented by Brecht and Piscator, and I don't doubt that all modern theatre bears the mark of the experiments of these two pioneers. I would argue, like Piscator, that all theatre, intentionally or not, is political theatre, in that it expresses a social standard and has content about class. It would be interesting, for example, to examine the American soap opera in terms of its persistent and often frightening class-consciousness.

When Brecht wrote, in a testimonial, that Piscator was "possibly the greatest theatre man of all time," it was because he realized how far-reaching Piscator's changes to the conventions were. There is scarcely a play on Broadway or London's West End today that has not in some way borrowed some of Piscator's inventions.

The development of high-tech scenery has of course come a long way since Piscator created *Hoppla, wir leben!* on a four-story scaffolding, and placed Rasputin inside a revolving globe. The multi-level setting of Broadway's *Les Misérables*, or the enormous moving scenery of *Cats*, as well as the actors' penetration of the audience, or the airplane that lands onstage in *Nixon in China*, are only a few examples of recent scenic innovations that can be traced back to Piscator's work, even when conceived by directors and designers who could hardly imagine actors in costume backstage pulling on ropes to make the stage revolve, as we did at The Dramatic Workshop.

Piscator's principal tenets are – and this is certainly what was taught at the Workshop – the dual paths of commitment and Total Theatre. The first is a matter of understanding and interpreting the content, the second the means of communicating this interpretation to the spectator.

The commitment of political theatre has varied with each decade since Piscator's first plays in the 1920's, and certainly since Piscator's work at the Workshop in the 1940's. The 20's and the 40's were post-war periods, when humanity's great hopes for peace called for expression, and visions of creating a better world were percolating. In the 1920's, the arts took up the political cause. The idealistic left furthered the communist cause, but was all too soon crushed by a combination of the Stalinists and the vicious forces of the right. By the 1940's and 50's the arts eschewed politics as unworthy propaganda, and the work of political artists was marginalized.

As I write this in the early 21st century, political art and political theatre have regained their dignity.

The Stadttheater of Germany, and the Maisons de la Culture of France, rarely announce a season without at least one overtly political play on their program, and this is also true of American regional theatres – be it a collective creation, or the work of a new playwright, or an ever-popular Arthur Miller work, or Genet or . . . more rarely nowadays . . . Brecht.

In Latin American countries, there has always been political art and political theatre, even under regimes of heavy repression and censorship, when they often continued to exist underground.

The effort towards collectivity was integral to Piscator, from the time of the first Piscator Collective in 1929. And though that vision was never completely realized, Piscator's work in this direction has inspired a whole generation to experiment with this creative aspect of the work, which has rarely been accomplished.

It is in the use of technology that Piscator's influence is most evident. Much of his technology was intended to "force" the audience to think and make decisions. Like the use of the narrator, it was a means of focusing attention on the social context and instructing an ignorant audience. It was, in my opinion, one of Piscator's weaknesses that he distrusted the audience.

It is astonishing that he believed the role of the Narrator was the essential solution to the problem of the audience's ignorance. Perhaps it is a German didactic idea, this notion that a wise teacher can make everything clear.

In today's theatre, and in today's film and television, the role of the Narrator is ubiquitous around the world. Sometimes the Narrator is one of the characters, sometimes there is a kind of chorus outside the action, and sometimes the disembodied character of the voiceover speaks.

The site-specific concept, and the deeper integration of the participating spectator, the realization of the production without scenery or costume . . . these and many other concepts of which Piscator wrote and spoke were left for the next generation to explore, and we are still exploring them.

On February 19, 1950, Piscator called a meeting of all The Dramatic Workshop alumni at The President Theatre. I wrote in my diary:

> Piscator talks. Some flame . . . revives. Among all the small voices, his clear, strong voice is alive with inner excitement . . .
>
> He speaks of his disappointment that The Dramatic Workshop has not produced a vanguard army of political theatres across America. He speaks derisively of certain alumni who have ignored his political inspiration. Tennessee Williams is cited. Piscator says, "I wish to make of every actor a thinker and of every playwright a fighter."
>
> And his regard and intentions seem to select me, to accuse me, to want to force me into willing action. But I doubt that he meant me particularly, for I doubt that he understands the seriousness of my intentions.
>
> At the end of the lecture we question Piscator about the next step, and he speaks of the need for mass action: "Individual action is not enough for our time." He speaks of Marx and says, "We must do our work, as a personal contribution, and join the party whose politics most nearly express our own as a social contribution."
>
> But that's not what Marx did at all. He formulated anew, as we must formulate anew. The individual action can inspire mass action when nothing else can.

What I did not know when I wrote this diary entry in 1950, was that Piscator was thinking deeply about the decision to return to Germany. Brecht was already in Berlin, and had opened *Mother Courage* there. Brecht and Wolf were urging him to come back to his homeland. He was about to lose The Rooftop Theatre. He was preparing his last New York production, of *Macbeth*. In a year he would leave America, never to return. He was, in effect, delivering his farewell speech to his alumni, urging us to do the work, so that his time spent in the USA would not have been in vain.

Piscator's Influence: The Work of The Living Theatre

There are many theatres through which the influence of Piscator can be traced, as in the work of the great Polish directors Tadeusz Kantor and Jerzy Grotowski, and of the Polish Gardzienice Company, whose work exemplifies the further fields of theatre that are still being explored.

There is Ariane Mnouchkine's reinvention of stage space, as in her use of a double-stage in *Mephisto*, in which the noble *Faust* play is performed on a vast opera stage at one end of the theatre, while at the other end there is the little stage of a satirical political cabaret. The audience, on swiveling seats, turns from one to the other.

And for many years now, she has focused on the dilemma of the displaced, even turning her theatre, the Cartoucherie de Vincennes, into a refuge.

The most impressive example of Total Theatre as Piscator envisioned it that I have seen was Victor Garcia's spectacular production of Genet's *Balcony* in São Paulo, Brazil. Ignoring the architecture of the auditorium, he constructed a spiral of seats from the stage level to the top of the wings, on which the spectators were seated. The revolutionaries were below and broke out through the stage floor. The entire central area was an elevator that rose and sank with the action. In the finale, when the revolution comes, the spiraling structures on which the spectators sit break apart and swing out perilously, while the revolutionaries, naked and gleaming with sweat, climb up the scaffolding, promising and menacing. It left no margin of doubt about the bond between the passionate and the political.

Among the many theatre directors of recent times whose political commitment reflects Piscator's influence, are the Brazilian Augusto Boal, whose Theatre of the Oppressed continues to engage the spectator in enactments of the controversies in the newspaper headlines of the day. Annet Henneman's Hidden Theatre in Italy began with productions by prisoners in the fortress prison of Volterra, and continues its work focusing on the plight of refugees and their quest for justice. And there is John Malpede's spirited LAPD (Los Angeles Poverty Department), a theatre of the homeless in downtown Los Angeles, and his site-specific work on the lives of the miners in Kentucky. In New York there is Fred Newman's brilliant repertory of political plays at The Castillo Theatre in New York, and its All-Stars project, which introduces the young people of the inner city to theatrical expression. And the bold experiment with a classic theme of Richard Schechner's *Dionysus in '69* can hardly be imagined without the pioneering work of Piscator that preceded it.

But because The Living Theatre is the theatre that I know best, the long-term enterprise of more than 50 years in which I have tried, with Julian Beck and Hanon Reznikov and a company of committed artists, to fulfill a version of Piscator's vision, I will set down here some examples of the ways that The Living Theatre has leaned upon, and tried to extend the work and ideas of Piscator.

Julian Beck and I opened our first theatre in our apartment in 1951. We called it "Theatre in The Room." Our first program consisted of four short plays and foreshadowed our later work. We began with Brecht's *He Who Says Yes / He Who Says No*, one of the best of his didactic plays. In the limited space, Beck created a small Piscatorean device. He placed a plank on the carpeted floor, and jutting up from it at an angle was a narrow stick from which a rock was suspended by a rope. When an actor entered the narrow pass, stepping on the plank, the rock swung back and forth, accelerating with each step, and reaching a climax when The Boy who says yes and no (played by that splendid dancer Remy Charlip) leaps from the cliff. In this simple way we were able to make use of Piscator's scenery in motion, without the need of huge stage machinery.

On the same program we performed Paul Goodman's *Childish Jokes*, a meta-comedy about the nature of theatre by the resident philosopher of The Living Theatre. And *The Dialogue of the Mannequin and the Young Man*, from *If Five Years Pass*, by Lorca, one of the best political poet/playwrights of recent times. And *Ladies' Voices* by Gertrude Stein, deconstructing and reconstructing the language.

Later that same year, we opened The Living Theatre at The Cherry Lane Theatre with Gertrude Stein's *Doctor Faustus Lights the Lights*, for which Julian Beck designed a set consisting of rectangles of various sizes and dimensions, covering three sides of the stage. Some were used as entrances and exits by actors, most were designed as light displays.

These onstage lights were controlled by an independent light-board, and were capable of performing what Stein's stage direction calls "A Very Grand Ballet of Lights."

This theme of the search for enlightenment, and its political consequences, was central to Piscator. In his efforts to equate the hero with the masses, he fell back again and again on the heroic individual, from Arkenholtz in *The Spook Sonata* to Orestes in *The Flies*.

The Living Theatre's second production at The Cherry Lane, Kenneth Rexroth's *Beyond the Mountains*, was yet another poet's retelling of the *Oresteia*, reaching back into the mythic, as Piscator did in *The Flies*.

In The Living Theatre's production of *Desire Trapped by the Tail*, by Pablo Picasso, the entire production had the collage quality that Piscator derived from his collaboration with John Heartfeld. Piscator's work in the 20's, when he staged several Dada spectacles, enjoyed the jagged quality that stirred Picasso, who shared the Dada school's daring.

Picasso's politics, long and hotly debated in the world of art and culture, reflect Piscator's thought in "The Cry of the People for Art": "I ought to say, 'From Art to Politics – and back' – oh let me be free from this politics which is first and last guided by chance – from this Art – which never succeeds in expressing the real truth. Yes, from these human beings who want neither politics nor art – without knowing what they ought to want."

Desire Trapped by the Tail shows us a group of surrealist artists trying to survive, and by the spirit of their art transcending their suffering, during the Nazi occupation of Paris.

For T.S. Eliot's *Sweeney Agonistes*, Morton Feldman, spiritual brother of John Cage, created a score that consisted of an amplified metronome that maintained the exact same rhythm throughout the dialogue, a subliminal message about being "stuck in time."

In *Faustina*, Paul Goodman's Roman Empress breaks through the role – in Pirandellian fashion – and like a pioneer Objective Actor, addresses the audience, introducing herself with her own name. She accuses the audience of allowing the horror of human sacrifice to take place, saying: "You should have circled round the stage and stopped the action."

But Julie Bovasso, the superb actress playing the empress, refused to play this final scene. When she objected that she could not identify herself by her own name and then not speak her own words, the playwright suggested that she write her own text for that scene, and that he would, if she wished, help to edit it, so that it would remain consistent with the style of the play. But she could not bring herself to do it. Other actresses were invited to play the role, but they too baulked at the final speech. In the end, Walter Mullen, who was an alumnus of the Workshop, dared to make the speech, in the persona of a surreal cross-dressing shaman who had a small, crucial role in the play. Walter Mullen understood what Piscator taught us about confronting the audience.

It is interesting to note how difficult the transition to Objective Acting is for the actor who has been trained to feel herself protected by the fiction and the safety-glass of the fourth wall. Piscator himself would never have risked such a challenge to the audience. What would he have done if, in fact, the audience *had* come up onto his stage?

Nowadays the theatre has gone far enough in breaking the barriers, that most actors could accept this breach of the fourth wall. And in performances of The Living Theatre's *Antigone*, *Mysteries* and *Seven Meditations on Political Sado-Masochism*, audience members have unexpectedly entered the scene. The Living Theatre ensemble always managed to deal with this on a dramatic level, though it became supremely challenging when the audience, as Goodman had suggested, actually tried to stop the torture scene in *Seven Meditations*.

Alfred Jarrey's *Ubu the King* is a play that Piscator should have done. His Dada-constructivism would have embellished Jarry's anti-authoritarian theme. Perhaps it was too anarchistic for him, though Maria Piscator called it "an explosion – the waves of which are still felt today, which liberated the theatre from realism."

In Auden's *Age of Anxiety*, the poet fulfilled Piscator's imperative that the Narrator is a necessity in modern theatre. Piscator's notion was, unfortunately, based on his disillusionment with the audience's capacity to think for itself, and its consequent need of a teacherly voice to help it to understand. But it is also the expression of the director's desire to make it clear, to make it ever clearer; and of the artist's eternal frustration that it isn't yet clear enough, that the communication is not yet, has never yet been, complete.

I played the Narrator sitting on a high stool, and read the lovely verses that guided the audience through the night adventures of four New Yorkers in a war-anxious world. It seemed appropriate that I was also the director, intersecting the roles of narrator and director.

Strindberg's *Spook Sonata* is a play that has a long history in this story. For its images of the infectiousness of social corruption, and the passing on of guilt from generation to generation, are relevant in every era. Piscator performed the leading role as a youth in 1920, in Königsberg. It was performed in two different productions at The Dramatic Workshop, one of them under my direction, in December of 1945, and once in Howard Friedman's staging in 1948, in which I played The Mummy and The Young Lady. Years later, in 1954, it became one of the milestones of The Living Theatre's repertory, when we produced it at our theatre on 100th Street.

At The Dramatic Workshop, Piscator praised my staging it with three ladders, from which the Spooks oversaw the action. But Julian Beck's cavernous, charred, black set was closer to Piscator's description of his set at Königsberg, where the infested old house, with its cobwebs and spiders, stood for the decadent society.

Piscator never directed a work by Cocteau, though he spoke of him often. The Living Theatre was fascinated by the ways in which Cocteau reused the Greek myths, and our production of *Orpheus* stressed the surreal elements of this approach: the talking horse, the angels of death, the miraculous occurances, the walls layered with images reminiscent of classical sculpture. In Maria Piscator's *Piscator Experiment*, she writes, "Cocteau did not interpret the house of Atreus in *The Infernal Machine*, he invented Greece anew." And we played his *Orpheus* as if he had invented the ancient Gods anew.

Claude Fredericks' *Idiot King* is a pacifist play of pure poetry and high idealism. For all its inventive forms, Piscator would not have approved of its political substance, about a king who will not kill, though his kingdom crumbles, and who has no social solution, except to insist that "where there is love there is only love." But it expressed a certain extremism that The Living Theatre insisted on, and that Piscator had to forgo since he always felt compelled to deal with the polluted waters of political corruption.

When The Living Theatre staged *Tonight We Improvise*, we were following directly in the Master's footsteps. Julian Beck's performance as the director had several of Piscator's characteristics, though Pirandello's Germanic director was based more on Reinhardt than on Piscator. In the intermission scene, during which the director constructs a setting which he calls "The Airport at Night," Julian created a cobweb of silver string, that criss-crossed the stage-space so that it became impossible for anyone to enter it. A glittering network catching the light. This was Pirandello's critique of modernist directors like Reinhardt or Piscator, who create sets that are impossible to play on, as interpreted through Beck's abstract expressionism.

174

With Racine's *Phèdre* we returned to the realm of classical myth, playing the corruption of the passions on a white velveteen stage floor which every human step threatened to pollute.

In *The Young Disciple*, Paul Goodman wrote a radical re-evaluation of the Christ story, a story of the unwillingness of the people to accept change, transcendence and enlightenment. Piscator, at the very end of his life, wanted to return to this theme. When he lay dying, in a clinic at Starnberg, Peter Weiss, the playwright whose *Investigation* Piscator had just staged, visited him and took notes at his bedside. Piscator advised Weiss:

> Drop everything you are doing – I say this with the full consciousness of a great responsibility – and let us give ourselves over to the Christ theme. Approached the right way it can shake up the world in many ways . . . Come here, let us discuss it! The time is ripe and it is urgent.
>
> (Haarmann 1992)

Haarmann continues:

> Concern with the Christ figure leads Piscator to the question of the necessity of cult theatre in the 20th century. A theatre of belief, of direct contact, of direct reaction, a theatre in which he wanted once again to enter the struggle against the repressive forces of his environment. Thus the modern political theatre returns to its origins. The religions promised and promise the unequivocal identity of stage and public. The communal aesthetic action is already political and vice versa. To shed new light on modern political theatre under the searchlight of cult theatre is the ultimate utopian vision, and in it all the world views and life philosophies of Erwin Piscator are finally united. It shows him as that which he always was: an enlightened moralist, in the 18th century sense, and a rationalist politician of the stage of the 20th century.

The Young Disciple, about the beginnings of Christianity, shed such a new light on our political theatre.

William Carlos Williams' *Many Loves* is a play within a play, or rather three plays in the framework of a discussion between a young playwright, his producer and actress, of the meanings and implications of the three one-act plays. These three characters serve as a sophisticated kind of narrator, explaining the action, not from one, but from several points of view.

The Cave at Machpelah was another play by Paul Goodman on a biblical theme, this time going back to Abraham and dealing with the roots of the patriarchal myth which to this day confounds our social structure.

The Connection, by a young playwright, Jack Gelber, was a milestone in The Living Theatre's history. Like *Many Loves*, it was a play within a play. Its subject was drugs and jazz, and the connection between these two levels of human experience. The Playwright and the Producer serve as Narrators, and there is also another dimension: two photographers are filming the junkies in their pad. The actors address the audience directly, as Piscator would have had it.

Working with the text of Alexander Dean's *Directing the Play*, Piscator emphasized the importance of our understanding the significance of stage space. Dean, with Piscator's approval, taught us that different areas of the stage carry various weights; that upstage left is a stronger position than upstage right, and that when a dramatic action takes place in a certain area – say a murder is committed in the first scene, downstage left – that area will bear the trace of its drama in all the following scenes.

In The Living Theatre's *Connection*, the musicians – piano, bass, saxophone and percussion – occupied stage right. They were, as it happened, all black. The white addicts, waiting for their fix, were stage left, and Sam, the one black junkie, lay stretched out on a day-bed upstage center, under a mural of a pyramid that bisected the stage. The balance was not immediately visible, but whenever an actor or musician crossed the stage, the audience felt a shift, as if a scale had found a different equilibrium. And when all the actors moved to one side, as they did when one character overdosed, the effect was vertiginous.

As Piscator had used real disabled people in *The Good Soldier Schweik*, when the war-wounded paraded before God, so we had real addicts among the actors and musicians in *The Connection*. This included some of the great jazzmen of the day. We were able to hire them because, at that time, the law prohibited anyone with a drug-related criminal record to perform in any club where liquor was served – that is, in nearly all the jazz venues.

The *Women of Trachis* is a translation of Sophocles into the extraordinary verse of Ezra Pound. Pound was not only imprisoned for many years as a traitor after the Second World War in St. Elizabeth's Hospital in Washington D.C., but he also remained throughout those years a propagator of violent anti-semitism, later followed by years of ambiguous silence. Could such a man write a play that The Living Theatre could produce? Yes, he could.

176

In *The Marrying Maiden* by Jackson Mac Low, The Living Theatre explored the limits of staging and language in a way that Piscator dreamed of and wrote about, but never ventured to stage, and we broke a few boundaries that even Piscator probably never imagined. Mac Low was a disciple of John Cage, and experimented with random structures. Using the text of the *I Ching*, he derived the script through an intricate system of dice throws. An onstage dice thrower gave the actors action cards, which contained randomly selected stage directions, and, using the dice, he controlled the playing of a score made by Cage out of a cut-up of the actors' voices reading the lines. These random devices demanded a great deal of discipline, as well as great flexibility, from the actors. It was not a form that Piscator was familiar with, except perhaps in his early Dada experiments – but this was without the satirical humor intrinsic to Dadaism. Nor were these theatrical experiments the "stylizations" against which Piscator spoke so vehemently . . . but rather an entirely different theatre form.

When Julian Beck and I visited Helena Weigl at the Berliner Ensemble in 1961, she greeted us with: "Ah-ha, here are the naughty people who are doing *In the Jungle of Cities!*" For when we produced it, it was during the hard-line days of the Party in East Berlin, and the play had already been refuted by the Ensemble as having outlived its validity since Brecht wrote it in 1922, before he had "studied Marxism." For us, its story of the corruption wrought by money was then, as now, an important theme. Piscator, perhaps at great personal cost, had no such limiting standards of what we would now call "political correctness," even though he was at other times too cautious in expressing his political opinions, leaving many of his American students under the impression that he was an apolitical artist.

Working with a Brechtian script gave us the opportunity to note the forms that Brecht learned from Piscator: there are scenes done in shadow-play, and in the original stage directions the playwright even suggested setting the play in a boxing ring to emphasize the combative nature of the story. Like Piscator, we did not heed the playwright's directions.

The Apple was Jack Gelber's second play. It takes place in a small cabaret run by a domineering figure played by James Earl Jones, and is obviously referential to The Living Theatre. Its realistic setting had a double, a journey through the bardos of *The Egyptian Book of the Dead*, the actors wearing elaborate animal masks by Ralph Lee, in search of what Piscator called "the secret behind the mask, where the truth lies."

The Brig was our first attempt at the form of political theatre that Piscator called *Zeittheater*, and sure enough we got busted for it, did jail time and had our theatre closed. Its realism is the realism of military madness. The actors entered into the madness of Artaud's sacrificial suffering which "signals through the flames," fortified by the rational humanism of Piscator. In my essay "Directing the Brig" I wrote, "*The Brig* is a structure . . . The immovable structure is the villain. The men placed inside this structure are intended to become part of this structure, and the beauty and the terror of *The Brig* is seeing how it succeeds and how it fails in incorporating those whom it has imprisoned into its own corporal being . . . Where Artaud cries out for madness, Piscator advocates reason, clarity and communication." (Malina 1965, reprinted in Brown 1965) Piscator said to me once in class: "We have gone back to what we can see, because although we know that other things exist, that which we can see is organizable . . . we will confront the dimensions of the structure, find its keystone, learn on what foundations it stands, and locate its doors. Then we will penetrate its locks and open the doors of all the jails."

Mysteries and Smaller Pieces was an invention that surprised its inventors. Intended as a one-time presentation at The American Center in Paris, It has remained part of The Living Theatre's repertory for over 40 years. A series of eight ritual actions, without explanations, six of them entirely without text, it takes the audience on a theatrical Eleusinian voyage. The first scene uses the words on the one-dollar bill, and another scene, called "Street Songs," uses the chants of the protesters in the streets, with the public first repeating and then inventing phrases relevant to the issues of the day. Both these forms were devised by Jackson Mac Low.

Piscator wrote:

> What I always wanted, is to play without scenery, without costumes, gowns, or props, naked – not physically naked – but naked in the soul. What I truly want is to find the secret behind the mask where the truth lies, the plain literal truth, which is at the bottom of our lives – the real why, the laws. Once we have recognized these laws, we can create accordingly.

> (Ley-Piscator 1967)

Mysteries is played without scenery, without costumes or props. As to "naked," that was still to come, not only for the soul, but physically, too.

The Maids is one of several masterpieces by the genius of the sexual politics of revolution. Genet's work was not yet known when I attended the Workshop, and I never heard Piscator speak of Genet. Not until 1962 did Piscator direct *The Balcony* in Frankfurt.

No one has given us so passionate a picture of the class system and the class struggle as Genet has. Piscator's great dilemma of how to make the social structure graphically clear and unmistakable, without losing the sensual and erotic aspects of human existence, is tragically resolved in *The Balcony* and *The Blacks*. And also in *The Maids*, where the fatal power-struggle between the mistress and her maids leads the maids to destroy one another while giving full allegiance to their real oppressor.

Frankenstein was created on a three-story structure scenically related to Piscator's *Hoppla, wir leben!* and *Rasputin*. It presents, in a graphic exposition, Mary Shelley's story of an artificial man, which she subtitled "The New Prometheus." The action takes place both inside and in front of the rectangular metal structure. Vertical metal tubing and horizontal platforms divide the area into 15 equal compartments. The play begins with a meditation and a promise which is not kept, that the person seated in the center will levitate. It is this deception that leads to a cycle of violence in which, one after another, each of the actors is gruesomely executed. The ensemble then forms a three-story tall figure of The Creature composed of all their bodies, its two red glowing lamp-eyes glaring at the audience.

In the second act we outlined the profile of a man's head in lights, on the metal grid. It was an image that recalls the famous silhouette of Piscator against the three-story structure of *Hoppla, wir leben!* Inside the head the names of the fundamental human attributes, as we defined them during the collective creation, were projected against a backdrop in true Piscatorean style. On the lowest level: Animal Instincts, The Subconscious, The Erotic. Above them: Intuition, Vision, Imagination, The Creative, and Love. And above that: the forehead, containing The Coffin (the awareness of Death), The Ego, Wisdom and Knowledge. The actors each portray one of the attributes, as the Ego passes through each of them and emerges as The Creature of Dr. Frankenstein, who learns speech as he recites Mary Shelley's wonderful monologue which begins, "It is with considerable difficulty that I remember the original era of my being." He then continues to describe first the hopes, and then the despair of humanity, leading to Death. It is the Piscatorean Epic *par excellence*, the story of humankind overwhelmed by its own technology, of the creation that turns against its creator.

Piscator's pioneering work in bringing modern technology into the modern theatre was for him only a method of clarifying the political commitment. He wrote in "Proletarian Theatre: Its Fundamental Principles and Tasks":

> . . . technical innovations were never an end in themselves for me. Any means I have used or am currently in the process of using were designed to elevate the events on the stage onto a historical plane, and not just to enlarge the technical range of the stage machinery. I do not say that new techniques will be the saviour of the theatre. I merely say that they can express new dramatic contents by liberating the creative forces of playwrights, directors and actors.
>
> (Piscator 1920, reprinted in translation in Howard 1972: 42)

With Brecht's *Antigone*, we swept the arena of Piscator's Epic Theatre clean. Not a shred of scenery was left, not a throne, not a sword, not even the board on which Brecht intended Antigone to carry her brother's corpse. Our response to Piscator's "What I always wanted was a play without scenery, without props, without costumes" surprised the audience in *Mysteries and Smaller Pieces*, which was a highly abstract series of rituals. *Antigone*, however, was a revered classic, and the family tree of its versions, Sophocles, Hölderlin, Brecht, were sacred cows. We followed Brecht's bold suggestion that there be only white light, evenly diffused across the stage. The actors wore their everyday clothes, avoiding bright colors.

We divided the space into Thebes and Argos. The stage was Antigone's city of Thebes, the audience was in the enemy city of Argos. At the very beginning we established this hostile relationship. We did it with the glance of which Piscator spoke. Each actor looked out into the audience, which was not in the dark but rather in half-light so that we could see them. When the actor met a responsive gaze she or he held the look for a long time with the subtext, "You are playing the enemy and we will destroy each other." It became the actor's obligation to return to this same spectator at significant points, especially when we went out to them and wept in their faces as we recited the chorus: "There is much that is monstrous, but nothing more monstrous than man."

Brecht added a prologue to the classical play. After the bombing of Berlin, two sisters, prototypes of Ismene and Antigone, discover the dead body of their brother, hanged, and dispute whether or not it's safe to cut him down. With Piscatorean boldness we replaced Brecht's prologue with a sound and movement piece in which we enacted an air attack, during which each of us went into the shelter-position which American school children are taught to adopt in air-raid drills.

Paradise Now! was The Living Theatre's contribution to the events of 1968. Piscator died in 1966, and did not therefore experience the fever and the fervor of that time, and I have personally speculated a great deal on how he would have responded to that wave of utopian optimism. Would he have risen up on the side of revolution as he did in his communist days? Or would he have been too discouraged by an uprising that was not guided by proletarian ideals and a Leninist certainty about the reorganization of society?

Piscator, I fear, would not have liked *Paradise Now!* even though it fulfilled the ambitions of his most ebullient rhetoric. In *Paradise* we tried to break as many of the traditions of the conventional theatre as we could. We rallied the audience to intense action; we stripped down, naked to the legal limits (and often beyond), challenging the audience to do the same; we embraced them, we pulled up the seats out of the auditorium and piled them on the stage, we burned money, and in the end we led them out into the streets, singing . . .

But this seeming disorder was based on a strict matrix, a careful path, to which the audience was given a map, and which made the whole spectacle an example of libertarian order, of which the world is afraid – with a fear that prevents the great social change that The Living Theatre calls The Beautiful Non-Violent Anarchist Revolution.

The program was a poster-size map, showing Ten Rungs, leading upward from The Rite of Guerrilla Theatre, outside the gates of Paradise, to the highest vision of the permanent revolution. Each rung consisted of a Rite, and a Vision and a Political Action in which the audience took part, or even invented. What looked like chaos was in fact a free-flowing movement toward more and more elevated forms. It was the great experiment of which Piscator dreamed, which was not given to him to fulfill, but which never could have taken place without his pioneering groundwork.

In Brazil, where The Living Theatre went in 1970 at the behest of Brazilian artists whose theatre work had been suppressed by the military regime, the company conceived a cycle of plays for the streets and non-theatrical environments called *The Legacy of Cain.*

Six Dreams about Mother was a play for Mother's Day performed in a school gymnasium by the pupils, with the assistance of their mothers and their teachers. The climactic moment when a pupil, held by a teacher, leaps into her comrades' arms, breaking in mid-air the crêpe paper tie that binds her to her mother, is a Piscatorean device. Its anti-authoritarian message so outraged the forces of order that the whole company was arrested. The men in the men's penitentiary managed to create a play for their fellow inmates and the guards and visitors, before the company was expelled from the country, after nearly three months in jail.

Upon returning to New York, The Living Theatre shared with Piscator his sense of homelessness in the United States, of feeling uprooted and alien. The first play we created in *The Legacy of Cain* cycle, after we returned, was *Seven Meditations on Political Sado-Masochism*, a response to our experiences in Brazil.

A series of political observations and analyses is spoken by the actors sitting in a circle at the center of which various oppressive and abusive actions are performed. One of these was a graphic demonstration of a form of torture practiced in the prisons of Brazil. To emphasize its cruelty we played it in slow-motion, a device we learned from Piscator.

Following Piscator's example of support for the worker's unions and their strikes, *The Strike Support Oratorium* was a street-play in support of the United Farm Workers' grapes and lettuce boycott. Using biomechanical actions derived from Meyerhold, a street procession showed the physical oppression of the stoop-labor of the underpaid migrant workers. The actors formed a human barricade in front of stores selling the boycotted goods, as if to stop such commerce with their bodies.

The *Legacy of Cain* cycle included a dozen other works designed for non-theatrical venues, among them *Turning the Earth*, a play in which neighborhood residents and children ritually planted community gardens, so that beans and even corn eventually grew along the streets and in the lots of Pittsburgh, the industrial city we chose for the first full version of *The Legacy of Cain*.

An all-day spectacle called *Six Public Acts*, a play in six acts and a pro-logue, which we subtitled "Changing the City," took place in seven different locations, linked by processions: from The House of Money (a bank), where we burned money, to The House of Violence (a police precinct-house), where we offered bread and roses to the police, urging them to greater gentleness, to The House of The State (a courthouse or state office building), where we first prostrated ourselves and then invited the audience to join us in drawing a drop of blood from our fingers and smearing it on the wall of the State house, dedicating it to those who were sacrificed to the State.

For the House of Property we built a portable, two-story wooden structure we called The Bastille, able to carry 14 actors – it was an altogether Piscatorean construction – from which Proudhon could expound on the meaning of property, while the company enacted his words. In The House of Love and Death we tied one another up in a sado-masochistic ritual, and waited for the audience to untie us. Piscator, alas, would not have trusted the audience with such a role, but in Brazil and Pittsburgh, in Italy, Germany and France, they always set us free.

The Destruction of the Money Tower is a dramatic structure closely related to the Jessner steps, which Piscator considered the ideal depiction of the social structure and the class struggle. The Money Tower is actually a three dimensional, in-the-round version of Jessner's setting. It is based on a drawing made in 1911 and widely distributed by the IWW (Industrial Workers of the World, an anarchist union, affectionately known as The Wobblies, of which The Living Theatre has been a member since 1971). The picture shows a five-tiered structure of platforms, at the bottom of which are the poor and the workers, crushed and desperate, even as they hold up the whole structure. They cry, "We work for all, we feed all." On the level above them are the working class, transforming the raw materials arriving from the bottom. Above them, the leisure class, seen dining in luxury and proclaiming: "We eat for you." Above them stand the soldiers, bayonets drawn, proclaiming, "We shoot at you." Over them the churchmen in clerical garb intone, "We fool you." And at the top, a pair of silver-suited capitalists who cry, "We rule you." Rising over all of this is a four-foot high green neon dollar sign.

Since The Living Theatre's *Tower* was to be performed at the gates of the steel mills of Pittsburgh, we made the lowest level that of the miners, the Third World and the *Lumpenproletariat.* We carefully studied the work of the steel mill, emphasizing in biomechanical language the role of the workers on the second story. Above the middle class busy packaging and marketing, we amalgamated the tiers of the church and the state, while above them were the rich, just below the neon dollar sign that shed its green light over everything.

After enacting a worker's death, the revolutionary spirit inspires a general strike which brings down the money system, and the whole 40 foot structure is dismantled, gracefully and with singing. The workers emerging from the steel mills appreciated our skill in erecting and dismantling the big structure. In Pittsburgh in 1975, out of 2000 workers leaving the mills at the end of their shifts, we managed to get 200 to remain and watch the play and talk with us about what it meant. Today, the Pittsburgh mills have all been shut down.

Returning, after eight years of street theatre, to the precincts of the theatre building, we created *Prometheus at the Winter Palace*, using texts by Aeschylus and Shelley and the events of the Russian revolution to make an Epic play, whose universal values encompassed the classical and the historical, as well as speaking to the plight of the political prisoners of our time.

When the audience entered it found the actors bound to the seats, immobile, until the audience realized that they had to liberate them for the play to begin. Then Hanon Reznikov, naked, as Prometheus, climbed to the apex of the Piscatorean metal scaffolding which spanned the proscenium, and began reciting the words of Aeschylus. At the end of the first act the audience is called upon again by Julian Beck, playing Lenin, to retell the classical story as the story of the Russian revolution. During the ensuing intermission, those whom Beck recruited to play the Red Army, the White Guard, the Tolstoyan pacifists and the anarchists, rehearsed in various parts of the theatre – on stage, in the aisles, backstage and in the lobby – in preparation for the dramatization of the Taking of the Winter Palace, which the audience enacted, using rolled-up Russian newspapers as guns. After their victory, the actors and audience sing *The Internationale*, just as Piscator's actors had famously done in no fewer than five of his early productions.

We drew a parallel between classical myth and modern history, so that Zeus became Lenin and Prometheus became Alexander Berkman, the anarchist who served 14 years in Western Penitentiary (in Pittsburgh). And Io, driven from shore to shore by The Gadfly (played by Tom Walker), Berkman became Emma Goldman, who lived much of her life in permanent exile. Piscator had set the example when he added the characters of Lenin and Trotsky (as well as the ex-emperor of Germany) to the cast of his Rasputin play.

At the end of the play we walked with the audience in a silent procession to the nearest prison, where we held a vigil, looking up at the prison walls, meditating on the end of punishment. Since we performed it mostly in Italy in 1978–79, the prisons were full of political prisoners, resulting from the suppression of the Red Brigades. This gave the scene a special poignancy.

In my diary of January 21, 1948, I wrote that "in Toller's *Masse-Mensch*, the best political play that I know, good and evil are clearly recognizable."

But it was not until 1980 that The Living Theatre staged *Masse-Mensch*, and we did it in Munich, where the events represented took place but where the play had never been performed. In 1921 Piscator had planned a production of *Masse-Mensch*, but the police chief of Berlin refused to re-license his Proletarian Theater and the Volksbühne produced it instead, without Piscator.

It remains the purest Piscatorean text, showing the conflict between the idealists of revolution, and armed struggle. I think Piscator would have approved of our staging. We made a set out of collapsible, folding metal gates that repeatedly became a prison. Mounted on wheels, they could be moved into any position to become walls, or even guns.

The Yellow Methuselah is a work by Hanon Reznikov that interfolded two very different plays, to create an epic of world history and beyond, into the future. George Bernard Shaw's *Back to Methuselah* is the story of humanity's search for immortality, from the Garden of Eden to 20,000 C.E. or "as far as the mind can reach," whereas *The Yellow Sound*, a "stage composition" by Vassily Kandinsky, is a singular concoction of figures, colors, sounds and other abstract elements. Taken together, the two plays transport us to a higher order of awareness. Shaw and Kandinsky both appear onstage as participants in a panel discussion on longevity. Julian Beck as Bernard Shaw went into the audience with a microphone and interviewed audience members about their hopes and fears regarding longevity and immortality. The spectators thought they were only being amplified, but they were also being recorded, and their responses were quickly edited backstage, so that at an appropriate moment later in the play the voices of the audience returned to resolve the debate. It is a technical innovation that Piscator could not have imagined . . . but no . . . he did imagine techniques beyond his time.

The Archeology of Sleep was Julian Beck's last play, a work about the depths of the mind and the abuses of science. It examines the dreamwork. Piscator said:

> But dreams have a reality in art. Part of my dream is to bring the theatre back to its real function as being the best educator in the world. Theatre owes its origin and character not to some exclusive qualities of the Greek spirit, but to the human spirit in general . . . Theatre interests me only when it is a matter of interest to society – when it expresses a meaningful universe . . . But there are times when we find

it necessary to relate experiences to even larger realities – those of the Epic Life.

(Ley-Piscator 1967)

In *The Archeology of Sleep*, an elevated track carried a "train of thought" across the back of the stage, carrying "The Sleep of the City" and many characters that enter into the sleeping minds of the actors, taking them to Piscator's "even larger realities." The audience is invited to participate and in the end to sleep, only to find themselves alone on stage with the actors gone as the lights come up. They are awake, and reality has shifted.

Us is Karen Malpede's drama about four people played by two people: a couple, his mother and her father. In order to underline the universality of the *Weltbild* that Malpede presents in this inter-generational, Oedipal story, I sketched a set which spread all the scenes across a tall, broad wall, a cross-section of life. It was difficult for the actors to maneuver along the shelf-like platforms that Ilion Troya erected in true constructivist style, but they, too, were an emblem of the relational difficulties that the actors were portraying. It was a device deriving from Piscator's *Hoppla, wir leben!*, *Rasputin*, and *The Kaiser's Coolies*, all of which saw him using multi-level sets designed by the innovative Traugott Mueller.

Poland/1931, Jerome Rothenberg's poetic evocation of Jews and Poles, immigration and assimilation, was played on a flat space with the audience seated in a single row around the walls of the space. Though our production made minimal use of costumes and props, the only scenic elements were six wooden benches, which the actors arranged differently in every scene.

In *VKTMS* by Michael McClure, the classical figures of Orestes, Electra and Pylades are transformed into war chariots, wheeled about by their slaves. It takes place at the moment of their bloody massacre, and they are all stuck in that moment forever. The terrible abuse of the class-structure, of the disabled and still unforgiving royals, and the slaves who hate them and yet continue to serve them, is a theme Piscator wanted the theatre to deal with, in both classical and modern scripts. Sartre's *Flies*, which Piscator produced at The Dramatic Workshop, tells the story in an existentialist version, in which Orestes is liberated from his furies. But McClure shows these figures still stuck in the old story, still not free from the fear and the guilt of their old crimes. Our chariots were beautifully constructed by the graffiti artist Rammellzee, demonstrating how today's iconography can breathe new life into myth.

Armand Schwerner's *The Tablets* represents yet another way of dealing with myth and history. Here, Piscator's Narrator is the central character, in the person of the Scholar/Translator. He is trying to understand the past, but the past – the meaning of the ancient tablets – gets the better of him, while the tablets speak directly to the spectators, telling us that we must go much deeper to understand their language and ours. *The Tablets* was originally written as a long epic poem, and Hanon Reznikov adapted it as a dramatic work, working in close collaboration with the poet.

Else Lasker-Schüler was a poet who, like Piscator, was a pioneer of the modern art movement, and though she remained marginalized all her life because of her eccentricities, she was a lodestone for a generation of modern artists. I don't know whether she ever met Piscator, but she was certainly part of the Berlin scene before she escaped, in 1933, to spend the rest of her life in Jerusalem.

And her play *I and I* seems to indicate that she knew Piscator's kind of theatre. A rich pastiche of the Faust story and the Nazis' machinations, the play is set in heaven and hell, and features the Nazis and the Ritz Brothers. Told as the odyssey of the poet trying to get her play produced, Max Reinhardt appears as her potential producer. The whole thing takes place in a cabaret in hell, with the German Army seen marching endlessly by means of a George Grosz-inspired Piscator device, a rotating wheel of soldiers, marvelously invented by Ilion Troya, a designer schooled in constructivist and expressionist art. Piscator should have done this play, but perhaps he didn't know of it. He always complained that there were no playwrights fit for his purpose.

The Body of God was a collective creation in the manner that Piscator advocated. The title is taken from Eric Gutkind, the Jewish philosopher, who intended "The Body of God" to mean the people – all the people – and we used it to focus the audience's attention on the homeless people who slept in the streets around our theatre on Third Street on New York's Lower East Side.

First, our company discussed the theme and collected a collage of texts. Then we invited eight homeless people, some of whom were staying in shelters nearby, and others who were out on the street, to perform with us. Their stories and their passions became the subject of our texts and enactments.

The audience was greeted by our homeless collaborators, and given a plastic bag to put their belongings in, and a piece of cardboard on which to sit on the floor, "anywhere . . ." In this way they had to make a decision about where to sit, and later, when they are asked to move to make way for the shifting geography of the performance, they may in a small way feel the embarrassed uncertainty of homelessness.

German Requiem is Eric Bentley's adaptation of Kleist's play *The Schroffenstein Family*. A poetic tract about the cycle of violence and historical animosity, the play seems timelessly relevant. We divided the room into two castles, separated by a mountain, with the audience seated as partisans of one of the two warring families. I wanted to go further, to have each side wear their family's colors or carry their banners, but I did not succeed in this. On one night the full impact of such a feud was made vividly clear. During the intermission, two rival street gangs fought a battle in front of our door. The audience watched spellbound through the lobby windows, thinking at first that it was part of the play, until the ambulances and the police cars arrived and took away the injured.

Rules of Civility and Decent Behavior in Company and in Conversation is a list of guidelines written by the young George Washington, which Reznikov transformed into an ensemble theatre-piece showing how the strictures of a misconceived morality lead to an ethical vacuum, in which the wars of our day are made to seem justifiable. At the end of the play, the two historical figures, George Washington the child and George Washington the man, lead the audience outside to a peace vigil in the street. When we performed it in Rome, we marched on the American Embassy, in theatrical protest against the first Gulf War. The police stopped us.

In *The Piscator Experiment*, Maria Piscator writes, "The intellectuals wrote about Epic Theatre, giving it different names, such as Political Theatre, Documentary Theatre, Engaged Theatre, *Zeitstück*, Piscator-stage, *Lehrstück* . . ." The Living Theatre's *Echoes of Justice* is in the true sense a *Zeitstück*, or perhaps even a Documentary play. It came about when Hanon and I and Exavier Muhammad Wardlaw, a member of our company, were guests on Bob Fass' program, *Radio Unnameable*, on WBAI. We took phone calls live on air, and one was from Larry Davis, a prisoner on Riker's Island, who told his story, describing how he was being viciously abused, because he had shot at the police when they broke into his home, where he was with his wife and children. Since we were talking about political theatre, he said, perhaps we would be willing to dramatize his story. Exavier went to work immediately, got the trial transcripts from the lawyers involved, and transformed them into the play *Echoes of Justice*.

In *Anarchia*, we showed how the editors and staff of a fashionable magazine were affected by a feature they did on the Italian anarchist Errico Malatesta, who made them aware that they were wearing chains, imprisoned by their jobs and limited lives. Some of the office workers at the magazine do a street play in agit-prop style in front of their building, to protest against war taxes. When they are confronted by a terrorist attack, they call upon the audience to save them. Some spectators respond and others do not, and so at the end of each performance there is a different distribution of corpses and survivors. How the play ends depends on the choices made by the audience. We like to imagine that Piscator would have approved.

The Zero Method juxtaposes a personal relationship with the seven propositions of Wittgenstein's *Tractatus Logico-Philosophicus*. In the middle of Hanon Reznikov's play, the actors stop to discuss what they're doing with the audience. "What do you think of this play?" we asked. "What do you think of our economic relationship?" "How many of you paid to be here?" "How many got comps?" "If you paid do you think it's worth the price?" In another scene, two actors recite and enact headlines from the day's newspapers. The use of newspapers as a text is not a new idea. It had inspired Piscator himself when Hallie Flanagan's Federal Theatre Project presented *The Living Newspaper*, "a committed documentary that informed the audience of the size, nature and origin of a social problem, and then called for specific action to solve it," as Lijntje Zandee describes it in *The Federal Theatre and the Living Newspaper*.

Maria Piscator writes in *The Piscator Experiment*, "The Living Newspaper technique was used in the early Piscator productions of the twenties. We can trace it still further back to the montage technique of Eisenstein and Meyerhold. Patterned after film documentaries, in swift-moving scenes, the Living Newspaper, successfully developed by Piscator, was used in England for adult education and propaganda in the armed forces during World War II, and of course has been adopted since by radio and television."

Augusto Boal and his company, The Theatre of the Oppressed, developed the Living Newspaper, at first in Peru for a literacy program and then in Brazil under the rubric "newspaper theatre." In February 1971, Boal was arrested and tortured in São Paulo. Boal's work, agitating and inventing new ways to carry political theatre forward, continues to this day, even after his death in 2009, thanks to his many followers.

In *Utopia* The Living Theatre made an experiment which it had long dreamed of: to make an entirely positive play in keeping with the universal wish to make a better world. At the Workshop, Piscator had asked me to make a compilation of the utopias in world literature, and I made a feeble attempt, starting with Thomas More and Campanella. I don't remember whether I ever finished the essay, or gave it to Piscator, but it whetted my appetite for imagining the distant landscape of the world we want to live in. In *Utopia* it was largely a matter of satisfying the audience's vision of fulfilling their own desires. In the course of the action we were able get them to articulate their desires, and the obstacles to these desires, and enact with us the overcoming of the obstacle and the achievement of the goal. In the end, the audience acted out, by means of a scene from Shakespeare's *Winter's Tale*, the conquest of death, the most utopian vision of all.

Not in My Name is a long-running protest play against the death penalty that has been performed many times on the traffic island in the middle of Times Square on days when there is an execution in the United States. In recent years there have been more than 3000 people on death row, and as many as two to three executions each week. At the end of the street play, we try to reverse the cycle of violence by each looking into one spectator's eyes, and making a promise/vow to them that we will never kill them. We mean that moment of contact to be the beginning of the reversal of the murderous cycle.

Piscator's emphasis on the economic basis of all dramatic works, whether classical or modern, Dadaist or realist, finally led us to do a play about the capitalist system, how it works, and how it came to be. Reznikov based his play on the text of Fernand Braudel's *Capitalism and Material Civilization: 1400 to 1800*, to illustrate the economic life of people of various statuses in various countries, during those 400 years. In order to give the audience a direct experience of the transactions involved, we created a stock market during intervals, in which the performers offered shares in the futures of their characters. They sold stock certificates to the public for real money, which would be redeemed at the end of the play. Some stocks rose in value, *but only at the expense of those that fell.*

Resistenza was a play inspired by its environment. Created in Rocchetta Ligure, a small Italian town that had been prominent in the resistance against the German Occupation and where the last of the aging *partigiani* still tell the tales of their valorous opposition to the Nazis. When we dramatized their struggle, the audience rose and joined us in the battle. As we worked on it, I often thought of Piscator's staging of *The Sheepwell*, with its dramatic groupings of the villagers against the tyrant. But I thought, too, of Piscator's oft-repeated story of the performance of the opera *La Muette de Portici* during which the rebellious song of the last act led the audience out into the street to start a revolution.

A Dream of Water, though couched by Hanon Reznikov in a fictional framework, is really a document about the building of the Three Gorges Dam in China, and the human suffering and ecological damage it is causing. It is also a hymn celebrating the substance on which all life is based. In the middle of the play we conduct an open forum with the audience on the subject of water management. Piscator, who always advocated making the theatre an open forum, though he only attempted it in his early plays, would have been moved by the profundity of the audience's discussion at these performances.

In *Enigma*, we paid homage to the thoughts and theatre of Julian Beck. The play, written down by Reznikov, is the result of a collective discussion over many weeks on Julian's work and the dilemmas of the artistic creation.

Maudie and Jane is a two-woman play about the disequilibrium in our society – the ageist prejudice against the elderly, and the economic imbalance between rich and poor, successful and disenfranchised. Piscator's emphasis on class-consciousness is tenderly resolved in the naked encounter between a beautiful, successful young woman and the helpless, aged body of an 80-year-old.

Eureka! was Hanon Reznikov's last play, which I completed after his death.

It comes closer than any play I've done to Piscator's vision of total audience participation and of vastness of theme.

There are no seats. When the spectators enter they are already in the play. They remain in the action throughout. They begin by enacting the beginning of the universe with the Big Bang, and end in a protest dance against the theory of the End of the Universe . . . In a dialogue between Edgar Allan Poe's and Alexander von Humboldt's respective views of history, the audience members perform together with the cast in conceiving the long trajectory of Evolution, Civilization, the dangers of militarization and ecological folly. At each performance I felt: *this* is what Piscator *really* wanted to do.

Since the audience participated from the very beginning to the end, performing, speaking, *Eureka!* is in a sense the ultimate Piscatorean play – and I am happy that I have at least this once fulfilled Piscator's vision of total audience participation.

Red Noir is a play written by Anne Waldman, depicting the desperate criminal world of the Noir films. A glamorous female detective is deeply involved in intrigues. Against this framework of negativity, The Living Theatre, following Piscator's utopian example, used the poetry of that same playwright to express the hope that joyous and anarchist and compassionate ideals can overcome the bleak landscape.

In *Korach*, The Living Theatre deals unmistakably with Piscator's ideas . . . A biblical figure who challenges Moses' authority is called by some "the first anarchist in recorded history." The question of power, poetical and spiritual, is the central theme, and a large cast of Israelites and Rebels enacts a struggle in a desert setting, in which the audience sits on a low platform around the action in the center, which takes place on a higher platform.

And in *History of the World*, each actor guides one or more of the spectator-participants through history, from the cave to the Beautiful Non-Violent Anarchist Revolution.

It is in the workshops that The Living Theatre has been conducting for many years that the fullest extent of our work on collective creation has been realized. We begin with a discussion with 20 to 80 people of the subject matter that constitutes that group's concerns. I speak to them of two principles that Piscator taught us at the Workshop: The Principle of Total Theatre and The Principle of Commitment. Then we ask groups to choose their subjects with Piscator's principles in mind. Once a theme is chosen, the group creates a text using the poetic method of the surrealists' Exquisite Corpse. Each actor writes two lines of poetry on the chosen subject; the next writer only sees the last line and continues the thought on from there. Then, using some of the techniques we have taught them in exercises, each group creates a scene based on their themes. And finally we put these scenes together, so as to make them a theatrical event that can be performed on the street or in any public place.

These plays, collectively created as well as acted by the workshop participants, include *A Day in the Life of New York City*, created in the aftermath of 9/11 and performed at the end of September and the beginning of October in public parks in Manhattan and Brooklyn; *The Code Orange Cantata*, performed at the street protests during the 2004 Republican convention; and *No Sir!*, performed in front of the nation's most famous military recruiting station on the traffic island at 43rd Street and Broadway, where a large screen on top of the booth plays a looped promotional video which repeats after about seven minutes. *No Sir!* was created to be performed below this screen during one run of this loop, turning the pro-war video into an element of our anti-war play.

So here is how one theatre, The Living Theatre, throughout its long history, has followed the precepts of Piscator's stagings to express its politics. But beyond all that, or rather underlying it in the sense that it is fundamental, is the spirit of Piscator's inexorable search for theatre forms that could serve his great cause: to make the world better through the art of the theatre.

Political Theatre, Theatrical Politics: Epic Theatre in the 21st Century

What has become of political theatre in the third millennium C.E.? The concept of "political correctness" has made it obligatory for major European theatres to include a certain number of plays with socially relevant themes in their repertory. But though many of these make use of Piscator's inventions, such as the breaking of the fourth wall, the use of narration and the Epic use of film and video, too many of them lack the essential element of a committed cast – of an ensemble that has probed the meanings and the interpretations of the drama and its characters, and analyzed the drama's social significance.

Where then is the new political theatre? It is not absent. Today I can say that I have seen it, and that we have participated in it. The new political theatre, as Julian Beck cried out in the last scene of The Living Theatre's *Paradise Now*, is in the street. Yes, that is where it can be found.

At the massive demonstrations that have been taking place in recent years, in the various cities where summit meetings of the G8 and the World

Trade Organization were deciding the fate of the world economy, and the consequent life and death of masses of people: there, we saw hundreds of thousands of activists come out to protest against capitalism!

Piscator would agree that our fundamental political problem is the capitalist system, "with its inequality and injustices and the poverty and the wars needed to support it." These demonstrations are pure theatre.

In July 2001, when the G8 met in Genoa, 200,000 people marched and performed. What made the biggest splash in the world media was, alas, a bloody splash, the killing of Carlo Giuliani, a young demonstrator who threw a fire extinguisher at a police car, and died for it. The commercial news media has a saying, "If it bleeds, it leads." Bloodshed means news for them; without blood, something is considered less newsworthy.

Piscator taught us that the purpose of theatre is to diminish or eliminate bloodshed. In "The Theater of the Future," which Piscator wrote in 1942 for *Tomorrow Magazine*, he says:

> War is hateful to me, so hateful that after the bitter debacle of 1918, I enlisted in the political struggle for permanent peace.

In Genoa, there were hundreds of groups representing various causes. There were feminists, anarchists, anti-militarists, communists, socialists, ecologists and save-the-whalers. The unifying theme was the failure of capitalism to address our needs.

Their efforts towards dramatic expression were even more varied: streamers and banners, costumes and music, chanting and singing, dramas and pantomimes, techno-tricks, confetti and audience contact, dances, acrobatics, drums . . . They were searching for the means of expression to say what they need to say, boldly, loudly and succinctly, so that it would communicate in the bustle of the street and the frenzy of the demonstration.

This effort and this search are the fruition of Piscator's work. He envisioned "a nationwide network of political theatres." Instead, he catalyzed an international network of theatrical activists. It is more than he could have hoped for.

During the huge parade of these 200,000 and their scenic paraphernalia, The Living Theatre performed an ambulatory piece which we called *Resist Now!* We created it together with 40 Genoese activists, some of whom had theatre experience and some of whom had none. We did a week of workshops with them in the open-air pavilions along the seafront of Genoa, where hundreds of other groups were preparing their protests. We formed a walking pyramid of bodies that recited the Moloch section of Allen Ginsberg's *Howl*.

In front of us was a contingent of the Argentinian *Madres de Plaza de Mayo*, moving with slow steps and sombre robes in the solemnity of their lament for their disappeared sons and daughters. Behind us was a group of Berlin transvestites on a float, awash with pearls and feathers and sequins and camping it up with cries and shrieks.

The beauty of it was that these two groups, the mourning mothers and the screaming queens, were aware of the motives of the other's demonstration, and aware that each had legitimate cause to protest against governments both for killing dissenters and for stifling sexual freedom. It is the epitome of Epic Theatre to see so many diverse issues enacted in the street at the gates of the meeting place of great powers. In 1930, Piscator wrote, in "The Cry for Art:"

> Perhaps the sense of Political Theatre has changed so that today we are permitted to act for "Theatrical Politics."

And 80 years later we begin to see this come to fruition.

In 2009, 2010 and early 2011, protestors demonstrated in Iran.

In 2011, we have watched courageous and non-violent street actions in Egypt, occupying Tahrir Square, forcing the resignation of the tyrannical government, and inspiring the Arab Spring of pro-democracy actions from Yemen to Bahrain, to Syria, to Libya.

In the fall, in New York City, thousands of people gathered on Wall Street to protest against the greed and the heartlessness of our whole economic system; not only specific "inequalities and injustices," nor only "the poverty and the wars," but the very system itself, which encompasses all those abuses within it. They adamantly refused to confine their protest to one or another abuse of the system, instead focusing on the entire structure and philosophy that uphold it. They brought into view our humanity, as a master–slave system with one percent gathering the profits and 99 percent in the struggle . . .

The ideal is enormous, "Abolish Capitalism." The smaller steps towards this great vision are not yet formulated . . . But it is pure and profound, as Piscator would have had it, and as the world needs it to be.

Whether this is indeed the beginning of a revolutionary movement that will change the world is not yet known. We may yet face the setbacks of violence and the impatience of the armed forces that are desperate to keep the social peace – but are so often the very cause of bloodshed. But as I write this, the leaderless movement that calls itself Occupy Wall Street has grown from city to city, and now from country to country, beyond Wall Street and New York City. It incorporates occupations and marches and street theatre.

We are performing an excerpt from *Seven Meditations on Political Sado-Masochism*, starting with The Meditation on Money, and ending with the question, "What can we do?" directed to the audience. We then, at the end of the play, discuss any and all possible routes to a better society. We are one of thousands (and counting) of groups and individuals working to theatricalize the cause.

Yes, Piscator, Julian Beck proclaimed your concept, "The theatre is in the streets!" And that's where it is now, and we thank our wise teacher.

Today, information travels faster than ever before in history. Today, the networks of communication outdistance the decision-making processes of lawmakers and the decision-makers themselves, in states and corporations. This is a new form of social and political life. We have no precedents. We are inventing the process as we proceed.

This is what Piscator taught us: not what it is we must do, but rather to become people who will know what to do in the changing culture, to grasp the facets of human nature that are not alien to ourselves, and to enact them. So that we will be able, as Brecht said of Piscator, "to serve humankind through all the means of the theatre."

New York City, October 2011

References

Brown, Kenneth H. 1965. *The Brig*. New York: Hill and Wang.

Cole, T. and H. K. Chinnoy, editors. 1949. *Actors on Acting*. New York: Crown Publishers.

Dean, Alexander. 1941. *Fundamentals of Play Directing*. New York: Farrar & Rinehart, Inc.

Drain, Richard, editor. 1995. *Twentieth Century Theatre: A Sourcebook*. London: Routledge.

Gassner, John. 1940. *Masters of the Drama*. New York: Random House.

Haarmann, Hermann. *Erwin Piscator und die Schicksale der Berliner Dramaturgie*. 1991. Munich: Welhelm Fink Verlag.

Howard, Roger, editor. 1972. *Culture and Agitation*. London: Action Books.

Kirfel-Lenk,Thea. 1984. *Erwin Piscator im Exil in den USA*. Berlin: Henschelverlag.

Ley-Piscator, Maria. 1967. *The Piscator Experiment*. Carbondale and Edwardsville: Southern Illinois University Press.

Piscator, Erwin. 1929. *Das politische Theater*. Berlin.

Reich, Bernhard. 1970. *Im Wettlauf mit der Zeit*. Berlin: Henschelverlag.

Willett, John. 1979. *The Theatre of Erwin Piscator*. New York: Holme & Meier.

Index

201

204